BARNUM & BAILEY

T MENAGERIE

THE GREATEST SHOW ON EARTH

RD BARBOUR ST.
SHOW GROUNDS

THUR. 6
JULY

OCT 1 3 2000

D0467225

x 5/01 √ 7/02
x 11/02 √ 9/03
x 4/05 √ 6/05
x 4/05 √ 7/06
10x 4/05 √ 11/07
13x 5/09 √ 11/89
13x 7/09 √ 4/11
13x 5-09/8-12

Also by Stewart O'Nan

A Prayer for the Dying

A World Away

The Speed Queen

The Names of the Dead

Snow Angels

In the Walled City

Editor

The Vietnam Reader

On Writers and Writing, *by John Gardner*

doubleday

New York
London
Toronto
Sydney
Auckland

WITHDRAWN

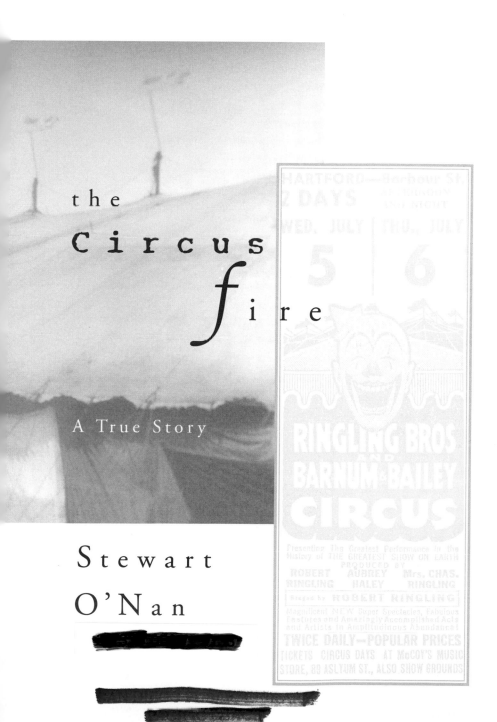

the
Circus
*f*ire

A True Story

Stewart
O'Nan

PUBLISHED BY DOUBLEDAY
a division of Random House, Inc.
1540 Broadway, New York, New York 10036

DOUBLEDAY and the portrayal of an anchor with a dolphin
are trademarks of Doubleday, a division of Random House, Inc.

Book design by Maria Carella

Diagrams on pages 21, 52, and 132 by Jackie Aher

Endpapers: Image reproduced with the permission of Ringling Bros.-Barnum & Bailey Combined
Shows, Inc. RINGLING BROS. AND BARNUM & BAILEY® and THE GREATEST SHOW ON EARTH®
are federally registered trademarks and service marks of Ringling Bros. and Barnum & Bailey
Combined Shows, Inc.

Library of Congress Cataloging-in-Publication Data
O'Nan, Stewart, 1961–
    The circus fire: a true story / by Stewart O'Nan. — 1st ed.
        p.   cm.
    1. Hartford Circus Fire, Hartford, Conn., 1944.   2. Hartford
(Conn.)—History—20th century.   3. Fires—Connecticut—Hartford—
History—20th century.   4. Ringling Brothers Barnum and Bailey
Combined Shows—History.   I. Title.
F104.H305   2000
974.6′3—dc21   99-42051
                                                                                     CIP

Copyright © 2000 by Stewart O'Nan
ISBN 0-385-49684-2

All Rights Reserved

Printed in the United States of America

June 2000

10   9   8   7   6   5   4

OCT 1 3 2009

This book is for everyone who went to the circus that day—
those who came home
and those who stayed.

Contents

Contents

Foreword

I did not want to write this book. Why I attempted it I'm not precisely sure. Certainly not because I had some personal connection to the circus fire or because I had something deep and meaningful to say about it. I suppose it was because I found the fire a strange and tragic event, one that had taken place in the city I had just moved to. In the beginning, writing about the fire was a way, maybe, of learning not only about the mysteries surrounding the fire but also the history that shaped the place I live.

I first ran across a mention of the fire ten years ago in an old *Life* magazine while I was doing research for a novel. The notion of a circus tent burning down and children dying inside it shocked me, as did the pictures accompanying the article.

I must have filed the idea and the images away in my head, as I often do with unsettling things, because years later when we moved to Hartford, I recalled the fire and its effect on me. I decided I should read more about it, so I went to the library and asked for a good history of it.

They didn't have one.

Maybe another library around town?

No, what they meant was, there wasn't one.

I thought that was wrong. The circus fire was the biggest disaster in the history of the state, and such a strange one. So many people had died, I couldn't believe no one had commemorated the event, set it in words for later generations.

I didn't want to write a book about the fire, I just wanted to know what happened. I started asking people around town what they knew about it.

Everyone had a friend or neighbor who had been there that day, a grandmother or a cousin. Everyone had a story. People of that generation knew exactly where they were that afternoon, just as, later, they could recall what they were doing when President Kennedy was shot. The fire had that great of an impact on the city.

By then I'd begun to do research, thinking—not realistically—that maybe I could interest someone who knew how to write nonfiction in taking on the project. I'd gather the material and hand it off to a professional and in a year or two I'd have that book I wanted to read.

Soon I had several notebooks full of photocopied documents, and the novel I thought would take me into the next century was finished. Suddenly I had the time and obviously the interest. I was stuck.

By choosing to write the book, I would assume the obligation of telling hundreds of survivors' stories. I would become—in a way I did not feel comfortable with—the custodian of the circus fire, implicitly charged with not only telling its story but also, in the method of telling it, in my choices as a writer, interpreting the fire, imbuing it with whatever meaning I felt it had. I did not want that responsibility, but at that point what I wanted no longer mattered. The fire had me, and I had it.

When I first told people not from Hartford that I planned to write a nonfiction history of the fire, they asked me why I didn't just write a novel. The question surprised me; I'd never thought of writing a novel about it. From the beginning, because of its vague, legendary nature, I felt it deserved only the most stringent, very best intentions of nonfiction, the idea being to tell the truth about an event that changed the lives of tens of thousands of people. I suppose I thought I might cheapen the fire by fictionalizing it.

As I dug deeper into the research, I discovered my choice of nonfiction was right for a simpler reason: the fact that truth really is stranger than fiction. Not merely weirder, but packed with coincidences, gaps and lapses that well-made fiction can't tolerate. The subject—the deaths of 167 people, most of them women and children—seemed to beg for a clear and definitive telling, yet the picture available to me was fragmentary and often contradictory.

The story of the circus fire, as Hartford already knows, is not just a tragedy but also a mystery, probably insoluble, which keeps it alive and vital in the city's imagination, an emotional touchstone. This mix keeps it fascinating yet frustrating. The answers we want nailed down can't be. Only in fiction could the story of the circus fire be made complete, its missing pieces found and fitted neatly into place. But then it wouldn't be true.

Even this is a best guess. Though I've tried to be careful in my interviews with survivors and the families of the dead, and diligent in my research of the existing files, the circus fire is essentially a mystery, now further obscured by time. This account cannot possibly contain the whole, complete truth of what happened without including all of the literally thousands of stories of that day and the hard days beyond. That book would be as wide as life and as long as memory.

This book contains just some of what I learned about Hartford and how it responded so heroically to a terrible and unique tragedy. As a history, it hopes to fix a time and a place long gone, to preserve it so readers can visit it and try to understand what the people of Hartford went through, how they faced the worst and bravely found ways to carry on, as people are asked to do every day.

Any errors or critical omissions in this book are mine. To all those who recognize them, I apologize.

A carnival should be all growls, roars like timberlands stacked, bundled, rolled and crashed, great explosions of lion dust, men ablaze with working anger, pop bottles jangling, horse buckles shivering, engines and elephants in full stampede through rains of sweat while zebras neighed and trembled like cage trapped in cage.

But this was like old movies, the silent theater haunted with black-and-white ghosts, silvery mouths opening to let moonlight smoke out, gestures made in silence so hushed you could hear the wind fizz the hair on your cheeks.

More shadows rustled from the train, passing the animal cages where darkness prowled with unlit eyes and the calliope stood mute save for the faintest idiot tune the breeze piped wandering up the flues.

The ringmaster stood in the middle of the land. The balloon like a vast moldy green cheese stood fixed to the sky. Then—darkness came.

—Ray Bradbury, *Something Wicked This Way Comes*

Cleveland, 1942

They played by the lake, their tops guyed out on the lot by Municipal Stadium. The Indians were on the road, and healthy crowds turned out for the big show. Only the Pennsy tracks ran between them and the shore, fenced them in along the bluffs. All day a breeze off the water snapped the flags of the big top.

It was August and hot. It was the first summer of the war and already they were short of men. Their owner John Ringling North had scaled back to a four-pole big top from the traditional six, but layout superintendent Leonard Aylesworth still had to recruit neighborhood kids to help his men erect the tents.

They were always late that summer; the engines they relied on to pull their trains were needed for the war. The Office of Defense Transportation decided when they went and how they got there—a problem only made worse by the oversized flatcars they used to haul their wagons. The curves on some routes were too tight and there were delays, hours spent stalled on sidings to let troop and munitions trains through. The jumps between cities took too long, and then setting up was slow, and the matinees got pushed back.

On top of that, the man who usually oversaw all these logistics, general manager George Washington Smith, was gone, off to the Army's War Show, an open-air mock-battle pageant designed to sell victory bonds by displaying the tanks and planes and howitzers the country was subsidizing.

Still, Ringling Bros. and Barnum & Bailey Combined Shows made their dates. Blowing a show was bad luck, and they'd had enough of that already. There was serious money to be made. War plants were running three shifts and everyone had a fat paycheck, not like a few years ago. Just two railroad shows had survived the Depression, and the Cole Brothers only remotely rivaled Big Bertha.

This was still the Greatest Show on Earth, with its tradition and glitter, a new elephant ballet scored by Stravinsky and choreographed by

Balanchine, and stars like Emmett Kelly and Alfred Court, the Wallendas and the Cristianis and the Flying Concellos, even menagerie draws like Gargantua the giant gorilla and his bride M'Toto, who did nothing but loll around in their air-conditioned cages until it was time for their twice-a-day staged wedding. One hundred clowns, the posters boasted, one thousand animals.

People came out to see them and forget the war, if only for a moment. There was a promotion where if you bought a bond you got a free grand-stand ticket, and the show this year was decidedly patriotic, the big specta-cle or "spec" a celebration of American holidays, the finale of the closing spec capped by the unfurling of four huge portraits of President Roosevelt. Servicemen in uniform were admitted free.

The '42 show had done well so far, opening strong in Madison Square Garden, following that with a good run at Boston Garden, then dipping down south to Baltimore to open under canvas. They played packed houses all the way up the eastern seaboard—Hartford was especially good, with Colt's Firearms and United Aircraft there—before turning inland across upstate New York. In Syracuse they played a straw matinee, the overflow crowd sitting on the ground, and then a turnaway that night, the big top so full even John Carson's opportunistic crew of ushers couldn't shoehorn one more rube in. Sellouts in Schenectady and Utica, a big house in Buffalo, but then when they hit Pittsburgh it rained.

It was a rough go. During the opening matinee, one of Alfred Court's lions attacked trainer Vincent Souday, laying his right thigh open from groin to knee. Court himself rushed in to finish the act, but the damage was done, the mood had been set. It poured. For the six-day stand the back-yard was mud, the girls in the spec hauling on boots, their rainy day cos-tumes clammy, never quite dry.

At the employment office downtown the circus requested permission to hire 150 more workers, but war industries had priority, and Pittsburgh, the steel capital of the world, was working round the clock, the mills churn-ing out clouds so dark the city kept their streetlights on all day long. The young, unattached men whom the glamour and freedom of circus life had always drawn were in dire short supply. The show took on anyone who signed up and was happy to get out of town.

Cleveland was a four-day engagement, August 3rd through the 6th, shows at 2:15 and 8:15 daily, doors open at 1:00 and 7:00, same as always. Like the army the circus operated by clockwork; every working person knew where they had to be and what they had to do. In the last war it was said the Kaiser had modeled his army's transportation scheme after Barnum's. The routine defined everyone's day; in a way it comforted them, gave them something solid to hang on to.

Opening day was unremarkable, the performances sharp, the weather mercifully clear. The lot had a view of the harbor, two stone jetties tipped with white lighthouses reaching into blue, blue Lake Erie. The tent was air-conditioned, another new-fangled idea of John Ringling North's. After the withering heat of the grounds and the stifling humidity of the menagerie tent with its ripe zebras and camels and elephants, the matinee customers appreciated it. That night the crowd was larger, swelled by families and workers finished with day shift.

The morning of Tuesday the 4th, the dew and the cool fog burned off and the day promised to be sunny. Kids who showed up early enough were hired for the price of a pass to scrounge around under the bleachers and re-trieve last night's empty Coke bottles. The lot was too small for the cook-house, so it was across the street from the big top. As the staff fried pork chops and bacon and eggs and toast for breakfast, cageboys bumped wheel-barrows piled with chunks of horsemeat between the big cats' wagons. The tethered camels and zebras tucked into piles of fresh hay. It was all clock-work, and after Pittsburgh, welcome.

Around 11:30 A.M. the flag on the cookhouse went up for lunch, and the hands left their charges grazing away. The first call for the sideshow was noon. The kid show, it was called, with the Doll Family of Tinytown, Percy Pape the Living Skeleton, and Dr. Mayfield the Fire Proof Man, among others. Pretty soon the towners would roll in, the midway would fill up, and the talkers would have to step out on the bally platform and turn the tip—convince the crowd to line up at the ticket boxes and fork over cold cash to see Mo-Lay the comedy juggler and Egan Twist the Rubber-Armed Man and Miss Patricia the hot-neon-tube swallower. A clutch of spielers and performers were waiting for their lunch orders when someone ran through the doorway and shouted that the menagerie was on fire.

They all ran.

What happened happened fast. As they dashed across the street to the midway, they could see black smoke pouring up and flames racing along the peaks of the menagerie top. Inside, the elephants were staked to the ground front and back with iron chains. They were trumpeting.

Two men ducked into the canvas marquee and began tearing the steel railings in front of the ticket booths out of the ground. The first came easily. As they tugged at the second one, a giraffe bounded past them and galloped across the lot.

Hands broke out water buckets and fire extinguishers, but the breeze from the lake fed the flames. Scraps of canvas floated free, rose like balloons on the superheated air. Luckily the wind was blowing from the northeast and pushed the fire away from the adjacent big top. Only the poleless gorilla top, home of Mr. and Mrs. Gargantua, separated the two large tents. Their handlers immediately cut the ropes, dropping the untouched canvas over their cages. A circus water truck arrived with a short section of hose and wet the canvas down, allowing a tractor to come in and haul the Gargantuas' wagons off, their air conditioners still humming.

Inside, flaming pieces of the tent dropped into the straw and hay. It went up like dry brush. Cageboys untethered their animals and led them out, then went back for more, hunched over from the blaze above. Big John Sabo, the menagerie super, made three trips before the heat drove him out. One zebra was running around wild, turning circles in the smoke; it shot out of the main entrance and zigzagged over to the grade by the railroad tracks where a number of hands closed in and wrestled it to the ground. An ostrich sprinted out, on fire; it took three men to tackle it and beat out the flames.

The elephants still hadn't budged and wouldn't until the boss of the bull men, Walter McClain, arrived. McClain was a giant of a man with an even greater reputation as a trainer. He knew his bulls would wait for him, so he led his men in even as the roof above them was coming apart. The men scampered around to the rear stakes and unlinked the beasts' shackles. At McClain's command the elephants reached down with their trunks and yanked their front stakes out of the ground. Another word from him and they marched out in procession, trunk to tail. Some were horribly burned, their flesh hanging in strips, peeled off like rind, but they were out.

Three they couldn't reach. One, Ringling Rosie, they freed from her chains, but she was spooked and refused to leave the burning tent. The heat

These camels never left their bed of straw. Workers stand about helplessly as Cleveland firemen mop up. In the left background, behind the now-empty rigging, rises the four-pole big top. PHOTO COURTESY OF THE CIRCUS WORLD MUSEUM

was down on them now, pushing them out. McClain stayed as long as he could (the right side of his face would be burned pink from his hairline to his collar), then ran. From outside, witnesses watched Ringling Rosie stomping back and forth as the flames enveloped her.

Likewise, the camels refused to move, balked at any effort to save them. They folded themselves down in their straw and the fire broke over them. The canvas was coming down, pieces burning in the dirt. In their cage wagons, the big cats roasted in their bedding, unable to escape.

The fire was mostly smoke now, the poles and wire rigging of the top charred and bare, yet still standing. The top was gone, consumed like tissue paper, nothing but scraps left. It had only been a few minutes.

The circus water trucks and the first Cleveland engine company to arrive played streams of water on Ringling Rosie. As police cordons held back the crowds, workingmen battled the fires inside the cages. Steam poured off of the charred wood. Inside, lions and tigers and pumas squirmed in the cinders, their coats smoking. Some lay still. The cageboys sobbed.

Firemen quenched what was left of the fire—hay and smoldering rope—while John Sabo and show veterinarian J. Y. Henderson took inventory. Two giraffes had been incinerated in their chain-link partition; how the third had escaped no one could figure out, but it was safe, just bruised and scratched from falling hard as workers corralled it. Another unlikely survivor was Betty Lou, the pygmy hippo; she'd saved her own life by diving into her bathing tank and staying submerged until a tractor driver snaked her wagon out of danger.

Few others were so lucky. Ringling Rosie stood among the bodies strewn through the charred mud and puddles of black water, pink bleeding patches where her skin had been stripped off. Dr. Henderson was hoping to spray her with an unguent called Foille, a new medication invented for industrial burns. When Walter McClain ordered his men to double-chain her for the treatment, she went berserk, and afraid she might break loose, a city detective had to shoot her between the eyes with his .45. The pistol wasn't enough gun. The shot knocked her down but she was still breathing. Dr. Henderson had to ask a police ballistics expert to use his submachine gun on her.

One of the three giraffes there that day. Only one survived—Edith, who somehow vaulted the corral. PHOTO COURTESY OF THE CIRCUS WORLD MUSEUM

The elephant line stood in the street, quietly receiving treatment. They were burned mostly on their heads and trunks, their thin ears crisped. Trainers daubed Foille on their raw flesh with paintbrushes.

The three other elephants McClain's men couldn't get to were hurting. Later that afternoon another policeman put down Little Rosy, who was just too badly burned.

The camels were the worst, and the big cats. Police and Coast Guardsmen brought over high-powered rifles and ammunition from a nearby armory. One camel handler begged them not to shoot his animals, others cursed them, but it was necessary.

Dr. Henderson went hopefully from cage to cage with his sprayer of Foille. The cats looked up at him, licking their burned paws, wisps of smoke still rising from their fur. The doctor asked a detective for his pistol. The Coast Guardsmen were there with their rifles for the larger animals. Together they had to shoot three camels, three lions, and a puma. The thing he would never forget, Dr. Henderson said later, was how, throughout, the animals were completely silent.

. . .

The Cleveland menagerie fire was a shock, even more so because it was wartime and the circus was supposed to be a diversion from that larger tragedy, but anyone who knew the circus knew it had a history of disasters.

From the beginning, American circuses seemed prone to fire—perhaps naturally, considering their early performances were lighted by either candles or oil lamps. In 1799, Rickett's Equestrian Circus, widely recognized as the first in America, lost their Philadelphia amphitheater when it burned to the ground.

P. T. Barnum seemed especially susceptible. Fire destroyed his American Museum at Broadway and Ann Street in lower Manhattan in July of 1865. Hoping to douse the floors below, firemen smashed the thick glass of the whale tank; the tactic didn't work, and the whales burned alive. Barnum quickly rebuilt a few blocks away, but in 1868 fire struck again. In 1887 the Barnum & London winter quarters in Bridgeport, Connecticut, burned, killing most of the circus' animals. It suffered another major blaze in 1900, and, though Barnum himself was gone by then, several minor fires almost yearly through the teens, capped by a $100,000 loss in 1924. In '27, the Combined Shows moved their winter quarters to Sarasota, Florida, ending his strange legacy.

The Ringling Bros. had the reputation of being ridiculously lucky, partly because of their competitors' perception of them as high and mighty, holier than thou. They ran what was known as a Sunday School show, going so far as to ban swearing on the lot. With no rigged midway games or salacious girlie acts, they continued to outgross other less savory outfits, often by promoting their squeaky-clean image. The Ding-a-ling Brothers, cynics called them, the Five Deacons. The first fire of note that struck them was in August of 1901 in Kansas City, Missouri; the sideshow tent burned, but, as their famous luck would have it, no one was hurt.

Barnum & Bailey—before the 1919 merger the sole and original Greatest Show on Earth—was possibly even luckier. In May of 1910, on a Saturday afternoon in Schenectady, New York, their big top caught fire with fifteen thousand souls in attendance. Fred Bradna, the big show's equestrian director at the time of the Cleveland menagerie fire, was about to blow his whistle for the opening procession when he saw a patch of flame

The 1910 Schenectady big top fire, as seen from a perch overlooking the midway, the sideshow top behind a wall of banners. PHOTO COURTESY OF THE CIRCUS WORLD MUSEUM

Schenectady. The cables of the rigging are visible, still attached to the tops of the quarter poles. PHOTO COURTESY OF THE CIRCUS WORLD MUSEUM

waving above the bleachers. He asked the spectators to please leave their seats in an orderly fashion, and they did.

There was no panic. The fire looked so insignificant that they climbed down the grandstands and bleachers and stood on the track and in the rings, watching as canvasmen climbed up onto the top and tried to cut out the burning section. A fire station directly across the street laid in hose immediately and focused water on the top, but soon it became apparent that they could not easily contain the blaze, and the crowd scurried out the main entrance and the back door and under the sidewalls, all without injury.

Witnesses at a country club overlooking the lot said they saw great masses of flaming canvas float up into the sky, the fire consuming them as they rose, a magician's trick. In minutes the poles were on the ground, though some of the canvas escaped untouched and the stands were saved. No one was hurt. The greatest loss was loss of face; once the fire was out, the crowd besieged the ticket wagons, demanding their money back. The ticket sellers were saved only when drivers hitched teams to the wagons and dragged them off.

The Ringlings' luck struck again in August 1912, in Sterling, Illinois. The big top was set up on a racetrack pasture. At one o'clock ten thousand people were waiting for the doors to open for the matinee when a barn a few blocks away caught fire. Al Ringling noticed the wind lifting burning shingles into the air and ordered the doors closed. As he feared, a brand landed on the roof of the top and the flames jumped up. The tent burned in minutes. By this time, Fred Bradna had moved to the Ringling Bros., so he was a witness again. Hook men calmly hustled the elephants away, as everyone feared a stampede. Again no one was hurt. The poles and stands needed only sanding and a new coat of paint.

The next morning the *Sterling Daily Standard* reported that the initial cause of the fire was either a spark from an engine or some boys seen smoking cigarettes around the barn. "The rapid destruction of the big tent has caused much speculation," the *Standard* said, "and people who witnessed it go up in flames today are still wondering what made the big tent go so quickly. The truth is the tent was covered with parafine to keep out rain and when the fire started this to melting it also added fuel to the flame and caused the more rapid destruction of the big tent."

The fire itself was a spectacle worthy of a circus. A picture of the burning tent won first prize in a photography contest held by a national magazine.

No other big top burned in the years between 1912 and the Hartford fire of '44, so it's not odd that the Sterling fire and the Hartford disaster are often paired in news stories. Both were matinees and both tops were the Ringling Bros. But the show had two other major fires very shortly after Sterling that are less well known.

The first was in Cleveland, this one also by the lakefront lot. In May 1914, forty-three railway cars went up while sitting mostly empty on a siding. The second was in October 1916, when the baggage stock tent burned in Huntsville, Alabama. Forty draft horses were incinerated; forty more had to be killed. According to witnesses, the fire took five minutes.

Even more than fires, train wrecks have plagued circuses over the years. The most famous wreck deserves mention here. It also occurred during wartime, in June 1918. At 4:00 in the morning, the crew of a train carrying the Hagenbeck-Wallace Circus stopped near Ivanhoe, Indiana, to fix a hotbox. The engineer pulled most of the train onto a siding, but the last five cars, including four sleepers, were still sitting on the main line. Miles away, an empty troop train blew through stop signals, its driver asleep at the wheel from a dose of kidney pills. In the old wooden sleepers, the circus workers and performers slept in their cramped berths, kerosene lanterns burning dimly above the aisles.

The crew of the circus train heard a distant chuffing and turned from their work to see the headlamp of the troop train bearing down on them. The driver had finally woken up, but it was too late for the brakes. The engine tore through the sleepers, driving them together, pitching them in a heap. The injured were trapped in the splintered wreckage, and as rescuers clambered in to help them, the pile of cars caught fire.

The crash site was between stations. The Gary and Hammond fire departments came as fast as they could, but the only water available at the scene was from a shallow marsh. Realizing the fire would not be put out, people climbed into the wreckage to pull out friends and loved ones. Some did; others died trying.

The Ivanhoe fire killed more than eighty-five circus folks, including animal trainer Millie Jewel, The Girl Without Fear; the number is purposely vague because many people were missing or burned beyond recognition. One Chicago paper wrote: "The two bodies recovered today were like several others which had been removed from the wreck, taken away in common water pails. They consisted only of burned bones from which every shred of flesh had been incinerated." In the end, fifty-six of the victims were buried in a large plot in Chicago's Woodlawn Cemetery, more than forty of them unidentified. Unknown Male No. 15, reads a typical grave marker. A stone elephant marks the plot, its trunk drooping, indicating sorrow.

By far the Ivanhoe wreck was the worst disaster in the history of the circus up to that time; the sheer number of people killed was staggering. Typically, other circuses pitched in and offered Hagenbeck-Wallace equipment and assistance, and in the great tradition of show business, Hagenbeck-Wallace accepted both and soldiered on. They missed just two stands.

Though Ringling Bros. and Barnum & Bailey had not had a major fire on the lot for many years before Cleveland, the show was not immune to tragedy. The year before, while they were touring the south, eleven elephants had died suddenly, most of them during their Atlanta stand. Autopsies revealed the animals had consumed large amounts of arsenic. At first a member of the circus train crew was arrested on suspicion of poisoning, but the charges were dropped. Police picked up several other suspects—including a recently fired worker—then let them go as well.

Old hands remembered that in the early thirties several elephants had fallen sick in Charlotte, North Carolina, from grazing near a chemical plant by the lot, and one of the last stands before Atlanta had been Charlotte. While many circus folk accepted this explanation, the connection was tenuous at best. The cause was never conclusively determined.

In a way, all of these tragedies could be said to fit the popular view of the circus as a dangerous and slapdash workplace, populated by shady transients and naturally prone to disaster. Our regular world, we figure, is much safer, being routine. And part of this attitude comes from our wonder at the daring, maybe even foolhardy risks we associate with circus acts like lion taming and wire walking. The danger involved is that much more exciting to us because we know it's real. Big cats can and do turn on their trainers; tightwire artists working without a net can and do fall to their deaths.

But these risks are painstakingly calculated by expert professionals, as are the rigid logistics behind the daily world of the circus. Likewise, both systems come from a long tradition, often propagated along family lines, and are practiced and perfected well before being taken out on the road.

Mostly though, the danger incurred by high-wire artists and animal trainers comes from trying to do a new bit, or trying to do more. In the case of these earlier top fires, it seems obvious that the danger was an old one, and never corrected. Schenectady, Sterling, Huntsville—all of these would be remembered after the Cleveland fire, and then again after Hartford.

· · ·

All afternoon tractors dragged the charred bodies out, the hooked chains clanking, then pulling taut. John Ringling North strode the lot in a brown leather jacket and cinnamon jodhpurs, directing the cleanup crew. He'd already called the sail loft in Sarasota for another tent and told his aides to scour area zoos for replacements. To the press he conceded they would have to cancel the matinee but vowed they'd play that night. The show would go on.

Dr. Henderson and his assistants worked on the survivors. The city donated the basement of nearby Public Hall, and they laid out a makeshift sick bay for two elephants, three camels and a Grevy zebra—all badly burned and in shock. Walter McClain asked for a squirt of Foille on his face and went back to take care of his other charges.

It could have been worse, everyone said. Besides the elephants, no performing animals were hurt, only menagerie stock. The ring stock top with hundreds of horses was right beside the menagerie; at one point a smoking pole had fallen on it. City firemen too late to save the menagerie concentrated their efforts there.

There was no chance of saving the menagerie top itself. It was 320 by 120 feet, with six poles. People said it burned in three minutes; others said ten. Like the tents in the earlier fires, it was waterproofed with the traditional mixture of paraffin and white gasoline. The *Cleveland Plain Dealer* reported: "One reason the tent was destroyed so swiftly was that its waterproofing was highly inflammable." The fire melted and then pyrolized the wax coating—turned it into flammable gas the same way the body of a lighted candle feeds its own flame. In essence, the tent burned like a giant wick. The breeze only made things worse.

David "Deacon" Blanchfield, the show's superintendent of trucks and tractors, testified at the state fire marshal's inquiry after Hartford: "I saw the one in Cleveland burn. You see one minute [it's] on fire, the next, there's no top. It's impossible to save a circus tent. There's no way to do it, unless you was right there and put it out with your foot. You ain't got the least conception of how quick a big top goes. That's as true as I sit in this chair. I wouldn't say unless I know, because I see two tops burn; and how hot it gets under there. That fire in Cleveland, it was over in less than twenty minutes, and it burned the hide off four elephants, completely off."

Initially Cleveland authorities thought the cause might be a carelessly discarded cigarette—the usual suspect in hotel fires of the time. One of the workingmen first on the scene thought the blaze originated on the roof of the tent, possibly caused by a spark from a passing locomotive. Another hand told a reporter for the *Plain Dealer* that he'd noticed a drunken worker lying in a pile of straw near where the fire started, smoking a cigarette. A third said he'd seen some boys with matches outside of that end of the tent. A fourth was telling anyone who would listen that the origin was a short circuit in a generator that was being repaired. The local fire prevention bureau would only say there was an investigation under way. "We may never know what happened," John Ringling North told reporters.

A truck hauled the burned giraffe wagon off to the runs. A local rendering plant disposed of the carcasses.

That night's show went on as scheduled; there was even an open-air sidewalled menagerie. They played to a crowd of eleven thousand, three thousand more than opening night. The biggest hand went to the elephant ballet, and especially to those animals who showed marks of the fire through their tutus.

In the basement of Public Hall, Dr. Henderson swabbed more Foille on the survivors. He had little hope: as with any seriously burned patients, animals are likely to contract pneumonia. He worked through the evening but in the end they were too badly hurt—they'd inhaled flames. One-Eyed Trilby the elephant died around midnight, then Rose the Grevy zebra. A last elephant, Kas, didn't live till morning. That left the three camels, Pasha, Tilly and En Route. They hung on, kneeling silently in their straw, unable to eat or drink. Early the next morning Dr. Henderson called on a detective to end their suffering.

The final toll was four elephants, all thirteen camels, all nine zebras, five lions, two tigers, two giraffes, two gnus, two white fallow deer, two Ceylon donkeys, one axis deer, one puma, one chimpanzee, and one ostrich. Publicly, the circus insisted there wasn't a dime's worth of insurance on the lot of them. John Ringling North estimated the loss at a gaudy $200,000. In private the circus filed claims with their carrier for the animals and cage wagons at just under $36,000.

The basement of Public Hall. Circus veterinarian Dr. J. Y. Henderson examines Pasha while Blackie Barlow paints on Foille. The three camels hung on the longest, but eventually they succumbed too. PHOTO BY THE *CLEVELAND NEWS,* COURTESY OF THE CLEVELAND PUBLIC LIBRARY

The night of August 5th, while the evening show was going on in Cleveland, Pennsylvania Railroad police at the Duquesne yards near Pittsburgh arrested a boy in his teens for illegally riding a freight. At first he refused to tell them his name. Railroad detectives found menagerie meal tickets in his pocket, and then at the Duquesne police station, he blurted out, "I know something about the circus fire."

The boy said he was sixteen and his name was Lemandris Ford—or Lemandria, or Lamadris (the papers couldn't agree). He'd quit school in Hazelwood the week before and signed on with the circus in Pittsburgh along with an older companion, Jess Johnson. The two had been let go Tuesday morning for not working fast enough.

Lemandris Ford then confessed to setting the fire, saying Johnson had convinced him to do it "to get even with the circus for firing us." According to Ford, Johnson lighted a cigarette for each of them, then held a knife to his ribs and threatened to stab him if he didn't throw his into a pile of hay where the animals were eating.

The fire itself Ford said little about. Later though, he admitted, "I felt pretty sorry when I saw all those dead animals lying around."

The circus timekeeper verified that Ford had been with them for those days, and Ford signed a confession. He had no previous police record.

Ford waived extradition, and circus police chief John Brice and two city detectives drove down to Pittsburgh to pick him up. By the next day the detectives were convinced Ford had nothing to do with the blaze. The boy was vague when questioned about the menagerie tent and the animals in it and was easily tripped into making contradictory statements. The man in the photo he identified as Jess Johnson was actually another criminal with a connection to the circus.

Police picked up Johnson anyway a few days later, but again the detectives thought him an unlikely suspect. By now Lemandris Ford had recanted his confession. The police publicly called his story a hoax and said the discrepancies in his statement made them suspect he was either seeking notoriety or else a victim of hallucinations. The boy alternately admitted and denied setting the fire right up to the time of his hearing.

Circus police chief John Brice had been with the show over thirty years. Though his hair was now a striking white, he still answered to the nickname Barnum Red. From his earliest days, he had a knack for spotting undesirables on the lot. Now his gut told him the kid was making it up. Medical records showed Ford had suffered a fractured skull in a car crash the winter before. The court ordered a psychiatric examination. Based on its findings, they returned him to Pittsburgh with the recommendation that he be committed to a home for the feeble-minded.

The origin of the fire remained a mystery, officially undetermined. While there was no proof beyond his confused confession, many still believed that Lemandris Ford was responsible, John Ringling North among them. By this time, *Life* magazine had already run a heavily illustrated story that stated the allegations as if they were fact, calling the accused "the young arsonist Alamandris Ford."

Later, other tall tales would crop up about the fire, including stampedes of elephants roaring down the streets of Cleveland, their stakes banging parked cars; the impressive weaponry (riot guns) and number of shots required to put down the animals; and the heartrending behavior of one lioness trying in vain to save her cubs by lying on top of them. As with Lemandris Ford's story, some people believed these and some didn't.

The circus had more practical matters to think of. They needed to restock their menagerie, and they did, partially, at least for the rest of the season. In '43 they would tour without a menagerie, and never again would they have the number of zebras and camels they had before Cleveland.

But the circus and John Ringling North would always find a way to profit, even from their own tragedies. Legend has it that the four elephants who died would later be displayed as sideshow attractions, much as Barnum showed Jumbo's remains in a special tent—untrue, it appears, yet testament to the public's perception of North's vaunted ability to find a silver lining.

The circus rebounded easily. It was sad, yes, but they were used to the fact that trouping was a hard and not always safe life and that accidents happened. Proof that it could happen to anyone was never far off. Walter McClain had pioneered the use of elephants in unloading flatcars and helping haul wagons from the runs to the lot. In November, as the show unloaded in the Jacksonville yards, he slipped and fell as he was trying to hop a moving baggage wagon. The front wheel crushed his skull, killing him. The circus mourned and carried on. That was circus life.

But while the razorbacks and canvas hands knew the dangers at the runs and on the lot, everyone with the show also knew the risks were theirs alone. The audience was never in danger. It was with great pride that even after the Cleveland fire Ringling Bros. and Barnum & Bailey could truthfully state that no spectator at any of their shows had ever been killed.

. . .

As terrible as the menagerie fire was, Thanksgiving of that year taught the public how bad a fire could really be. The Cocoanut Grove, a crowded nightclub in Boston, burned in seven minutes. Exits were few, some of them blocked by doors that opened inward, and 492 people died, most of them not from burns but by asphyxiation. The smoke from materials used to decorate the club proved to be toxic, poisoning hundreds. Many of the bodies seemed untouched, just sleeping. All 492 were identified.

The Boston press made much of the Grove's employees knowing the way out while customers groped blindly in the smoke. How the fire started was never firmly established, though a teenaged waiter, having lighted a match to see a lightbulb he was supposed to change, was tried in the papers. The courts cited the inflammable materials, lack of exits and well-past-capacity crowd as criminally negligent, and sentenced the club's absentee owner to prison. The courts also tried the city building inspector who had licensed the club, but while they found him derelict in his duties, he didn't see time.

Survivors of the dead sued, but the owner's pockets were not deep. Each claimant received as a death benefit only $160. Immediately, cities around the country changed and then began to strictly enforce their fire codes. Insurance companies clamped down. We would learn from the Cocoanut Grove, officials said.

*J*uly 4, 1944

It was Christmas in July, a circus tradition, the one day the whole family of the Big Show threw themselves a party. In Providence they'd be celebrating, the cookhouse decked out with flags and crepe-paper streamers, the canvas wall segregating the workers from the performers and management taken down just this one day, everyone digging into fried chicken, with cake and ice cream for dessert and seconds for all who wanted them.

But no, the twenty-four-hour man was here in Hartford, ahead of the show, laying out the lot, telling the mowers how to do their job, ordering all the hay and grain and fuel and food the show would need during their stand and then making sure it would all be here by morning when the first section of the train pulled in. Rationing made his job that much harder, and forget about getting anything delivered the night of the Fourth.

His first concern was the lot. He knew it well; they'd played on the Barbour Street grounds for ten years now, moving over from Colt's Meadows in the early thirties. The city had bought the land back then, hoping to build a high school on it, but that didn't happen, and they turned it over to the Public Building Commission, who rented it to carnivals and circuses. The show had played here around this time every year since, only missing once, during the '38 strike season. Most of the year the land stood empty, a grassy meadow.

It was a long, rectangular lot stretching east from the street—the only real access. The ground was level enough, but dusty, the grass dry; it hadn't rained in days. To the right as he came in was the McGovern Granite Company who made tombstones, their long yard filled with blank, polished samples. Farther in on the same side a maroon snow fence protected a tract of victory gardens. Neighborhood kids used the middle of the lot as a ball field, and the twenty-four-hour man could see the ruts of the batter's box on both sides of home, the grass trampled between the dust pits of the bases. The left side and back end were lined with trees, and beyond the trees at the back, a dirt road rose over a gentle hillock and connected with Hampton Street, a square block empty save a plot of shade tobacco and the barracks and spotlights of an army antiaircraft unit.

Around town, banners herald the yearly appearance of the circus. PHOTO BY WILLIAM DAY, COURTESY OF ROBERT F. SABIA

From past years he knew where the tops were supposed to go, and he knew there wouldn't be room for the menagerie tent. It was just as well—they'd been late several stands, so shorthanded, and anything that cut their set-up time was welcome.

Officially they had the lot from this evening till the morning of the 7th. The show's contracting agent had made the arrangements back in February, supplying the city with the circus's standard lease form and dropping off thirty or so passes with the superintendent of buildings. The rent was $500, to be paid by draft at the money wagon the day of the show. It was the standard deal.

And everything here on Barbour Street seemed fine to the twenty-four-hour man, business as usual. The advance men had done a good job of getting their bills up. Every mom-and-pop Italian grocery and barbershop and package store in the North End had a lithograph picturing the Panto's Paradise spec in its front window, the owners happy to have free passes in exchange for displaying the posters. The lot was in good shape. The weather was clear and expected to stay that way.

In Providence they were having Christmas dinner. Not the twenty-four-hour man; he had to order ice and fish and fresh bread, eggs and bacon and milk. It would be a long, hot day. When he left, the mowers were still working.

· · ·

The show had hired John Sponzo to cut the grass and cover the side-walk on the east side of Barbour Street with dirt so the trucks and wagons wouldn't break it up. Sponzo owned a brick company on Main and a fair amount of land by the corner of Cleveland and Hampton Streets, a section of which the circus would use for their horse top and cookhouse. Later he testified that he and one of his men were on the lot the 3rd and the 4th.

They had a pair of horses and a mowing machine and a one-horse rake. They had some trouble with cans and wire fouling their blades. Where the tent was, he said, the soil was sandy and the grass didn't grow much. They cut the lot and raked the grass, saving half for bedding and half to feed the horses.

Was enough dry grass left, in his opinion, to start a fire?

"I would say no," John Sponzo said, "because we did a fairly good job of it."

Principals

**The Cook party,
Southampton, Mass.**

*Mrs. Mildred Cook
Donald Cook, 9
Eleanor Cook, 8
Edward Cook, 6*

**The Norris / Smith party,
Middletown, Conn.**

*Mr. Michael and Mrs. Eva Norris
Agnes Norris, 6
Judy Norris, 6
Mrs. Mae Smith
Barbara Smith, 12
Mary Kay Smith, 6*

**The Kurneta / Erickson party,
Middletown, Conn.**

*Mrs. Frances Kurneta
Mr. Stanley Kurneta
Miss Mary Kurneta
Betsy Kurneta, 10
Tony Kurneta
Raymond Erickson Jr., 6*

**The Gale / Grant party,
East Hartford, Conn.**

Mrs. Hulda Grant

*Mr. Frank Golloto
Donald Gale, 10
Caroline Brown, 8*

**The Smith party,
Vernon, Conn.**

*Mrs. Grace Smith
Joan Smith, 12
Elliott Smith, 7*

**The Epps / Goff party,
Hartford, Conn.**

*Mrs. Mabel Epps (pregnant)
William Epps, 7
Richard Epps, 3
Mrs. Maurice Goff
Muriel Goff, 4*

**The Bocek / Marcovicz party,
Hartford, Conn.**

*Stella Marcovicz
Francis Marcovicz, 4
Dorothy Bocek, 13*

**The LeVasseur party,
Bristol, Conn.**

*Marion LeVasseur
Jerry LeVasseur, 6*

July 5, 1944

They were late out of Providence and blew the matinee. They'd been late all season—in Bridgeport and Fitchburg and Manchester—but this was the first show they'd blown.

They blamed the trains. According to the front-page story in the *Hartford Times:* "There was a divergence of opinion between circus and railroad officials as to what occasioned the delay. A spokesman for the show said the 72-foot flatcars needed to transport the main tent were 'unable to negotiate sharp curves in the railroad' between Hartford and Willimantic. Railroad dispatchers (with the New York, New Haven & Hartford) said the train was never scheduled to go that way. 'It came up the main line via the Cedar Hill yards in New Haven on schedule.' "

It was a different show this year. John Ringling North was out, replaced by Robert Ringling, seemingly at the whim of his mother, Mrs. Edith Ringling, widow of Charles, one of the original five brothers.

The struggle for control of the show seesawed between two sets of heirs: John Ringling North and his brother Henry, who were nephews of John Ringling; and Mrs. Edith Ringling and her son Robert, joined by their ally Aubrey Ringling, widow of Richard (son of original brother Alf), and newly married to James Haley. The state of Florida also factored into the equation, since the childless John Ringling had left it his mansion, his art museum and 30 percent of the show. At first his will provided handsomely for the North boys and their mother—who along with her son John was named his executor—but when John Ringling had a falling out with them late in life, he signed a codicil taking away everything except $5,000 for their mother. The mistake John Ringling made was never removing the Norths as his executors. They took the will to court and in the meantime as trustees of the estate voted the 30 percent of the stock. To thwart John Ringling North's sometimes overwhelming ambition, Edith and Aubrey Ringling entered a pact known as the Ladies' Agreement; on all top-level matters they were legally bound to vote their shares together.

In this manner, Edith's son Robert—an opera singer with no circus

(Left) Flamboyant showman John Ringling North was out of power at the time of the fire, but would soon scrap his way back. (Right) Robert Ringling's brief reign as president of the Big Show had been successful on all counts until Hartford.
PHOTOS COURTESY OF THE CIRCUS WORLD MUSEUM

Newly married Aubrey Ringling Haley consults the great animal trainer Alfred Court. Court was in Hartford, but did not perform that day. PHOTO COURTESY OF THE CIRCUS WORLD MUSEUM

experience—came to replace the flamboyant John Ringling North. He pledged to return the show to its roots, doing away with North's blue four-poler and bringing back the pre-1939 six-pole white top. There was nothing as fabulous as Balanchine's elephant ballet during Robert's reign, but the Broadway-style pageantry North favored remained, as did their problems with the Office of Defense Transportation, war rationing and a serious lack of manpower.

The war needed everyone; industry had even requisitioned some of the little people among the performers to work in tight spaces on aircraft assembly lines. In Providence, George W. Smith had 670 workingmen, well below the usual complement of 960, and it took three of these, he complained, to do the work of one good man. For the ushers and ticket sellers and concessionaires there was lots of "cherry pie," the circus term for the extra work of setting up the grandstand's wooden folding chairs. Troupers did double duty, helping tear down and set up, proving they were "with it and for it."

Maybe the lack of manpower was the reason they were late getting into Hartford, or maybe it was the Christmas celebration. It was only a matter of time before they missed a show. They'd been doing more evening-only dates since the beginning of the war, often performing just a late show on the day they arrived or just a matinee on the day they had to jump to another city. But the jump from Providence to Hartford was only ninety miles, and their schedule gave them more than six hours to cover that distance. It's possible that the circus fell back on its usual excuse of the trains out of sheer habit.

It was bad luck blowing a show, and show folks were notoriously superstitious. Since the great aerialist Lillian Leitzel's fatal fall, Merle Evans, the conductor of the band, refused to play "Crimson Petal," her theme music. Scranton, where the show closed in the strike year, was a jinx town. Whistling in the dressing room was bad luck, and peanut shells on the floor, and the old camelback trunks, but blowing a show was the worst.

The first section arrived at the Windsor Street siding at 9:45 Wednesday morning, nearly five hours late. The Flying Squadron, it was called, and it carried the menagerie cages and cookhouse wagons and the trucks and tractors and elephants to move them. A crowd of towners—adult circus buffs and children—watched the razorbacks unload the flats. Most followed the procession of elephants and wagons up North Main and across Cleveland to Barbour Street. People waved from their porches.

On the lot an even larger crowd waited, and the bosses of each department pulled stacks of passes from their pockets and hired on as many

Unloading the flats at the runs. PHOTO COURTESY OF THE CIRCUS WORLD MUSEUM

Elephants in harness, hauling a menagerie cage wagon onto the lot in Portland, Maine, June 30th, 1944. PHOTO BY MAURICE ALLAIRE, COURTESY OF MR. ALLAIRE HIMSELF

able bodies as they could find. The cookhouse went up first, with its long picnic tables and red-checked tablecloths, and then the horse tent. Hammer gangs drove stake lines for the big top, and for the sideshow, dressing and shop tents.

The second section had arrived by now, and the six poles of the big top were going up, fifty-seven feet tall and capped with flags. Roughnecks rolled out the canvas sections on the ground and began lacing them together with rope from the centerpoles out to the stake lines. The sun was higher now, and the men smelled like work.

Around 11:00 A.M., city building inspector Charles Hayes arrived on the lot but saw the big top was nowhere near ready. The city didn't legally require Hayes to inspect the tent; it was a custom. He left, saying he'd return in a few hours.

The crew finished lacing and inserted sidepoles around the edge of the tent, then with the help of two elephants straining against their padded harnesses hauled the canvas to the top of the centerpoles. Inside, in the suddenly welcome shadow, teams placed two rows of shorter quarterpoles around the oval and a half-dozen elephants working solo raised them, shoring up the roof. Once done, the canvasmen came back outside and tightened or guyed out the ropes holding the sidepoles.

The big top that was now up was new this year—the largest tent in the world, the circus claimed. It had come out of the sail loft the first week in May, and like its predecessors had been waterproofed with six thousand gallons of white gasoline and eighteen thousand pounds of paraffin. Seventy canvasmen had helped to melt the wax in cauldrons, thin it with gas, stirring it with paddles, and then sprinkle the mixture on the laid-out sections and spread it with brooms. The process was cheap and effective. The show had treated their tops like this for years.

Now that it was up, John Carson's ushers started setting out the jacks and stringers and bibles for the red grandstand chairs, the planks of the blue bleachers seats. In the grandstands they marked the row numbers on the risers with chalk, 1 through 18.

As the circus worked, city police nosed around the lot, searching for runaways, eyeing the teenaged hands. A detective collared one boy and hauled him away. He'd just signed on in Providence; now he was going back home. The cops were also looking for a runaway from Portland with a history of mental problems. Roy Tuttle, his name was. It didn't mean anything to the men they asked; there were too many transients coming through, and some of the hands prized their anonymity. One man knew his longtime partner on the canvas crew only as Reefer and liked it that way, the fewer questions the better. The cops kept wandering, leaning in to show the picture of Tuttle.

Even more annoying to the men were the towners who turned up to watch them sweat, getting the most out of the show without spending a penny. They saved a special name for these rubes: lot lice.

Meanwhile, out on Barbour Street, Department of Health officials were checking the hot dog and orangeade stands residents had set up on the sidewalk. The North End was solid blue-collar, Italian and Jewish families crammed into three-story tenements. People turned their yards into parking lots for a few extra bucks. It didn't look like the circus was going to make the matinee, and everyone was disappointed, not just the kids.

Downtown, the ambassadors of the circus were taking care of business. Legal adjuster Herbert DuVal called on the superintendent of buildings at city hall and paid the $500 rental fee in cash. John Brice met with Hartford police chief Charles Hallissey and arranged for both uniformed and plainclothes protection on the lot and a traffic detail on Barbour Street. He informed him that the matinee had been canceled because of a detour they had to make leaving Providence.

No one made arrangements with the Hartford Fire Department; neither did the department send anyone to inspect the grounds. Executive officers of the department would later say they could not recall nor produce any records to indicate ever providing protective measures at any circus showing in Hartford over the past thirty years.

Later, Herbert DuVal also met with Chief Hallissey, paying him $300 for a license (two days at $150 each). The form was not dated. It had spaces for whom the license was granted to and for what type of event, where and for what period, but the spaces were left blank. At the very bottom the form said: "Subject to the direction and control of the police department and to the laws and ordinances of the state and city covering such performances." The only ink on the entire thing was the signature of Chief Hallissey. DuVal gave him forty or fifty passes, which he distributed to his associates.

Back on the lot, the ushers were fitting the stands together. Leonard Aylesworth's canvasmen fastened the sidewall around the edges of the top like a curtain. It was not treated with the paraffin mixture, and the upper part could be lowered to let in the breeze. John Brice walked around the outside, making sure the bottom was tied down tight to the stakes so no one could wriggle in for free. If some determined person did, there would be seatmen under the bleachers to catch them.

The tractor or cat drivers were spotting the menagerie wagons, getting them into position to the right of the main entrance. There wasn't room to raise the menagerie top, so they snaked the cages in along the back of the

Philadelphia, June 11th. The big top, fully rigged for the show with spotlights and trapezes. Three animal cages are in place. In Hartford, Alfred Court did not perform, and the center cage was omitted. PHOTO BY ROBERT D. GOOD, COURTESY OF THE CIRCUS WORLD MUSEUM

sideshow tent and circled them with a sidewall. Deacon Blanchfield explained: "You can honeycomb the cages in but you couldn't line them up in their respective order under a top." They "did what's called corralling the menagerie."

At the runs, the performer's section had arrived. They came up on the circus bus and made straight for the cookhouse. With no matinee to get ready for, they stayed in the backyard, writing letters or catching up on wash, hanging their wet clothes on guyropes. Chess was the rage in the dressing tent, and there was always checkers. Some of the "bally" girls from the aerial ballet were knitting. Jugglers and tumblers practiced in the grass. The Wallendas checked their rigging. May and Harry Kovar inspected their cats. The heat was awful and there was nothing to do.

People turned up expecting to be let in. Some had come in special from the outlying towns, driving in or sitting on hot buses, and now they had to tell their kids there was no show. The bosses said they were sorry. Come back tomorrow, they said.

The health inspector poked around the juice joints in the front yard, making sure the orangeade was covered and that they were using paper cups. He'd been waiting all day to check the men's toilet, and finally it went up, a khaki tent just to the right of the main entrance, one wall butted up against the big top. There were three toilets to the right of the door, and a trough like a halved hot water heater for a urinal with solid disinfectants hung from wires. It passed.

Traffic on the lot had been heavy for hours now, the grass crushed and matted. The elephants tromped up dust, and a crew went around spreading wood shavings, followed by a water truck trailing thin, even streams from its sprinkler bar, darkening the ground. The layer of mud created was so thin it would stick to your shoe and leave a perfect footprint of dust behind.

At 3:45 Charles Hayes the building inspector returned as promised and found work progressing on the big tent. He stayed for about an hour, walking the track around the rings, checking the bleacher sections at the ends. When he left, everything wasn't complete, but he was "satisfied that the erection of the tent, construction of seats and exits complied as in previous years." There was nothing unusual, nothing new that he could see.

. . .

The big top as it stood June 30th, 1944, in Portland, Maine.
PHOTO BY MAURICE ALLAIRE, COURTESY OF MR. ALLAIRE HIMSELF

The circus missing its show was front-page news. Just the circus being in town was front-page news. In the age of radio, during a war that limited not just travel but the everyday amenities, the circus was a diversion all of Hartford looked forward to, a hardy perennial. The *Times* and the *Courant* gave it space, aping the stories they'd received from publicist Roland Butler's pressbook. The band was all brass this year, the oompah of the tubas replaced by the much classier, more exotic Bayreuth tuben—invented, Robert Ringling said, by Richard Wagner himself.

The ballyhoo was unnecessary. Hartford had always loved the circus. The first, Rickett's Equestrian Circus, had shown here in 1795; the first elephant in 1826, for a steep 12½ cents. P. T. Barnum exhibited his Wild Men of Borneo in 1855. For the rest of the century Hartford was considered Barnum territory, being so close to Bridgeport, but there was room and time for Dan Rice's Circus and Melville's Australian Circus and Nixon's Royal Circus and Old John Robinson's Circus and the Hippozoonomadon Circus and Nathan's Big Bonanza Circus and the Great Forepaugh Show and even Buffalo Bill's Wild West Show. Hartford had seen Jumbo and the Sacred White Elephant and Barnum's $25,000 Behemoth Monster Hippopotamus; they'd seen Grizzly Adams in his cage of bears and Tom Thumb and Alice Montague the $10,000 Beauty and Chang the Chinese Giant and Zip the What Is It? and come back for more.

Tickets were on sale at McCoy's Music Store, 89 Asylum Avenue, and at the circus grounds—at "Popular Prices," the ads bragged. The cheaper grandstand tickets were $1.20, the most expensive $2.20. And the bond campaign was still on, a $100 bond entitling the buyer to excellent seats.

Mildred Cook bought four reserved tickets for Thursday's matinee, one for herself and one for each of her three children. She and her husband had separated, and the children were living with her brother and his wife back in their hometown of Southampton, Massachusetts. She figured Donald and Eleanor and Edward needed a stable home with two parents. Mildred worked two jobs—days as a claims adjustor at Liberty Mutual insurance and part-time as a housekeeper at the Hartford seminary—and rarely had time off. She'd invited the children down, and the circus was part of the lure.

They'd come down earlier in the week. Wednesday the four of them

went to the duckpin lanes on Farmington Avenue and then to Church Hill

Park in Newington. While they were there, another little girl drowned. The lifeguards lifted the body out of the pool and laid it on the hot concrete in front of everyone. The next morning Eleanor Cook, who was eight, would write her aunt Marion Parsons: "Dear Mom, We are getting ready to go to the circus now. When we were at Newington a girl got drowned. We just got to the bus in time." Tonight, though, Mildred Cook just wanted to get her children dinner and forget all about it. The circus would help.

The evening show went on as scheduled. The crowd was large, partly due to the matinee's cancellation. Hartford police detective Thomas Barber drew his usual assignment, mingling with the midway crowd and keeping an eye out for pickpockets. Barber was a widower and a single father—an anomaly for the time. His daughter Gloria watched the two boys while he worked the night shift. On Monday she was getting married; her fiancé Orville Vieth was in the service and shipping out, so she'd still be home to help, but the war would be over soon and he'd be left with the boys. His youngest, Harry, was supposed to go to the circus with his uncle Boots tomorrow, and Barber had taken the day shift so they'd be at the same show.

As the performance started, the lighted midway cleared out, and Thomas Barber noticed fellow detective William Dineen waiting by the marquee. MAIN ENTRANCE, it said. THE GREATEST SHOW ON EARTH. They passed through the iron railings leading to the ticket boxes, flashing their badges at the sellers. It was even warmer inside, the scent of so many people and animals cloying. The kids were in shorts, and Barber was hot in his jacket. The two stood there in the shadows between the bleachers, hands folded in front of them, watching the crowd, only peripherally taking in the show. At the rear entrance by the bandstand stood another pair of detectives doing the same.

The Wallendas got the biggest hand, according to the morning *Courant,* wowing the crowd with their three-level pyramid—Karl Wallenda and Joe Geiger riding bicycles across the wire, a pole between them on which Herman Wallenda stood on a teetering chair, and atop his shoulders, arms out wide, Karl's wife Helen. The clown firehouse, an old favorite, garnered the most laughs, Emmett Kelly standing by dolefully while Lou Jacobs and his crew of buffoons squeezed out of a miniature red convertible and ran around frantically, menacing the front rows with hoses and buckets full of—it turned out—confetti.

Philadelphia, June 11th. The Panto's Paradise spec plays to a packed house. Note the Wallendas' bicycles and chair hung from the platform to the right above center ring.
PHOTO BY ROBERT D. GOOD, COURTESY OF THE CIRCUS WORLD MUSEUM

The show ended with the big spec—The Changing of the Guard—the elephants, their handlers and the bally girls done up in plaid like Highlanders. The crowd jostled their way down the stands and out into the midway again, satisfied, then back to Barbour Street to wait for the bus or, if they were lucky, to retrieve their cars from whatever lots they could find. It was still the war, their headlights just eyelike slits in layers of blackout paint as they crawled along the dark streets. Soon the midway emptied of customers, the PA speakers clicked off, the lights died. From the air, enemy bombers would see nothing more than what had been there this morning—an empty field.

Anna Cote would go to the circus the next day with her sister Iva. That night the two of them were sleeping when Anna woke up and saw a man standing on the steps to their parents' room. She huddled closer to Iva. The man looked at her and said, "Don't be afraid," then disappeared. When she described the man, her father knew who it was—his father, long dead.

July 6, 1944

Circus day

A month after D-day, the city woke to the radio: WTIC, property of the Travelers, broadcasting from "the Insurance Capital of the World"; WTHT, owned by the *Hartford Times;* and WDRC, the Doolittle Radio Corporation, which had ties to the *Courant.* Among the war news and ball scores, spots for the circus greeted first-shift workers heading off to Colt's and Royal Underwood Typewriters and Fuller Brush, and to Pratt & Whitney and Hamilton Standard and Sikorsky, all part of United Aircraft in East Hartford.

There were so many people working at the Aircraft that the city's population had grown beyond its housing capacity. Residents were renting out sheds and garages and getting good money for them. Relatives doubled up; lodgers on different shifts split the cost of a single room. The new population was unattached and making good wages, and social workers worried about the rise in prostitution and syphilis. With so many fathers and brothers and husbands off at the war, more women were working, leaving their older children alone or in the care of aunts and grandmothers.

The government discouraged absenteeism, a growing problem, especially now when the country was so close to victory. Most people with war work didn't give the circus a second thought. And it was going to be scorching; at 8:30 Thursday morning it was already seventy-six degrees, the humidity even worse than yesterday. People coming off graveyard shift would have trouble sleeping, the sheets sticking to their skin.

The kids who'd seen the posters around town didn't care about the heat. Today was the last day. For months their parents had been promising to take them, and now they called them on it.

On the lot, a water truck chugged up the midway, sprinkling the matted, dusty grass. The concessionaires had eaten breakfast and were tending their Kewpie dolls and fake lion-tamer whips. Even as they readied the front yard for the crowd, the roughnecks were counting the hours till teardown. Already, department heads were preparing for the next stand. Leonard Aylesworth, the boss canvasman, gathered a stake crew and headed for Springfield to start laying out tomorrow's lot.

In Middletown, the four Norris and Smith girls piled into the back of the Norrises' big black Oldsmobile sedan. It was a '41, one of the last made before the war. Michael Norris drove, his wife Eva beside him, Mae Smith against the door. The families had lived up and down in a duplex together, but a year or so ago the Norrises had moved out after a fire on their sunporch. Michael Norris, a circus fan, had been planning the trip since the dates were announced; he'd taken a half day from his job as proprietor of the Russell Company's company store to take everyone to the show.

In back, the Smith girls were dressed for the weather—twelve-year-old Barbara in shorts and a sleeveless top, six-year-old Mary Kay in a sunsuit. People often mistook Mary Kay for Judy Norris, with their dark brown hair the same length; even their faces looked the same straight on. Agnes Norris was slightly older, and still sickly from an early kidney condition. The drive was about an hour. They rolled the windows open for some air.

At the same time the Norrises and Smiths were coming up Route 9, an even larger group from Middletown was getting ready. The Kurneta and Erickson clans were related through marriage but close as blood. Eight of them were supposed to go, but Joann Erickson had a summer cold and her mother stayed home to take care of her. Nineteen-year-old Mary Kurneta took a day off to go—as did her older brother Stanley, to see the circus with his son Tony, their mother Mrs. Frances Kurneta, niece Betsy Kurneta and nephew Raymond Erickson, six. Before they left, Raymond broke his shoelace. His mother tied a knot in it and tucked the knot inside his sneaker so it looked right. She waved them away, then went back inside to tend to Joann.

By 10:00 A.M. the temperature in Hartford had reached the eighties. People who'd been mulling over going now decided maybe an air-conditioned movie was a better choice. One grandmother declared it was simply too warm for walking.

On Grandview Terrace, six nephews and nieces of State Police commissioner Edward J. Hickey waited impatiently for the big black Cadillac of his driver Sgt. Adolph Pastore to pick them up. Sergeant Pastore and

Commissioner Hickey had been together many years, and the children considered the sergeant another uncle. They loved the stately car, always polished, and secretly nicknamed the commissioner "185," after the Caddy's license plate number. The press called the former detective "Bull" Hickey, for his stocky build and legendary tenacity. A perfectionist, he'd worked his way from mailman to Pinkerton detective to naval intelligence officer to state trooper, county detective and finally state police commissioner, solving hundreds of cases from petty theft to capital murder, sending cop-killer Gerald Chapman to the gallows and blowing the Waterbury Conspiracy wide open. For the children it was enough to know Old 185 would be waiting for them at their aunt Isabel and cousin Billy Hickey's house on Barbour Street, close by the circus grounds.

In East Hartford, ten-year-old Donald Gale was kicking around Mayberry Village when Hulda Grant, a friend of his mother's, asked if he wanted to come along to the circus with her boyfriend and her daughter Caroline. Sure, Donald said, but first he needed to check with his parents. His father worked third shift at Pratt & Whitney, and Donald had to wake him up and then beg him, please. It worked.

At Fafnir Bearing Company in New Britain, one woman received a call from her mother. She and her father had just been invited to the circus by their neighbor, whose daughter was an aerialist with the show. Did she want to come too? In minutes the woman had contracted a mysterious illness and was given permission to leave work.

Bill Curlee was originally from Hartford but was working in Cleveland as an inspector for one of Pratt & Whitney's vendors. He'd saved his gas ration stamps to come back east and visit his family. He and his brother-in-law were going to take their children and some neighborhood kids to the circus. He was a big fellow, always joking around. He was lounging precariously on the porch rail that morning, making his mother nervous. "You don't get off of that thing," she scolded, "I'll send you home in a coffin."

The sun was high now and the humidity didn't seem to be dropping. The streets baked, tar gone soft. Shortly before noon Hartford Hospital received its first case of heat prostration, a thirty-seven-year-old man overcome on the job. On the lot, the water truck was supposed to sprinkle the midway one last time around noon, but things were running late so they skipped it.

The normal use for the four Mack water trucks.
PHOTO COURTESY OF THE CIRCUS WORLD MUSEUM

In the backyard, fourteen-year-old John Stewart of Barbour Street supervised a crew of North End boys hauling hay for the horses and elephants. It was dirty work but fun once a year, and they'd promised him six passes. John Stewart made the most of the job. He lorded his authority over his employees, a real straw boss.

Doors would open at 1:00, giving seven-year-old Elliott Smith and his mother and sister Joan time to shop at Brown Thomson downtown. Grace Smith bought two pieces of summer-weight material for dresses she could have never found out in Vernon and was so pleased she treated the children to lunch at Sage-Allen's cafeteria. Elliott was a fussy eater, and the menu didn't include peanut-butter-and-jelly sandwiches, so his mother suggested English muffins. It was the first time either he or Joan had had them. They finished in time to catch the North Main Street bus up to Barbour Street.

Some survivors remember taking trolleys that day, possibly because Hartford had only recently gotten rid of them, the last one running in July of 1941. By '44 all traces of them were gone. The city tore up the tracks, took the overhead wires down and shipped the iron poles to Baltimore and other cities that needed them. They stripped and then torched the old cars, salvaging the steel. Private citizens bought a few lucky ones and turned them into chicken coops, hauled them across the city to be used as diners or down to the shore for beach cottages.

It was all new buses now. People coming from out of town had to change at the Isle of Safety at State and Main by the Old State House. Nine-year-old Edward Garrison and his grandmother, aunt and two cousins boarded a bus on Burnside Avenue in East Hartford with two sailors. When they changed at the Isle of Safety, the sailors followed them on.

Eighteen-year-old Spencer Torell also worked for Fafnir Bearing, on graveyard, as a parts-in-process inspector. He and his friend Wally Carlson took the bus in from New Britain. At the Isle of Safety they transferred to a trailer coach, a wartime invention. Since industry had stopped making new cars for the duration, car carriers were obsolete. The Connecticut Company modified them, enclosing the trailers and adding benches for seats, even pot-bellied stoves for heat in winter. The one flaw was that, being a two-piece combination of a cab and a trailer, a trailer coach required two workers: a driver to drive and a conductor to collect fares. Today they were running expresses up to the circus grounds without conductors.

The aisles were full, and people waiting at stops farther up Main watched as bus after bus passed them by. There was still time though, and it really was much too hot to walk.

Mildred Cook and her children finally caught a bus and were lucky enough to get seats. Don hung his elbow out the window and watched the unfamiliar three-deckers of the North End slide by. Southampton was a quiet little New England village, and just the sheer number of people—the sprawl and chaos of the city—intimidated him. Everyone was sweating, the air ripe, a real body to it. It was sweltering, and the breeze stopped dead every time they missed a light.

Mabel Epps from Bellevue Square had to convince her sister Maurice Goff to go. Mabel was seven months pregnant and needed help looking after her boys, William, seven, and Richard, three. And Maurice's daughter Muriel wanted to go, so the five of them went. It would be the children's first visit to the circus.

Despite gas rationing, many people drove. From the street you could see the sideshow tent with its three flags flapping on high, and behind it the massive big top. The sidewalks overflowed, kids scampering off the curb to slip ahead. Neighborhood teenagers guided cars into the yards, collecting 50 cents for the afternoon, $1 for all day. Mrs. Dewey Howrigan at 386 Barbour Street had a full lot in her long backyard, thirty at least. Some people parked their cars at McGovern's, joking about the nameless gravestones. The Norrises chose the closest lot, a house right near the grounds. The girls piled out of the backseat, squealing, all but Barbara Smith, the oldest, who'd had to cut short a Girl Scout outing. She wasn't thrilled with going and quietly let everyone know it.

The orangeade and frankfurt stands on the sidewalk were doing a land-office business, underselling the official versions inside, but enough people bellied up to the Midway Diner and the other grease and grab joints to keep the circus happy. The midway was mobbed with mothers in linen print dresses, girls in pinafores, boys in knickers, even a few elderly gentlemen with their jackets folded over their arms, hats in hand. Lines ran deep at the white, yellow and red ticket wagons.

Robert Onorato from Plainville was a shutterbug. He had one reel of 16mm color film left, and his son's birthday was coming up, but he decided he'd only have one chance to shoot the circus. He took a long shot of the big top and then wandered about the crowd, catching the wagons and the hot-dog stands and people milling in front of the marquee.

The bug men were out with their boards, hawking chameleons on string leashes for 50 cents. Comedian Charles Nelson Reilly, who grew up on Vine Street, remembered buying one. Hulda Grant bought one for Donald Gale. It was supposed to turn the color of your shirt. Donald checked after a few seconds; the lizard wasn't doing much.

There was everything to buy: pink balls of candy floss bigger than kids' heads and candy apples so sweet they made one's teeth ache, striped boxes of popcorn and bags of peanuts, and the big seller today, ice cream fished from a Borden's truck, wisps of clouds licking out the door. There were balloons and circus pennants and buttons and pictures of the sideshow and big-top stars, miniature sombreros and monkeys on a stick—but only if children could convince their mothers or fathers or aunts or grandmothers to buy one for them.

Mildred Cook didn't have a lot of extra money to buy things, and Donald and Eleanor and Edward knew it. She bought them two bags of popcorn to share between the three of them.

"More than an hour's time is given patrons before the performance begins to visit the Mammoth Menagerie and the International Congress of Freaks," the program boasted. Being a Sunday School show, Ringling Bros. and Barnum & Bailey had none of the lucrative games of chance less reputable circuses and carnivals made the staples of their midways. There were no sharps playing the nuts (the old shell game) or tossing the broads (three-card monte). There were no mitt readers or palmists, no peelers or cooch shows, only the sideshow panels shifting in the breeze, the spielers dealing out their patter on the bally platform, the ticket takers lazing in the shade of their umbrellas.

Even their sideshow was tame compared to some of the truck shows. There were no gruesome oddities like giant Amazonian rats or double-headed fetuses in jars. The freaks on exhibit that season—once the spieler enticed folks to give up their money and enter the tent—were decidedly traditional, not shocking at all: Mr. and Mrs. Fischer the giant and giantess; Baby Thelma the fat girl; Rasmus Neilsen the tattooed strongman. Anyone—like William Epps—who paid to circle the hot interior and gawk up at them on their raised stages must have felt taken. Yes, Percy Pape was

Tattooed strongman Rasmus Neilsen wows them on the bally platform.
PHOTO COURTESY OF THE CIRCUS WORLD MUSEUM

tall and gaunt, and Frieda Pushnik the armless and legless girl might upset some younger children, but Hanka Kelta the long-haired girl was hardly remarkable, and the troubadours, midgets and minstrels were frankly old hat.

The menagerie was much more interesting. Guests elbowed into the marquee and took a right through a roofed opening show folks called the connection. Even before they reached the ticket taker, the smell of elephant dung hit them.

Hard by the connection stood the air-conditioned wagons of Gargantua and M'Toto under their own small canopy, surrounded by children and their parents. Circus publicity touted Gargy as the largest gorilla ever exhibited (doubtful) and the most famous animal since Jumbo (quite possibly true). His lack of romantic interest in his bride and his love of Coca-Cola were common knowledge. According to show lore, he hated humans, the permanent sneer on his face the result of a keeper's cruelty. He reportedly crippled several trainers and nearly strangled John Ringling North, who once unwittingly stepped too close to his barred cage in winter quarters. The Carrier Corporation had built his new cage with double panes of glass that kept the interior "jungle-conditioned" at seventy-six degrees and 50 percent humidity and had the added advantage of stopping Gargy's old trick of peeing into his hands and then tossing it through the bars at the customers.

In Hartford that afternoon condensation fogged the glass, making it

Lions in their menagerie cage wagons, Portland, Maine, June 30th, 1944. PHOTO BY MAURICE ALLAIRE, COURTESY OF MR. ALLAIRE HIMSELF

The sidewalled menagerie in Hartford the day of the fire. The house in the background is 353 Barbour Street; the flag to the right crowns a peak of the sideshow top. PHOTO COURTESY OF THE *HARTFORD COURANT*

hard to see, but he was in there all right. Gargantua the Great, The World's Most Terrifying Living Creature, The Largest and Fiercest Gorilla Ever Brought Before the Eyes of Civilized Man, was on his back by the tire he sometimes played with, sacked out like a hound dog.

The sun welcomed visitors to the menagerie proper, making them squint. The ground inside was strewn with wood shavings to keep the dust down. Beyond the white canvas corral of sidewall, just south of the big top, a diesel generator drummed, its rich fumes combining with the smell of crushed grass and the dung and musk of the animals.

The elephants drew people to the middle, the big cats and black bears and lesser monkeys in their wagons strung along the back wall of the sideshow tent on one side and the big top on the other, just outside the stake line. Numbering an even thirty, the herd was still formidable. Reeking, the massive beasts stood on a carpet of hay, flicking their thin ears, occasionally shoveling in a mouthful with their trunks. A single rope strung between bent metal stakes separated them from the crowd, and children lined up to warily offer them peanuts, marveling when their palms came away wet.

Betty Lou, the pygmy hippo who survived the Cleveland fire, wallowed contentedly in her bathing tank. She'd become a darling of the cageboys, who secretly slipped her her favorite treat, chocolate. In fact, most of the animals in the menagerie were survivors of the Cleveland fire. Edith the giraffe over at the far end by McGovern's was the one who'd come dashing out of the front entrance. Beside her cage, a half-dozen brand-new camels sat in their hay, oblivious of history.

Showtime

It was almost 2:00, and people started thinking of going in, patting their pockets and searching their purses for their tickets. As hot as it was in the sun, it would be worse under the big top, sardined into the seats and bleachers shoulder to shoulder and hip to hip.

Out on the midway, one family was about to head in when the mother suddenly faltered, bent over and fell to the ground. Something was wrong with her legs; she couldn't move them. The woman's husband tried to help her up but her legs wouldn't respond. They had to find a doctor. He picked her up and carried her back to the car. She wouldn't regain the use of her legs for a year.

Another woman from East Hartford had taken her three-year-old nephew. She'd brought the boy into the sideshow with her and naturally the performers scared the toddler. She tried to quiet him with ice cream and orangeade, but the child would not stop crying. The night before, the woman had dreamed of her dead sister, dressed in black and seated on the bleachers. Though she'd already bought tickets, she returned to the yellow wagon and cashed them in. SAVED BY SIDESHOW FREAKS, the headline screamed the next day.

The lore of the fire is chock-full of these near-miss stories, generally attributed to the hand of providence. For everyone inside the tent that day, there are five who were going to go but somehow didn't end up there. The bus was late or they got off at the wrong stop. Older children took the money with which parents had entrusted them to buy siblings tickets and spent it on ice cream sundaes and war movies and forbidden penny poker games. One woman was going to take her grandchild but, waiting for the bus, remembered she might have left the iron on and went home to check. And of course, afterward, everyone who'd planned on seeing the canceled Wednesday matinee claimed they were saved. Fate, or God, had intervened.

No such presentiments or foresight stopped the crowd now pouring through the marquee, bunching up at the iron pipe railings leading to the ticket takers. Just outside the front door, people with free passes for buying war bonds had to stop at the tax boxes and pay the government its share. Only servicemen in uniform were exempt.

The public toilets, or donickers, were off the main entryway, just past the menagerie connection, the last exit before going in. Boys and older gentlemen who had filled up on Cokes and pink lemonade took a right into an opening in the canvas; girls and women headed left. At the commissioner's inquiry, several men testified that everything in the men's seemed in order—no trash or toilet paper on the ground, just the three toilets and the trough, the overpoweringly sweet creolin disinfectant hanging by its wire. One recalled three empty metal pails by the urinal, but nothing was made of them. The commissioner didn't call any women to hear about their side.

The lines moved steadily, people taking baby steps, kids climbing the pipe railings like monkey bars. Elliott and Joan Smith's mother gave their tickets to the maroon-blazered attendant and they walked between the two blue bleacher sections at the end and into the big tent.

The heat was like a wall; it was stuffier in here, muggier. A black iron cage filled the near ring, another one down at the far end. Poles rose all around them, ropes and rigging hanging like vines, bright lights shining down. The blue quarters were thick as telephone poles and seemed to lean dangerously over the slowly filling stands, each ending in a blue or red star stitched into the tent roof. Elliott and Joan gazed all around as their mother led them along the hippodrome track—a fancy circus term for no more than the lot's natural grass strewn with wood shavings.

Usually frugal, Grace Smith had splurged on reserved seats. They went left, toward the north side of the tent—the six-bit side, it was called. They had to cross a barred iron chute that ran from the round animal cage and between the bleachers and the grandstand, beneath a canvas sign with EXIT in large red letters and outside where the animals waited in their cages. *49*

The chute was taller than Elliott and came up to Grace's chest. They had to climb over a set of wooden stairs five steps high and a yard wide, imagining lions and tigers pacing under their feet. The stairs had no railing, and an attendant took Grace Smith's hand to steady her coming down the other side.

Iron pipe railings fronted the grandstand sections, preventing anyone from the cheaper bleachers from sneaking in, and keeping people off the track during the specs and the clown walkaround. Gatemen perched on camp stools manned the narrow openings. Grace Smith presented their tickets to one. He handed the stubs to an usher inside the railing, and that man guided the Smiths to the proper aisle and led them up the grandstand to their seats.

There were eighteen rows, three of those on the ground before the risers started. The Smiths were about halfway up, in the middle of their sec-

A mother helps her child over the stile across the northwest animal chute. In the background, the southwest blues are jammed. To the left, the last two letters of an EXIT *sign are visible over the southwest exit.* PHOTO BY CARL WALLIS, COURTESY OF THE *HARTFORD COURANT*

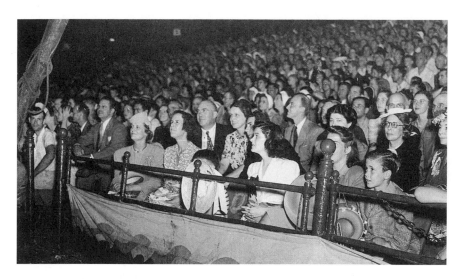

At the foot of a grandstand section, undated evening show. The railings keep the crowd off the track, only the narrow open gateway to the left for access.
PHOTO COURTESY OF THE CIRCUS WORLD MUSEUM

tion. Each row was supposed to have sixteen of the tomato-soup-red wooden folding chairs, but an enterprising usher could overlap them and fit more in, offering the extra premium seats to customers unhappy with their original tickets and then pocketing the difference. As one usher said at the inquest: "Sometimes you can pack them in and get a lot more than an ordinary sitting." Ushers in the best sections—those closest to the center ring—regularly fit in so many chairs per row they would stick out into the aisle. From testimony and the few photos available, it seems on the day of the fire at least some ushers overlapped their chairs.

Finally seated, perspiring freely, Grace Smith flagged a Coke vendor and bought one for each of the children. Elliott lifted the bottle to his lips, but instead of a cold, sugary shock to the teeth, the soda was thin and warm and bitter. He drank it anyway.

The Kurneta-Erickson party from Middletown was also in the north grandstand, farther down, in section S, the fourth row from the top. Stanley Kurneta was pleased. They were great seats, directly in the center and high enough for even the smallest, six-year-old Raymond Erickson, to see everything. The sidewall behind them had been lowered a couple feet, and a breeze dried the sweat on their necks. Around them, men had shed

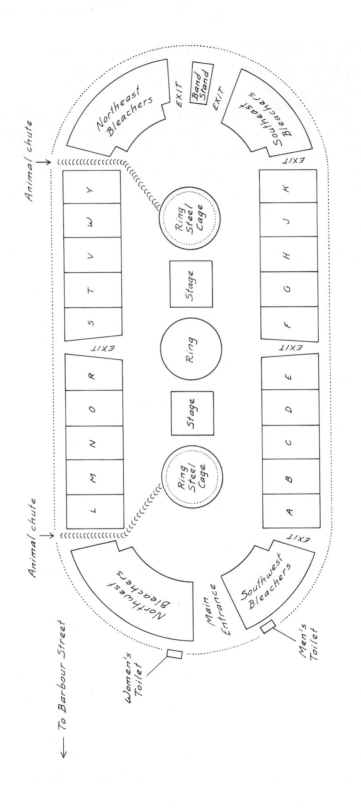

their ties and laid their jackets over their laps. A vendor stalked the aisles, hawking paper fans. Most folks made do with their programs or just one hand.

Donald Gale from East Hartford was here too, after crossing the chute, even farther down toward the bandstand with his neighbor Hulda Grant, her daughter Caroline and the boyfriend. The chameleon he'd bought still wasn't doing much, but now there were the trapeze platforms to look at, the rope ladders, the highwire strung in a half silver, half invisible line above the center ring. He was glad he'd woken up his father, and glad he'd said yes.

Elizabeth de la Vergne was scared of heights. She'd gone with her husband and son and some friends, but when the usher showed them where their seats were, she balked. They were reserved seats; it wasn't like the bleachers, they couldn't just sit anywhere. She was sorry, she said, but she was not sitting all the way up there, she simply couldn't. After a brief discussion, the usher managed to squeeze her into the front row of the section, down on the ground, right by the railing. Her husband and son took their assigned seats up high. She looked back at them and waved.

Mabel Epps and her sister Maurice Goff bought general admission bleacher seats. Once they came in, they could choose between the two sections right there by the main entrance or walk the length of the tent and try one on either side of the bandstand, where the performers entered. Being seven months along, Mabel chose the closest one, the northwest bleachers, just to the left of the front door. William and Richard tagged along after her; Maurice had little Muriel by the hand.

There was no flooring, and they had to climb from seat to seat, carefully placing their feet on the narrow boards, pushing off and catching their balance like the Wallendas. They picked an open spot a few rows from the top and sat down, their legs dangling into empty space beneath them.

The Cooks' tickets were in the south grandstand, a few sections in. They walked the track, on this side free of any chutes. In the exit between the southwest bleachers and the grandstand sat a soldier in a wheelchair. Beside him, filling the first two rows of section A, were a group of twenty or so fellow convalescents from Bradley Field Station Hospital, all in uniform, some wearing slings. Escorted by a Red Cross volunteer, they were recovering from combat injuries—and one of them from a dose of malaria picked up in the South Pacific. The Cooks passed them and then another section before Mildred Cook handed their tickets to the gateman. They sat near the top with a good view of the west animal cage. They'd just gotten themselves settled when Don realized he had to go to the bathroom; luckily they were sitting on the aisle. He gave up the popcorn and headed back toward the main entrance.

The Norrises and Smiths from Middletown were a few sections over from the Cooks, Barbara Smith still gloomy and unimpressed, her sister Mary Kay and Agnes and Judy Norris fidgeting in their chairs. Michael Norris basked in the atmosphere—the cages and rings and stages, sawdust powdering the ground. Propmen were scurrying about, making last-second adjustments. Candy butchers plied the aisles, waving boxes of Cracker Jack. It was definitely worth taking a half day away from the store.

At the east end of the south grandstand, a few reporters in suits and ties dotted the sparsely occupied press section, sweat pouring down their foreheads. Yesterday the circus had been news, but tomorrow the show

Philadelphia. This shot of the Changing of the Guard spec shows the bandstand layout as it was in Hartford—at the east end, raised, with twin exits separating it from the bleachers on both sides. PHOTO COURTESY OF THE CIRCUS WORLD MUSEUM

would be gone, and these unlucky cubs had been stuck with the mop-up assignment.

At the end farthest from the front door, marooned on their eight-foot-high island in the middle of the performers' entrance, Merle Evans and his twenty-nine-piece band waited like the rest of the tent. A few years ago they would have struck up a tune, the horns and drums punchy, almost martial, but the pre-show concert had gone the way of the old living statues act back in 1941.

Merle Evans was circus through and through. He'd briefly been bandmaster for Buffalo Bill with the 101 Ranch Show, and in the twenty-five years since the 1919 merger, the Greatest Show on Earth had known no other conductor. Legend was, he'd never missed a performance, even when hit with ptomaine poisoning. He had a weakness for popcorn, and publicist Roland Butler loved to claim he could play his silver cornet while chewing a mouthful.

One of his favorite stories was from when he was a young man playing the Midwest with a medicine show. Near their gig, a tent revival had set up. After his show, Merle hid in a ditch near the meeting, and when the preacher said, "The world will end when Gabriel blows his mighty horn," he let loose a blast. The sinners knocked over their chairs and ran, the tent coming down right on top of them.

When the show started, Merle Evans would turn away from his windjammers to check with Fred Bradna and watch the rhythm of the acts, conducting with his left hand and playing with his right. Each performance there were more than two hundred cues, many of them split-second and crucial to directing the audience's attention to a new act or away from one just finished. The cat act itself was a quilt of rumbas, fox-trots, marches, cakewalks, vamps—anything that fit the particular movements of the animals. Trickier were the horse acts in which the animals supposedly danced to the music; the illusion actually worked in reverse: the horse led while the band followed. Entrances, exits, segues—they all had to be on the dot. And if something happened, if a liberty horse should stumble and miss a trick or a clown discover a wonderful ad-lib, Merle Evans and the band were there to punctuate or save the bit with some improvisation. Once the show began, they were on alert, but now they were just part of the crowd, bored and hot in their white-and-gold uniforms, passing the time.

Emmett Kelly and Merle Evans tootle a duet; both would prove to be heroes in Hartford.
PHOTO COURTESY OF THE CIRCUS WORLD MUSEUM

Behind the bandstand, in the performers' entrance, or back door, Hartford police officers James Kenefick and Henry Griffin stood guard, detailed to provide that afternoon's protection for the dressing tent.

All the way across the big top, by the front door, Thomas Barber and two other detectives waited with a state parole officer, outwardly joking but all the while scanning the rings for a parole violator who was rumored to be a helper in the cat act. Barber's six-year-old Harry was supposed to be here with his uncle Boots, using free tickets Barber had been given for working the circus—possibly from the same batch Herbert DuVal had given Chief Hallissey—but so far there was no sign of them. The wedding was on his mind; he couldn't help thinking of giving his daughter away. She had kept the family together, stepping in for her mother, and the loss seemed double to him. Mary, now Gloria. Before he knew it the boys would be gone too, and he would be alone. The way of the world, he supposed.

Beside Barber, the two old police chiefs, John Brice and Hallissey, were cutting up jackpots—swapping their favorite stories, telling them better every time.

Outside it was blazing, eighty-eight degrees, anything metal left in the sun painful to touch. An attendant roamed up and down the midway, hollering that the show was going to start in five minutes, and new lines formed at the front door.

Commissioner Edward J. Hickey waited on the porch of his sister-in-law's house on Barbour Street, wondering what was taking Adolph Pastore so long. The residents were cleaning up their orangeade stands, stacking the cups and counting their pennies.

Under the big top, the crowd was restless and loud. Mothers checked their watches; it was past starting time. From the top of the southwest bleachers people could see over the dropped sidewall the menagerie elephants lined up along the fence in front of the victory gardens. Below, straight down between the planks, a full fire bucket sat in the grass. One boy was tossing peanut shucks between his feet, trying to hit the water. A man near him dropped his sunglasses and couldn't catch them in time; they tipped off the shoulder of the person in front of him and fell into the shadows below. Seconds later a hand holding the glasses reached up from beneath, almost giving him a heart attack.

The man under the bleachers was William Caley, seatman. His job was to watch the jacks that held up the stringers and make sure the structure was solid. The bucket was there in case anyone dropped a cigarette and caught the grass on fire or made a glowing pinhole in the sidewall. A pinhole wasn't quite a fire, just the orange embers slowly eating the canvas, spreading like a grease stain. They'd doused a fair-sized one in Providence, no trouble. Occasionally a lady would drop her handbag or a child might lose a souvenir—or like this fellow and his glasses—and Caley would retrieve them. Mostly though, he squatted there among the hundreds of calves hanging down like shod salamis, watching the slow snow of popcorn and trying to avoid getting hit with pop bottles and wads of gum. Compared to Caley's recent experience in the dangerous, sometimes explosive coal mines of Pennsylvania, it was not such a bad job.

The show was going to start, everyone hoped. The band was in position, the rings and stages were clear, but there were still people streaming in. The northwest bleachers where the Eppses and Goffs were sitting were jammed tight, the southwest too, even some kids sitting on the ground out in front. But it wasn't a complete sellout. Though the circus said afterward the reserved tickets had all gone, the very last grandstand sections down at the east end—Y on the north side, K on the south—had rows that were close to half empty.

Most papers nowadays quote the attendance as 6,789, the figure given by circus vice president James Haley at the commissioner's hearing, though

Haley, being relatively new to the show, was consistently sketchy on other details of the setup. Head usher John Carson estimated 6,000, but one longtime local circus expert called it "a sellout, a packed house." Contemporary accounts placed the crowd at somewhere between 4,000 and 10,000. Commissioner Hickey cited 10,048 as capacity "from information and records that were furnished me at my hearing," yet in his testimony General Manager George W. Smith stated that typically with this setup they sold 6,048 grandstand tickets and 3,000 general admission. Smith's math was off on both counts, but just barely. The official physical capacity of the grandstands (twenty sections, eighteen rows, sixteen seats per) was 5,760, the bleachers (thirty-four lengths at one hundred customers per) 3,400, for a total of 9,160. Of course, the house for the Fourth of July Providence show under the same top was widely publicized as a nice, round 10,000, and the Ringling program itself bragged that the World's Largest Tent sat 11,000. One survivor remembered numerous empty reserved seats, with ushers near the center ring selling these at a discount. Another woman in the southeast bleachers thought section K was empty.

The true attendance, like so many other things about the circus fire, will never be known. From the capacity, the few existing photos, and numerous eyewitness accounts, it seems the house that day was near but not quite full, with approximately 5,500 fans in the grandstand and 3,200 on the blues, for a total of 8,700.

All of them were getting impatient in the heat—the children for the show, the parents with the children. As Don Cook returned from the men's room, George W. Smith did one last reconnaissance of the midway. He came back through the front door, past Thomas Barber and chiefs Brice and Hallissey, and gave Fred Bradna the high sign to start the show. It was 2:23 Eastern War Time, only eight minutes late.

Over the PA, the announcer asked the crowd to please stand for our national anthem. As the grandstands rose, the unattached chairs scuffed and squeaked against the risers. All faces turned to the flag, way down at one corner of the bandstand, hanging limp on its pole right beside Merle Evans. The planks of the bleachers were so narrow it was hard to stand on them—especially for pregnant Mabel Epps. At both ends, people sang along with the clear brasses of the band, swaying, knees locked, a hand on the shoulder of those in front of them.

Out on Barbour Street, a man and his son were late. The man swung his car into the sole available parking spot, right across from McGovern's, thinking he was lucky. He'd killed the engine and started rolling up his windows when someone on the sidewalk called, "Hey. Back up. You're too close to that fire hydrant." The man backed up.

Not long behind him came Adolph Pastore in Commissioner Hickey's big black Caddy. From the porch, the commissioner called inside to Isabel, who grabbed Billy. Pastore popped the back door and the kids scrambled out, the whole crew headed up the street, double-time—all but Sergeant Pastore, who stayed with the car. They were late but none of them had eaten; it was for just this reason that the circus strategically placed the grease joints along the midway, the scents of frying wieners and bubbling caramel impossible to ignore. Hickey dug his wallet out and sprang for hot dogs and Cokes all around.

Inside, everyone had sat down, the legs of the chairs protesting again. Fred Bradna strode out in his huntsman's red tailcoat and white jodhpurs and black plug hat and blew his whistle to open the show. Merle Evans cued the band.

Some people remember a clown driving around the track squished into his tiny car, or an endless succession of clowns bounding out of one, but that never happened. Others say that the usual first three acts were canceled because of the threat of bad weather—that's false also.

The show followed the program exactly: "Display 1. Novel and highly amusing introductory presentation in which the art of wild animal training is given a reverse twist. A Frolicsome Forerunner of the Magnificent Display of Perfectly-Schooled Man-killers Which Immediately Follows."

To a flourish of trumpets, a man dressed in a lion suit bounded onto the west stage, follow spots from both sides picking him out. He turned somersaults and prowled the edge of the stage, menacing, jabbing his paws at the crowd. After him came a dozen bally girls made up as lion tamers in skimpy yellow dresses and high boots, their skirts showing a generous length of thigh, their hair tucked severely under black Cossack hats. They circled the lion as he turned, the music murky, dangerous, until with a clash of cymbals the lion produced a whip.

He flung it about his head, feisty as Clyde Beatty himself, running the girls through a number of acrobatic tricks and poses as the crowd laughed and the band broke loose with a goofy vamp. The burlesque was just a short warm-up to catch the crowd's interest and build tension for the real cat act, the shift from silliness to real fear that much more breathtaking.

As the girls were going off to applause, Commissioner Hickey and his brood handed their tickets to the ducat grabber at the front door and went right, along the south side, the children clutching their hot dogs and Cokes. They turned into section G, just past the side exit halfway down, and clumped up the aisle.

The commissioner was surprised to find his dear old friend and associate, former state's attorney Hugh M. Alcorn Sr., also seated in G. Back when Bull Hickey had been county detective, he'd been an expert witness for the prosecution, his memory perfect, and together the two of them had convicted hundreds of suspects. Now Alcorn's son, Hugh Jr., had taken over as state's attorney. Today Alcorn was with another son, Harold—a judge— and his wife and two children. Seeing Hickey was busy, he gave him a wave, figuring they'd catch up later.

Their seats were in row 18, all the way up. Impossibly, it grew hotter as they climbed, until they reached the breeze slipping through the dropped sidewall. As they were shuffling in sideways, trying not to drop their hot dogs or step on their neighbors' feet, the top of Hickey's head bumped the angled canvas of the roof. Finally they were seated and he could eat. A question from down the row: Could the boys take off their T-shirts? The commissioner gave them permission, and they balled up their shirts and stuffed them into the back pockets of their jeans.

Again, Fred Bradna blew his whistle, Merle Evans cued the band, and the announcer introduced the cat act. Those following their programs read some of Roland Butler's typically mellifluous prose: Display 2. Natural jungle enemies educated beyond belief performing together in new and exceptionally exciting exhibitions. Great New Mixed Groups of the Most Treacherous and Ferocious Wild Animals Ever Assembled, Presented Under the Direction of ALFRED COURT, Master Trainer of the Ages. Berber Lions, Abyssinian Lions, Royal Bengal Tigers, Berber Tigers, Siberian Tigers, Polar Bears, Black Bears, Black Jaguars, Sumatran Spotted Leopards, Himalayan Bears, Black Leopards, Pumas, Ocelots, Black Panthers, and Great Dane Dogs.

This was not exactly what they got. The trainers listed in caps at the bottom included May Kovar, Joseph Walsh and Harry Kovar, but May's husband wasn't working today. When the show opened in New York, they'd shown three cages of animals, but since leaving the big arenas they'd cut back to two and Alfred Court hadn't performed. He was sixty-one and not as strong as he'd once been. Damoo Dhotre, his number one understudy, was off in the army. Court's specialty was mixing species that were natural foes, a very risky business. He'd never been hurt in the ring, but the trainers who worked under him sometimes weren't as lucky.

The year before, May Kovar had been badly mauled at Boston Garden by a jaguar. In the middle of her mixed act of jags and leopards, one leapt from his perch, going for her throat. Equipped with just a light bamboo wand, she fended him off with one arm. The crowd thought it was part of the show. Only when he backed off and charged again, snarling, ripping her costume, did they scream. The jag knocked her backwards, digging its claws into her chest. By then, attendants entered the cage and drove the cat back with clubs, but May Kovar would need dozens of stitches. It was the second time that season she'd been attacked, the first during a practice ses-

Trainer May Kovar shows off her closer—the same used by Gunther Gebel-Williams decades later. PHOTO COURTESY OF THE CIRCUS WORLD MUSEUM

sion at Madison Square Garden. A trouper, she saw the circus doctor and made the late show, replacing the bad jag with one from the menagerie and playing with her arm bandaged.

While the circus pushed May Kovar as exotic and glamorous, she was just one of several women trainers following in the tradition of the great Mabel Stark. For years Harriet Beatty had trained cats alongside her more famous husband, and this season Dolly Jacobs regularly stepped into the cage for the pick-up Victory Circus. May Kovar was not as well known as either of them, partly because, being English, she'd been working in Europe and had only recently come over. Today, as the announcer boomed to the crowd, she would be in the west cage with her small cats and Joseph Walsh in the east cage with his bears and lions and Great Danes.

As the handlers prodded the leopards and panthers and pumas through the northwest chute, Thomas Barber watched them, trying to match a face to that of the picture the parole officer had passed around. As each cat came in, a handler slid a board through the chute so it couldn't back up, separating it from the one behind. When the lead cat moved for-

May Kovar in action in Philadelphia, June 11th. She wore the same outfit in Hartford and used the same short wand. PHOTO COURTESY OF THE CIRCUS WORLD MUSEUM

ward, the handlers lifted the boards and the rest moved up. To cover the progression, a bear lumbered out from the entrance between the north grandstands and into the center ring on its hind legs, guzzling a bottle of milk and stumbling around as if drunk as the band played a wobbly melody. The crowd ate it up yet never fully took their eyes off the cats, wondering what would happen if Walsh's bears and dogs and lions got into it.

The acts were mostly posing, the animals changing places, moving from perch to perch in measured steps. Walsh's Great Danes were in the east cage very briefly, pretending to herd the lions onto their various stands before going through the chute to a relieved hand from the crowd. The polar bears, black bears and lions did nip-ups together in pyramids, sitting erect on their haunches, front legs up and pressed to their chests as if begging. Walsh sent the bears off—more applause—then set to work with just six lions.

In the west cage, May Kovar wasn't alone. Standing by the junction of the chute and the cage proper, an assistant waited to send the cats off when she was done with them. All told she had fifteen, the choreographed routine breaking them into different pyramids, running them up and down the perches, the tallest of which was twelve feet high. The cats hissed and bared their teeth at one another as she maneuvered them through their paces, armed with just her trusty wand.

Though the two cat acts received equal billing, Walsh's, with its big cats and audacious combination of different species, was tacitly featured. May Kovar finished first and then waited as he wrapped up the lion act with his third pyramid, kneeling gingerly astride a lion while the other five held their poses above him.

Hartford police officer George Sanford, on the south side of the tent, had the day off and decided to take the family. He had his 8mm movie camera rolling as the cat acts closed, hoping to catch something special.

Under the front end blues, John Cook had joined William Caley. Cook was a First of May—a greenie in his first season with the show—and had just been given the position of seatman; today was his first day. Before this he'd been a stakeman, driving stakes for the big top, and was now laboring under the misapprehension that his new job consisted mainly of stopping kids from sneaking in. No one had told him to look out for fires.

Just before the end of the cat act, Caley left his position under the

May Kovar's assistant stands just inside the northwest chute during her act in Hartford. She can barely be made out over his left shoulder. Note the boards tipped against the chute. The woman in the foreground is most likely watching Joseph Walsh and his lions.
PHOTO BY CARL WALLIS, COURTESY OF THE *HARTFORD COURANT*

Joseph Walsh's last pyramid in the east cage—his big finale. Section Y, in the background under the belly of the rightmost lion, is partly empty. This was taken a minute or so before the fire broke out. Rescue workers later discovered most of the dead piled at the corner of section Y's railing and the northeast chute. PHOTO BY SPENCER TORELL, COURTESY OF THE CIRCUS WORLD MUSEUM

bleachers, Cook following him across to the northwest blues. They stood there between the bleachers and the chute, waiting for the cat act to break. As a rigger, Caley needed to watch the propmen tear down the chutes and make sure they didn't bump the jacks as they dragged the heavy sections out. Cook officially had no business here, but with manpower short the propmen were understaffed and paid 50 cents to anyone who would lend a hand.

Kneeling in the east cage, Walsh had the cats hold their pose until the applause had peaked. Merle Evans switched tunes, and Walsh stood and took his bows. The spots in the west end caught May Kovar. She acknowledged the applause in all four directions, smiling wide.

As the ovation disintegrated, the lights dimmed, and in the dusk the announcer introduced the Wallendas, world famous yet still touted in the program as if they needed the publicity: "The Last Word In High Wire Thrillers. New, Hazardous and Hair Raising Feats By World Acclaimed Artists Who Shake Dice With Death At Dizzy Heights."

A beam captured a group of four above the center ring in their leotards, the last still hustling up the rope ladder hanging from the north platform thirty feet up—Helen, Henrietta and Herman Wallenda and Joe

The Wallendas finish with their three-tier pyramid in Madison Square Garden earlier that season. In Hartford, they never got the chance. PHOTO COURTESY OF THE CIRCUS WORLD MUSEUM

Geiger. With them they had three long balancing poles, a specially designed chair and a bicycle with wheel rims designed to cup the wire and no handlebars. Karl Wallenda waited on the opposite platform with a similar bicycle. The heat of the tent had gathered here near the peak. The wire was temperature sensitive, and Karl checked the tension with one foot. Merle Evans and the band started the first bars of the lilting waltz from Gounod's *Faust.*

Afterward, witnesses would come forward and claim they saw strange things here. One man high in the southwest bleachers noticed dark pieces of broken glass—possibly from a Coke bottle—lying on top of the canvas above him. A woman not far from him saw two birds walking on the tent.

Outside, a motorist driving by on Barbour slowed and stole a glance at the big top, only to see "a shimmering appearance such as the sun on frost. It was not fire. At the top of the tent there was a haze that looked like heat waves, appeared like heat rising from pavement. It was not smoke."

Not all of these last-second stories were bizarre. One man sitting near the top of section A said he'd smelled rags burning. He looked out over the sidewall and noticed smoke rising between the elephants and the houses on Barbour Street. He thought someone was burning papers and had a rag among their rubbish and paid no more attention to it. Another man in the bleachers beside him smelled "something like paper burning."

A vendor went through the aisles waving a fistful of paper fans, chanting, "It's going to get hotter and hotter." At the foot of the southwest bleachers a Coca-Cola vendor was stopped, making change for the crowd around him, his tray jutting from his waist like a cigarette girl's.

The waltz went on. High above center ring, Herman and Karl Wallenda carefully placed the front wheels of their bicycles on the wire. Below, already forgotten, May Kovar sent her cats through the chute one by one, the cageboy prodding them on, propmen working the boards. Joseph Walsh broke down his last pyramid, the lions leaving their perches like clockwork.

· · ·

It's rare that people witness the beginning of any fire, even in a crowded place. Accidental fires, by their very nature, are always sudden, unexpected events, and catch people unawares. They can't be anticipated and therefore initially elude detection by the simple mechanism of surprise.

Psychologists who have studied disasters talk about the difficulty of breaking out of patterned behavior and responding to a new situation. One natural reaction to a fire is to flee, yet often people will look right at a fire and not register the information, simply because their minds are on some other task or caught up with some other expectation.

One surveillance videotape from England shows a small fire near the entrance of a corner shop, set by petty thieves as a distraction; while the flames jump from a foot high and then up to the ceiling, customers calmly walk in, select their merchandise and stand in line by the register, some even pointedly glancing over at the fire yet doing nothing. Only after two customers notice they've both marked the blaze—agreeing by a nod that it does in reality exist—do they alert the clerk. Though no one was hurt, the shop burned to the ground.

. . .

On the sidewall behind the southwest bleachers, a flame sprang up. Absolutely new and therefore invisible, unnoticed for a few precious seconds.

The fire was small at first, about the size of a silver dollar, depending on who you talked to. Nearly everyone who was there that day would claim they were the first to see it. As with the Cocoanut Grove even the people closest to the point of origin disagreed as to precisely where it was, either on the sidewall or the roof.

The fire was the size of a baseball, a football, a basketball, a dishpan, a briefcase, a small window, half a tablecloth. It was circular, it was triangular, it was shaped like a horseshoe.

One thing people agreed on was that it was small at first, so small that most people beyond that corner of the tent didn't see it. Detective Paul Beckwith, standing beside Thomas Barber, saw it beginning. "I remained silent," he said later, "hoping that no one else would notice the flame before it was extinguished, as I had no doubt that it would at that time. I had every confidence it would be put out."

The detective's lack of reaction fits with the rigidity of patterned behavior. He was there to catch a parole violator and was working hard at staving off all distractions. Once he realized there was a fire, he assumed someone else would put it out—an irrational assumption psychologists say is shared by most of us (not having the means ourselves of stopping a fire), but one which a police detective, trained to respond to emergencies, would be more likely to overcome.

Across from the detective, a girl in the bleachers felt heat behind her and turned around. She turned back to her mother and asked if the tent was supposed to be on fire.

An usher in front of the bleachers saw the blaze and pointed toward it—as did a man coming back up the bleachers with a Coke he'd just bought from the vendor. Pointing with his bottle, the man yelled, "Fire."

Some twisted around to see, but most people kept their eyes glued to the Wallendas high up in the spotlights. They didn't want to miss one second of their death-defying act.

The point of origin

The fire was still on the untreated sidewall behind the southwest blues, directly in the center, right where the men's toilet abutted the big top, about six feet off the ground. It hadn't involved the roof yet. There was a chance if people got water on it, they could stop it here.

A trio of ushers from the north side cut behind the bleachers and grabbed the fire buckets underneath. There were four in all; each held four gallons of water, filled before every performance by a guy named Chief. The buckets were full. The first usher there hefted one and chucked it, the water splashing across the bottom of the flames.

It did nothing.

The fire was at eye level, a yard wide and five feet high. Another usher tried one bucket, then another. The third usher threw the last one, but the fire was out of reach now. They tried to pull down the sidewall. It was too late; the flames were eating the roof, finding fuel. All they could do now was help the people at that end get out.

The blues right by the fire had already started to clear. Anna Cote remembered: "I looked up to the right over my shoulder and saw the fire. By the time I turned back around my sister and her girlfriend were gone."

The Wallendas' concentration was locked on their pyramid, the waltz playing softly so as not to startle them and upset their timing. With one wheel of the bike on the wire, Karl sensed the commotion below. From his vantage point he saw the flames creeping up behind the bleachers. Just as Henrietta on the far platform said, "Look," he signaled the others down.

Merle Evans, alert for the slightest deviation in the program, saw Karl's signal, followed where Henrietta was pointing and spotted the flames. He stopped the waltz with a flick of one hand.

From the east end, even from the north side, the fire seemed tiny, "a little ray of light across the tent." There was a moment of stunned surprise, but many in attendance had the same reaction as Detective Beckwith.

In the bleachers right across from it, William Epps said, "Look, Ma, there's a fire over there."

"Don't worry," Mabel Epps said, "they'll put it out."

Surely some circus person would come up with an extinguisher and snuff it. Yet it continued to burn.

Others thought it was part of the show, some kind of joke or surprise. Again, many failed to respond to what they could clearly see, trapped in their own anticipation of the show. They had come to see the circus, so this must be part of it. With no external cues or guidance, they fell back on their original, very narrow goals. Their failure to break out of their routine, despite evidence to the contrary, mirrors the behavior of the crowd at the Beverly Hills Supper Club in Cincinnati in 1977. Though a busboy came out on stage well before that fire had spread and used a microphone to tell everyone to leave, only a few did. They thought the warning was part of the opening comedian's act. One hundred sixty-four people died.

At the far end of the tent, Merle Evans knew the fire wasn't a joke, and he could see Joseph Walsh still had cats in his cage. Evans leaned over the bandstand and yelled to Fred Bradna, "Get those lions out—the tent's on fire."

Bradna saw the smoke by the front door and immediately whistled, calling the Wallendas down and alerting the others. His wife Ella headlined one of the equestrian acts coming up next; he ran for the back door to warn her.

Merle Evans cued the band and they struck up the disaster march, Sousa's "The Stars and Stripes Forever," a signal to show folks that something had gone seriously wrong. Evans chose the tune because every musician knew it by heart. The rest of the tent had no clue.

A policeman at the west end hollered at the exiting bleacher crowd, "Be calm. Walk slowly." Most were. A man halfway up with a boy shouted, "That dirty son of a bitch just threw a cigarette butt!" He dropped the boy over the side to the officer and jumped. "It was a cigarette," the man said, and ran off, the boy in tow.

One of the Wallendas' bikes fell and bounced off the sawdust.

The flames leapt up the roof, and now everybody could see the fire. No one was going to put this out.

The crowd gasped and then let loose a roar. The grandstands stood, and the chairs went over with a deafening clatter, Coke bottles rolling down the risers. Grace Smith grabbed Elliott's hand. Donald Gale stood by Hulda Grant, unsure just what was going on.

The plumed high-school horses were waiting by the back door, getting ready to perform their dressage when Fred Bradna dashed out and ordered them back to the paddock. The Ostermaiers, Los Asveras Troupe and the Bradnas tugged at their reins and whirled their mounts around. Ella Bradna's white charger spooked and backed into the dressing tent, tangling his legs in the guyropes, almost throwing her before she got him under control.

In clown alley, Felix Adler was preparing for the walkaround. "We heard a roar like applause," he remembered. "Only we knew the animal act was over and there shouldn't be applause. We knew then something was wrong. Then we smelled smoke. I got my daughter Muriel out of the danger zone. Then I thought of my pet pig and went back to get him."

Knowing the cat act had just finished, a number of performers thought a lion had gotten loose.

Emmett Kelly was in his little dressing tent, enjoying a cold beer before his star turn in the Panto's Paradise spec. "I heard someone say something about a fire. We were always very conscious of fire. I didn't see any fire. I thought at first it was the sideshow." He ran outside and saw smoke curling up from the front yard. He hoped it was only a straw fire in the menagerie, but the smoke was black—just like the smoke in Cleveland.

Inside, the Wallendas on the north platform hit the rope ladder, Helen and Henrietta first, then Joe, and finally Herman, who thought he had time to lash his bicycle fast but gave up halfway. Karl spidered down his ladder easily.

In the west cage, May Kovar still had five panthers on their stands waiting to go out. In the east cage, Joseph Walsh was breaking down his pyramid as fast as he could, keeping an eye on all six lions.

Fred Bradna ran back to the center ring, hollering for calm. Ushers and gatemen did the same. "Please keep your seats," they urged. "We know about the fire, we will take care of this."

In escape mobs, psychologists say, the behavior of a few people turns individualistic and antisocial. Lacking guides, others under extreme stress and therefore more suggestible than normal are unable to judge the situation critically and imitate these few, the effect spreading through the crowd in a process the sociologist Gustave Le Bon called a "contagion." Psychologists believe these others succumb to an "impression of universality" and, seeing the rest of the crowd all making for one exit, jettison all reason and pursue the same goals with even more fervor. The larger the crowd, the harder—necessarily—people will fight others to get out. Sociologists refer to this breakdown of societal constraints and the reversion to fight or flee behavior (and other people be damned) as "demoralization."

One reason why people panic and become a mob is a lack of leadership. In the Hartford circus fire, at least early on, Fred Bradna and the ushers and gatemen provided the crowd some exterior direction. Reassured by the voice of authority, many people in the grandstands stayed where they were. As in the Our Lady of the Angels fire in Chicago, in which the nuns told their students to pray rather than flee, people believed in the leadership of these men, and discipline held. This may have been due to the time—the war era, with its voluntary surrender of individual rights for the good of the country as a whole.

The people in the southwest bleachers needed no exterior direction. They bolted away from the flames, running east, toward the performers' entrance. The ones in the low rows had it easy, with nothing in their way— if they ran when they first had the chance. Those who hesitated were buried in the wave coming down from above.

People lost their balance on the narrow boards and fell, taking down those in front like dominos. Some went through the spaces between the seats, banging their heads on the stringers, getting wedged in between. The next wave stepped on them.

Anna Cote, who'd had the vision of her dead grandfather, said: "I couldn't stand up and walk down the bleachers so I put my hands on the bleacher and slid down to the next one. I remember doing that a couple of times and then my mind goes blank until I get outside." In fact, her sister Iva, already outside, came back in to save her. How she found her in the crowd Anna could only call a miracle.

Some people were still not moving, sitting or standing there entranced, as if none of this was actually happening—a reaction psychologists call "collective disbelief," another way of mentally minimizing or dismissing the danger because it doesn't fit with previous expectations. One survivor remembers sitting in the stands and watching a little girl trip over a rope and fall down, then get up and keep going—all of it far away, disconnected, drained of any urgency.

Above the southwest bleachers the fire suddenly flashed—like the striking of a giant match, some said. Or as one woman described it: "It was as though someone punched a button and a light went on."

The wind took the flames and pushed them up one seam. It streaked up the laces, a spear of fire headed for the top of the westernmost centerpole.

Across Barbour Street, at number 353, a neighbor was sitting on his front porch watching people mill about the grounds when he saw the fire breach the roof of the big top.

Hartford police sergeant Frances Spellman was coming up the midway, just fifty feet from the marquee, when he saw it.

Outside the front door, another policeman was talking to the man in charge of reserved seats. He heard someone yell fire and ran inside, finding circus police chief John Brice. "Yes," Brice said, "it's a fire." The policeman told Chief Hallissey he'd run for a cruiser he'd seen parked on the lot and send the alarm. As he started for Barbour Street, he could see Sergeant Spellman far down the midway, sprinting.

Circus general manager George W. Smith had gone to the yellow ticket wagon to check if the line for reserved seats had broken. He saw people coming out from under the sidewalls and thought an animal had gotten loose. He ducked inside the marquee, spied the fire and ran out through the connection to warn the elephant men.

The cruiser parked on the lot was Sergeant Spellman's. Its radio was broken, and he knew it. As he ran toward Barbour Street, he tried to figure out who would have the closest phone. He had a choice of two houses directly ahead of him. And he had a back-up plan. If neither had one, McGurk's or McGovern's would.

Our boys in uniform

The flames blazed up the laces, windblown, shooting to the roof. When the fire reached the top of the westernmost centerpole, it split, forking in three directions—straight across the top and spreading down both sides at the west end, possibly along the seams, following the richest fuel. Now the canvas itself was involved, the paraffin turning to gas and burning.

People were screaming—women, children—and the chairs banged and clashed as the grandstands began to react.

Over the PA, the announcer asked the audience to please leave their seats in an orderly fashion. The power went out, cutting him off.

The track near the front door filled with people. They'd come in that way; it was the only door they knew, and they made for it, running past other, easier exits—typical fire behavior: a reversion to the comfort of the familiar when faced with the strange. Above them, the top was solid flames, making them duck, yet still they surged, bottling up between the bleachers.

Under the marquee, a policeman yelled for the attendants to tear up the iron piping. Chiefs Hallissey and Brice pitched in. "Cut the ropes," the cop ordered, "never mind anything else." Thomas Barber had a jackknife and hacked through the one next to the ticket booth. Paul Beckwith yanked down a set connected to the bleachers, and the people poured through.

At the foot of the grandstands, it wasn't that simple. The crowd coming down piled up at the gates and pressed against the railings. "Fold 'em!" the ushers shouted, trying to jerk the rails out of the ground, but the crowd knocked them back. Gatemen came to their aid, holding the people off as long as they could. Some succeeded, some failed. They were a handful facing thousands.

Up in their assigned seats, Dr. Paul de la Vergne craned to catch sight of his wife in the crush below. He didn't see her. He should have never let Elizabeth sit by herself. He should have sat down low with her. He took his son's hand and fought his way down.

"Take it easy, take it easy, walk out quietly," the ushers were saying. Some people listened. In school, the children had learned what to do in case of an air raid, and parents pretended this was just another drill.

The Norrises were already gone. The first stampede had taken them away, leaving Mary Kay Smith beneath a pile of chairs. Mrs. Smith and Barbara were busy extricating her. The girl looked up at them, dazed, eyes wide yet not crying. Below, their neighbors were stuck at the gate. For now maybe they would be safer here.

It was a common tactic. Some people needed time to think, needed to know more information in order to assess the situation before acting— a kind of rational paralysis found in all unexpected disasters. Others still didn't consider the situation desperate yet. A man in the south grandstand explained: "I pointed it [the fire] out to my mother, and we discussed what to do with the pregnant woman who sat in front of us with one or more children. Realizing that the tent was held up by three gigantic poles [actually six], I said that we should get out of there. I feared that if the fire got to the top of the tent, the tent would collapse on all of us. The woman in front decided to stay, because she believed that the fire would soon be put out. We always wondered what happened to her."

An older gentleman sitting alone on the bleachers kept repeating, "If everybody would only keep their seats, we'll all be all right"—a denial of the reality before him, but, according to psychologists, a common reaction when presented with an unchangeable situation and no immediate options.

As the fire ate its way east, more people scrambled, bunching up, the bottom of the grandstands mobbed. One mother took her young son and wrapped his arms around her neck, his legs around her waist, and told him not to let go. Another man had his daughter stand on the riser above him and climb on his back. In S, Stanley Kurneta held his son Tony's hand and led his family down into the crush. Behind him followed Mrs. Kurneta and Betsy, Mary Kurneta and Raymond Erickson.

Outside of the railings, on the hippodrome track, it wasn't so bad early on. Folks going out the east entrance from the low rows in the middle of the south grandstands said the shoving was less than they'd experienced at baseball games. Mothers and aunts and grandmas hurried their charges along, strong-arming them when necessary.

In this first wave, the Red Cross volunteers started to move their convalescent soldiers out but then turned back to help. The canvas above the front door was fully involved, heat radiating down on top of people leaving. The men, while hampered by their injuries, could not be stopped from leading at least thirty children to safety, many of them burned. Dressed for the weather, the children were mostly exposed, their skin the bright red of sunburn. One soldier took a boy by the arm and made him cry. His hand came away wet. The child's skin had blistered; in gripping him, the soldier had ripped the blebs so they wept fluid. Outside, the Red Cross volunteers had to restrain their patients—even some in slings—from running back in.

An East Hartford mother was the beneficiary of similar heroics. She lost her six-year-old, knocked from her arms as they ran for the exit. A sailor scooped him up and carried him out, barely bruised.

There were rescues throughout the top. In the southwest bleachers, an older woman had somehow fallen through and gotten her foot caught so she was hanging upside down, her face a foot from the ground. Thomas Barber and another detective freed her and helped her outside.

On Barbour Street, Sergeant Spellman saw a woman on the far sidewalk and called to her. Where was a phone? Who had a phone around here?

There was one next door, she told him, pointing to the house on the left, 345 Barbour Street. He ran past her for the porch stairs.

In the tent, the main entrance was flooded with customers. Afraid they'd injure themselves at this rate, a ticket seller tried with some other circus employees to control the flow of people. They barreled him over, knocking him clear of the marquee.

One West Hartford father was leading his two daughters and his grandmother's nurse out the southwest exit between the bleachers and the grandstand. Several hundred people had already gone out that way. When they were about twenty-five feet from the exit, a man dressed in a circus uniform held up his hands to the crowd and shouted: "You'll have to go out another entrance." Scraps of flaming canvas were falling now, and there was

(Left) For some, early on, escape was as easy as ducking under the sidewall. This is outside of the northeast bleachers, the seats farthest from the point of origin. (Right) The same spot behind the northeast bleachers. Most of the top is still in good shape, only the west end fully involved. PHOTOS COURTESY OF THE *HARTFORD COURANT*

a fair crowd behind them. The father realized that to go back might mean death. He shoved to the front and told the worker, "You damn fool, we're going out this way," and pushed him aside. Fewer than twenty-five people followed him, assuming perhaps that worse disaster lay that way.

In the south grandstand, George Sanford's movie camera continued to roll.

The roof over the main entrance was driving the crowd back now. One man sitting in the southwest bleachers made it to the track before the swell swept him out the northwest exit, dragging him along the animal chute that ran through there. When he got outside, he stood there watching other people come out. Two little boys asked if he was hurt badly, and he discovered blood on his sleeve. The back of his shirt was covered with it. He felt himself for a wound, but the blood wasn't his. Someone must have rubbed against him in the crush.

The fire burned eastward, the band playing over the shouts and screams, the crashing of grandstand chairs. Everyone was getting out now;

there was no more heed for authority, no more waiting—even if there was nowhere to go but down into the piles at the railings. One woman pitched her high heels, dropped her pocketbook and headed down, hanging on to her son's belt. A man wrapped his daughter in his jacket.

They had to climb over piles of seats. The chairs collapsed as people tried to step on them, the wooden legs bruising and cutting shins. A foot caught in a seat, and people tripped and fell. Some stepped on the thick Coke bottles and twisted their ankles. And still there were people behind them, and more behind them, all coming down. A Hartford man explained: "There was nothing we could do. Others just walked over them in the rush."

The larger the crowd, the quicker panic spreads. Group ties in a random gathering like a circus audience are tenuous at best, and under stress people tend to react even more so as individuals, in this case with, perceptually at least, mutually exclusive goals. To the person trapped in the mob and barely moving, it seems certain that not everyone will get out. As the possibilities of escape visibly diminish—as the threat becomes larger, allengulfing, and as more people join the crush—the more violent some people become. Those in the way become not merely obstacles but deadly enemies.

Men were flinging chairs out of the way, the discards hurtling down to strike others below. The chairs seemed deceptively light and flimsy; they each weighed eight pounds and were built to last. One husband wielded one like a machete, swinging it to clear a path to his wife. Someone surged out of the crowd and pushed him down.

Donald Gale wanted to run for it, but Hulda Grant told him to stay with her. She took his hand, and the two of them made their way down through the chairs. The boyfriend had Caroline. The crowd funneled everyone into the aisle, pushing and shoving, but they got to the bottom of the section all right.

Here the wave of people smashed against the railings, a wrack of chairs tossed off to one side. They were going nowhere when a husky sailor in a blue uniform broke through, beating his way to the front. He punched Hulda Grant in the jaw and she pitched into the chairs. Donald lost his footing, and then the people were on top of him, heavy, and he couldn't see anything.

Blue sky

The same thing was happening all over the tent. Someone bowled an elderly man over from behind and he landed in a tangle of seats. He got up only to be knocked down again. The younger and stronger pushed the older and weaker over chairs, knocked them down and stepped on them. As one witness politically admitted: "It is fair to say that many people were trampled by those who had the brawn to carry it off."

Yet some did look out for others. A young mother from Hartford hit the railing of section C with her two-year-old and couldn't break loose. A thin, thirtyish man in shirtsleeves reached over from the track and lifted both of them out so they could escape. He seemed calm, and his calmness heartened her. As she ran off, he stayed there to help those remaining.

In another section, the aisle had jammed up. Some man at the bottom was holding everyone back until his wife could work her way down to him. He wouldn't let anyone out; he just kept calling to his wife. A girl ducked under the railing and gave him a good shove, and everyone started to come out.

A man from Middletown described a similar incident from a strikingly different point of view: "The people in back of us were surging down from the higher seats and I had to hold some of them back to let [a neighbor's wife] get out. This was when I hurt my leg." Once the woman and her daughter reached him, he put his elbows out like a blocker and cleared a path for them to the exit.

Don Cook took his sister Eleanor's hand and began down, but his mother caught her other hand. Now she had Edward and Eleanor. I'm going to be very calm, Mildred Cook thought, I'm going to take my time. "You go along," she told Don.

He dashed down toward the crowd but they were running over each other, and he didn't see an easy way around. He headed back up the grandstand and to his left—east, away from the fire, skirting islands of wrecked chairs.

Mildred Cook hesitated before following Don's initial move downward and lost him in the throng beneath her. "We waited a minute," she would say, "and I guess we shouldn't have." She led Edward and Eleanor down; as Don came across the top of the grandstand he looked back and saw them, part of the crowd now, surrounded. And then they were gone, lost among the others.

Across the tent, Joan Smith noticed all the seats behind her were empty. She told her mother she was going *up* the grandstand, not down. Joan was twelve and her mother trusted her. Go ahead, she said. The last Joan saw of her mother and Elliott, they were struggling down the aisle. She was halfway to the top when she realized she still had her Coke.

She tossed the bottle away and scaled the risers. The top edge of the sidewall hung right in front of her, partly slack from being let down for the breeze. She took hold of it with both hands and pushed off, swung clear and hung there a second before letting go.

She was a country kid, a tomboy who knew how to climb trees. When she hit the ground she relaxed, knees bent, and went with the impact. She was fine.

In G, Commissioner Hickey jumped up at the first sign of fire and hollered, "Be calm." Of course, no one paid any attention to him. One nephew responded by throwing his hot dog up in the air. Hickey quickly got the children under control and implemented a plan. The four boys would go down the sidepole right behind them. The two nieces and Isabel and little Billy he would accompany down the aisle and through the middle entrance on the south side. They started off, but one niece refused to move, evidently paralyzed with fear. Isabel came back and slapped her face. The girl moved.

The Alcorns chose to go over the back, the seventy-two-year-old former prosecutor leaping first, then catching the children as his son dropped them down. They met up with the Hickey party outside, Hugh Sr. realizing he'd forgotten his jacket in the rush. He'd had his wallet with $150 in it.

Going over the back of the grandstand was the best chance for those in the top rows. Parents tried to make it a game, and some children laughed as they shinnied down the poles and ropes. Adults at the bottom held the sidewall like a slide so kids could jump into it.

In the west end, the flames were overhead when one man, his wife and their five-year-old daughter jumped down. Impressed, the little girl kept saying, "It's a shame, it's a shame. The big tent."

Some people tried to catch others jumping. One terrified woman leapt from the top; her body caught a man across the head and shoulders, toppling him, almost knocking him unconscious. "If she had been a bigger woman—she weighed only about one twenty-five—I'd have lain right there and probably have been burned to death."

The Eppses and Goffs went over the back of the northwest bleachers. Mabel Epps told her older son William to climb down a pole, then dropped Richard to him, then little Muriel Goff. Once William had the two children in hand, Mabel Epps shouted, "Go! Get out of here!" He lifted the folds of the sidewall so the other two could crawl out.

Another mother was with five children in section H. Three men below caught the children as they dropped. Thinking they were all safe, the mother leapt, but outside, counting noses, she discovered she only had four. She ran back into the tent and found one boy sitting on the edge of the grandstand, stiff with fright. She ordered him to jump, and he did, but there was no one to catch him, and he injured his back.

The northeast corner of the tent. Inside, the animal cages are visible. In the foreground to the right, two people are running; the search for loved ones has already started. PHOTO COURTESY OF ART KIELY

Outside, another man had been strolling around the grounds while his wife and two kids were inside. He saw the flames and ran for the big top.

Molly Garofolo ran a beauty salon a couple of blocks south on Barbour Street, on the corner of Westland, right beside Jaivin's Drugstore. She was giving a customer a perm, the heated rods in her hair, when they saw black smoke rolling up outside. "My two boys are at the circus!" the woman screamed, and ran out the door. The hairdresser caught up with her and made her sit on the curb while she removed the rods—another few minutes and her hair would have burned.

Inside, the band played "The Stars and Stripes Forever" over and over, as if the song might calm people knocked through the bleachers or buried under chairs. Fred Bradna pleaded with the people in the east end to leave through the side flaps, but they all clotted helplessly at the bandstand exits. Children fainted in the crush.

All the while the fire was crossing the top of the tent. It spread like a grass fire, a haystack fire, a giant orange wave. Central Connecticut residents were familiar with shade tobacco tents, how a blaze on the sheer canopies could outrun the fastest man; it was like that.

Everyone had a metaphor. The tent went up like cellophane, like tissue paper, like a fuse. A Roman candle, a sheet of newspaper. It was like tossing a piece of paper in a fireplace, like putting a match to a celluloid collar.

The wind took the fire on top and whipped it across the east grand-stands. The west end was still in flames, but now people trapped in the seats and on the floor could look up and see beyond the orange and yellow line of fire—bright, strange as a vision—the clear blue sky.

Animal acts

Once the fire breached the roof, the tent became a chimney, sucking cooler air in through the exits and shooting it hot out the top. The paraffin acted as a constant accelerant; the vast area of the canvas provided an endless supply of fresh oxygen. The temperatures inside were rising, and likewise the panic.

One man in the middle of the grandstands plunged forward, knocking over chairs, women, children and other men indiscriminately, stepping on them when they fell. When last seen, the man was fighting and pushing his way to get ahead of everybody else.

A Manchester woman had gone with her husband and granddaughter. The husband lifted the girl over the railing into the arena and she ran for the exit. The woman was making her way when she "was suddenly confronted with one of those heartrending problems inevitably part of such disasters. Her path was blocked by the prostrate body of a woman. [She] hesitated to step forward and walk over the body. The press of other people behind her and around her kept her from bending to be of possible aid to the fallen woman. But her sensitive indecision was ended when the burning canvas of the big top came down upon her back, badly burning her back and arms. Then she forced her way forward."

The rush was like a human waterfall, like being hurled along by a huge wave breaking. A cadet nurse at St. Francis Hospital and a friend were able to lift up an elderly woman who had fallen to her knees and to drag her along. The two held her tightly until the flow carried them far enough into the open to stumble free. They left the woman in a safe place and redoubled their rescue efforts.

The fire shot right over top of Edward Garrison and his grandmother. The crowd knocked his aunt down and people helped her up but by then they were separated. The swarm tore his grandmother's hand from his and swept her ahead of Edward. She turned around to see where he was and was dragged backwards, her eyes locked on his.

One woman remembered her mother praying out loud as they held each other, drawn along by the tide.

And still the grandstands bunched up at the gates. At one, a chair was stuck across the opening and the pressure from behind toppled those in front over it so no one could get out. Even when the gates were clear, they were purposefully narrow. Trying to squeeze through, one woman found herself caught and crushed against a steel post, half in, half out. She stretched a hand to her companion and he yanked her free, the crowd squirting through the gap, falling across the track.

Ushers continued to urge the audience to exit in an orderly fashion, though the crush was so tight that people were losing shoes. Some lost their footing and others walked on them. A woman with a child in her arms went down and the crowd closed over her. The jostling was hard. One woman dropped her pocketbook but knew if she bent down to retrieve it she'd be run over. A girl let go of her program; she wanted to stop but the current pushed her on. A boy lost his glasses and stooped over to retrieve them. A man fell over him and they both went down.

Many saw women and children being trampled, but, as a girl from West Cornwall explained: "If I stopped to pick up one of them I would have gone down in a second. We just kept going and were pushed until we got clear of the tent."

Parents had no such luxury, and took advantage of any handhold. When one mother's little boy got knocked down, she snatched him up by his overall straps. But more often when a mother bent to rescue a child, the surge buried her.

A Plainville mother had her two children and a nephew with her as she made for an exit. In the crush an unknown man suddenly reached out and took her youngest son from her arms. She managed to make her way to safety with the other two, but once outside she could find neither her son nor the man.

A Meriden man lost his wife in the scramble, then found her in a mound of bodies and hauled her off. "As I pulled [her] out I found there was a woman under her, and I believe she was dead. The fire was crawling to the center of the tent, overhead, and the heat was unbearable. By this time, the howling and yelling was beyond description."

Ushers selflessly rushed children to safety and came back for more, while at the same time other circus personnel were deliberately smashing people's cameras. They asked a *Saturday Evening Post* photographer there on assignment not to shoot, and he agreed.

Children were running around crying, trying to find their parents. Some dashed straight back into the thick of the fire.

One man hugged his son to his chest and ran past the bandstand and out into the underbrush at the east end of the lot. "Here and there could be seen men, women and children horribly burned, many wandering aimlessly about, oblivious to advice that they try to get to a doctor as soon as possible. One woman, apparently unaware that she had suffered severe burns to her arms, was trying to comfort a 9 or 10 year old youngster who was also badly burned, mostly about the legs. The child was shrieking in agony and the woman kept telling him that he would be all right as soon as his parents found him. When told by those who had just left the tent that she and the youngster should get to a doctor so that medical care could be administered, she replied, she couldn't until her family was located—she didn't know where they were. She still didn't seem to know she was badly burned. There were indications that the tents which backed up to the main tent would also go up in flames so those who escaped through the rear entrance started down through thick underbrush below, trying to find a way out. A road off to the right about 300 yards from the fire proved a haven for hundreds. From this vantage point, thick black clouds of smoke could be seen billowing skyward. Here also many men, women and children could be seen, some burned rather seriously, others superficially."

Back in the northeast corner of the lot, way off in the woods, sat the show's water trucks. Deacon Blanchfield was supposed to make sure they were on hand during the performance with their engines turning, but somehow he'd forgotten.

The *Hartford Times* reported that the first alarm for the circus fire was turned in by a West Hartford man who detected smoke when he was buying tickets for the evening performance, but the first signal box that came in was number 82 at the corner of Clark and Westland, a good half mile from where he was standing. It rang downtown at 2:44 P.M., sending

Engine Companies 2, 7 and 16, and Truck Companies 3 and 4 to the scene.

In the same minute, box 828 at Barbour and Cleveland tripped, six hundred feet from the front door of the big top, scrambling Engines 14, 4 and 3 and Truck 1.

Sergeant Spellman reached 345 Barbour Street and ran inside, only to find another officer already on the phone yet saying nothing. Fire HQ's line was busy, he explained. The woman who lived there saw the fire and rushed in from outside, thinking she'd call the police. Her seventy-seven-year-old father was at the circus. Spellman took the phone from the other officer and dialed the operator, who told him the line was busy. He explained what the trouble was and she gave him the line.

Spellman told the switchboard that the main circus tent was on fire and to send in two or three alarms. The dispatcher said apparatus was already on the way.

Spellman next called police headquarters and told them that the circus was on fire and to send all available policemen and ambulances there. Without hesitation, HQ relayed the message to the cruisers: Proceed immediately to the circus grounds—pick up every man you can and take them with you. All officers on beats to be picked up and brought to the fire.

At 2:45 box 821 at Charlotte and Barbour and box 836 at Cleveland and Hampton signaled, sending Engine 5.

John C. King, Hartford's veteran fire chief, was in his car when word came over the two-way shortwave. He was about three miles from the scene and directed his driver to go full speed through the streets.

The department's response was immediate and strong. Engine Company 16 on Blue Hills Avenue near the Bloomfield line had four men dressed and ready. In seconds they hopped on a truck and rolled.

The *Hartford Times* was wired into the fire department's signal boxes. In the city room, the alarm went off. Being an evening paper, the *Times* asked its regular reporters to work mornings so they could make deadline. They all got off at noon. The city room was empty except for a few summer interns and other cubs. Another box called in, making everyone look up from their desks. It was going to be a big one. The circus, the police confirmed. The night editor grudgingly assigned a cub to the grounds with two photographers. As they grabbed their jackets, a third alarm went off.

The bravest girl I've ever seen

Don Cook ran across the top of the south grandstand. There was no one up where he was, just chairs and popcorn and Coke bottles. He reached the edge of section E and skipped across the board bridging the narrow entrance below, keeping the flames far behind him, headed for the east end of the tent where the band was still playing the same song. He glanced across the rings and saw people going over the northeast chute, vaulting the bars, crawling on top, the one pair of stairs jammed.

When Edward J. Hickey raced back in through that same narrow opening on the south side, he witnessed the same thing, but they were too far from him and the heat was too much.

The chute was chest high, the iron sections curved at the top and bolted together. Walsh's lions were still in it, even as people frantically clambered across the bars. The propmen never had a chance to move it.

A Middletown man and his family had been seated in W and hit the chute early, before the heaviest crush. As they started over, three attendants on the far side stopped them. The men had sticks to prod the last three lions through. "Get back, get back!" they yelled, waving the crowd off.

"Come on," the father yelled to his children, "go over anyhow."

He'd helped everyone across but his youngest son, who was shorter and heavier than the rest. He set him on top of the chute but the child's foot slipped through the ribs and when the boy looked down, right beneath him was a lion, snarling up, its jaws wide. The boy shied back and slid into his father's arms.

The father tried again, setting his son on the bars, but this time an attendant stopped him, shoving the child and saying, "Get back there." Why, the boy thought, would the man do something like that? The boy slipped between the chute and the edge of the grandstand, and someone knocked him to his knees.

His father reached down and with his arm around the boy's chest and one hand gripping the seat of his pants, hoisted him to the top of the chute above the lions and said, "Never mind what he says. Get over there." He gave the boy a push in the back, and he landed on the far side of the bars.

At the northwest chute, the scene was even worse, the fire almost overhead. May Kovar remained in her cage to drive her five panthers out. Embers were dropping, and she was afraid the cats would turn on each other.

As people pounded down section L, the railing at the end of the grandstand gave way. A woman fell and dropped a child she was carrying on top of the chute. The child's arm dangled between the bars. An attendant prodded the nearest panther, trying to distract him, to keep him moving past, but the cat turned and clawed the child's arm, ripping off part of his sleeve. A man standing on the ribs lifted the screaming child off and passed him to someone on the far side.

The first four went easily, but the last panther in the cage turned on May Kovar. The fire was above her, flaming scraps of tent raining down. The cat was spooked by all the commotion. May Kovar circled it with her wand, giving it room to make a decision, then, when it made for the chute, closed in on it. This time the cat didn't turn. She rapped it with her wand and shoved it in, shutting the door.

The White Tops, the magazine of the Circus Fans Association of America, would report that the pressure was so great at the door of her cage that May Kovar had to follow her panthers through the chute, but that's just a story, a dramatic image they couldn't resist. In reality she stepped out of the arena door and joined her cageboys shooing the cats back to the wagons.

At the rear of the grandstands, where the chute entered the tent, it changed from iron bars to wooden slats. The wooden section connected with the ramp that led to the individual wagons. Usually the animals came out one by one, separated by boards, but not today. Two panthers with a long-standing feud were surprised to find themselves together in the wooden part of the chute and decided to fight. Another cat raced back in, toward the cage, running under the fire and flaming debris, singeing its fur.

Back inside, May Kovar helped the people caught at the chute, picking up children and boosting them over, but no one would remember this. The papers focused solely on her heroics inside the cage, fighting her panthers beneath the blazing roof. A retired fire captain from New York City called her "the bravest girl I've ever seen."

But while her cats were out, and safe, the chutes were still there, and the crowd was larger now. Men tossed children across and then vaulted over, but others struggled to get a grip on the bars, catching their knees and feet. Some failed and slumped back, swallowed by the next wave. The heat from above was like being stung all over by bees.

One man on the far side caught children thrown to him, then pulled the mothers over, but that kind of cooperation was rare. Each time one young mother tried to pull herself over, people behind her searching for purchase dragged her back. She kissed her boy and told him to run, then tossed him over the top of the cage. Hands hauled her down again. When she looked up she saw her son had caught his foot between the bars. He dangled upside down, his hands not quite touching the ground on the far side. She started to pull herself up and over, but, upside down, the boy reached between the bars and untied his shoe. It fell into the chute and he was free.

The seventy-seven-year-old man whose daughter's phone Sergeant Spellman was using to call the fire department managed to crawl over the chute and stumble from the tent, but took a drubbing from the crowd. In the confusion his earphones had been yanked out and crushed. In silence, he hobbled down the midway toward home.

A couple from Meriden were sitting on the aisle down low. They hesitated, and the first rush trampled the husband. His wife helped him crawl through the narrow gap between the chute and the grandstand. Outside, they had to climb over the tongues of the animal wagons holding the big cats, who roared and paced in their cages. May Kovar stood guard over her leopards, a cageboy soaking them with a hose.

Beyond the line of wagons, people streamed back and forth along the north side, searching for neighbors and family members. Edward Garrison and his grandmother wandered among them, hoping to find his aunt and cousins. His grandmother wanted to go back inside. Just then the two sailors who'd followed them all the way from East Hartford on the bus came out of the tent, supporting the aunt and the cousins.

Inside, the fire burned east. Officers James Kenefick and Henry Griffin toiled on the far side of the northeast chute, telling people to jump, then reaching over and tugging them across. The north grandstands held nearly three thousand people, and with the west end in flames, several hundred ended up here. It was a battle, the whole crowd trying to come at once. Griffin remembered: "Boys stuck their feet through the bars, got them turned so they couldn't get away. Others were stuck or jammed so they couldn't move." They piled up on top, blocking the people behind them.

A fifteen-year-old West Hartford girl and her younger sister came tumbling out of the grandstand and into the scrum at the northeast chute. The older girl saw the officers running up and down the far side, pulling people over, and pushed her sister up on top of others who'd already fallen. As she lifted her sister, she looked down into the face of a young man slightly older than herself, unable to get up because of the layers pinning his legs.

An officer helped the younger girl across and was about to move on to someone else, but the girl held on to his hand and pulled him back toward her sister. He had to save her too, she insisted, and he did. They never knew what happened to the young man.

The Wallendas crossed the northeast chute. Herman Wallenda: "When the flames hit the roof, we saw we had to get down fast. We slid down the ropes and headed for the performer's exit, but people were so crowded there that we saw we didn't have a chance. So we climbed over the cage that lines the exit. That was easy for us—we're performers. But the public couldn't get out that way."

Herman's teenaged son Gunther was with him; they climbed over the northeast chute right by a quarterpole and headed out of the tent. When they looked back, people seemed to be getting out.

Fred Bradna, veteran of several top fires, saw the confusion at the northeast chute and ran over there. He pulled children from the pile and carried them to safety.

Dorothy Bocek, thirteen, had been sitting in the north grandstand with her married sister Stella Marcovicz and her nephew Francis, four. All three made for the northeast chute. Dorothy asked Stella what she should do. Stella, holding Francis's hand, said, "Just take care of yourself."

At the chute they got separated. Somehow Dorothy made it over, she didn't remember how. Outside, she couldn't find Stella and Francis.

The band played on, but not loud enough to drown the screaming. "They all sounded like beaten dogs," Emmett Kelly said.

Rich black smoke rolled up from the canvas. Pieces fell and caught in women's hair, ignited their light summer dresses. The unpyrolized paraffin became a flaming liquid that rained down like napalm, burning skin on contact, staying aflame until the fuel was all gone. It sizzled as it hit the skin of children in sunsuits, blisters dotting their arms like chicken pox.

The fire consumed the roof pole by pole, the heat on top of the crowd like a giant broiler, making people duck and flinch away from it. Still it found them. One girl's arm burned where she had it wrapped around her father's neck. Hair burned, and bald spots—not from flame but radiated heat. It literally cooked people.

The roof over the center ring evaporated. Ropes holding heavy tackle and trapeze equipment burned through, sending everything crashing into the rings below.

Mildred Cook lost Eleanor in the mob at the bottom of the grandstand. She hoped her daughter had followed Don. She ran with Edward for the front door, toward the fire, hoping to sneak under it.

Or, according to the missing persons report, the three of them headed for the main entrance together. The heat descended on them, making them groggy. Edward said he was tired and wanted to lie down. He did, passing out immediately. Mildred then fell unconscious, but Eleanor walked on.

After saving the lady caught in the bleachers, Thomas Barber retreated with her out the front door. There was too much heat to go back in there, so he patrolled around to the north to make sure the animals weren't loose. He'd seen May Kovar's act and unsnapped the flap of his holster just in case. That his service revolver might not stop a leopard never occurred to him. When he turned the corner, the cats were all safe in their cages.

On the midway, police cruiser number 8 nosed through the crowd streaming around it and stopped by the white ticket wagon. Chief Hallissey got on the radio and told headquarters to detail as many men as they could to the scene. One of the men headquarters then radioed was Det. William Dineen, who knew his two children were inside the tent.

Hallissey called the city authorities, and through them the War Council. They'd need to mobilize everybody on this one.

Downtown, Engine 4 turned up Ann Street and saw a pillar of heavy black smoke rising into the sky. The men on the truck wondered what the hell it could be.

This ain't no time to faint, lady

The fire drove the crowd ahead of it, down toward the bandstand. People who'd thought they had time now realized they'd underestimated its speed. It was moving too fast and the east end was too crowded to get out that way. The fire was going to cut them off.

A girl was running around with her blouse on fire, batting at it. Another woman heard someone say her shirt was on fire. She felt the heat, and then a man struck her in the face and said, "This ain't no time to faint, lady."

One girl had gone to the circus for her eighth birthday. Her mother couldn't take her because she was eight months pregnant, so she went with an older neighbor. They came down the north grandstand after the first rush. People were walking on others trapped under chairs, crushed and screaming.

"We've got to help them," the girl said.

"We don't have time," the neighbor said, and she was right.

When they reached the chute, the woman took one look at the crowd and said, "We'll never get out this way," and turned around, leading the girl back up the stands, all the way to the top, right by a sidepole. There was no one else there, and the girl balked. The drop seemed far.

"You've got to jump," the woman said.

"I can't," the girl said. "I can't even climb the pole in gym."

"If you don't, I'm going to push you."

The girl jumped, grabbed on to the pole and slid down, the friction ripping the skin from her arm. The woman climbed down right behind her.

Now the crowd realized they'd never make the east end and stormed up the grandstands on both sides, searching for poles and ropes, any lifeline. At the edge, parents instructed their children to run outside and wait for them. People remember the jump as being twenty-five, thirty, even thirty-five feet, when actually it was only between ten and twelve—but they were children then, and twelve feet to a six-year-old is a long way down.

Adults at the bottom gathered to catch children, but there weren't enough of them for everybody. One man climbed down a rope with two children on his back. People leapt for the sidepoles, slid down halfway and caught their hands on the rough guyropes. The ropes burned their palms raw, and they let go from the shock and fell.

Some people jumped, not bothering with poles or ropes. One group of boys had a favorite game called paratrooper; they'd climb up on garages and—Geronimo!—fly off, bending their knees and rolling on landing, just like in the newsreels. Now they had a chance to use their new skills. But the very young and very old hadn't practiced. There were scores of bad falls. One woman went over nearly headfirst. Little girls landed on their hands and broke their wrists and arms. An older gentleman broke his leg and had to be helped away.

And there were injuries among the catchers—black eyes and strained backs, scratches and bruises from being kicked. A minor price.

But even there behind the stands people weren't out of danger. In some places the sidewall was staked down to the ground so tight there was no way to struggle under it. This was especially true behind the northwest bleachers just to the left of the marquee and the ladies' room—a natural place for kids to sneak in.

Thirteen-year-old Donald Anderson saw the column of blue sky as the fire tore above his section. He hung from the top row and dropped down. He'd come with Axel Carlson, an older man, a distant cousin of his grandfather. When Donald reached the ground he couldn't find him anywhere. A mob of people were trying to squeeze out the northwest exit beside the chute, crawling all over one another—dog eat dog. Donald wanted no part of that. He had a fishing knife with him, with a good sharp blade. He unfolded it and tried to cut the rope holding down the tent; it was so thick he would have needed a hacksaw. He stuck the knife into the middle of the wall and worked it down, sawing the tough canvas until he had a fair-sized slit. Left and right at the bottom, left and right at the top, and it was a door big enough for him to get out.

He was thinking of nothing but self-preservation, but when the crowd saw it, hundreds poured through behind him. Outside now, he scanned their faces, trying to find Axel Carlson. When he didn't see him, he took his knife to the next panel, cut another door and went back in.

The old man was right there, and a little girl no more than three or four, trampled. Donald picked her up and followed Axel Carlson out.

Donald Anderson—along with May Kovar—would be remembered as a hero of the circus fire; he'd even get a medal. But all around the tent, fathers slashed at the canvas with penknives, boys wearing HiJacks paratrooper boots whipped miniature jackknifes out of their scabbards, and people dashed into the cool air.

Most of the sidewalls were not staked down, however; people ducked underneath the folds into sunlight, some of them getting stepped on as they crawled out. On the north side they had to scrabble under circus wagons to get clear. On the south they had the light plant and the menagerie animals to deal with. The camels were uneasy, tethered along a rope fence tied to a wagon.

One family came out in the middle of the elephants, chained and swaying, some of them rearing. They trumpeted and shook their heads from side to side menacingly. Ralph Emerson Jr. was eighteen, an animal trainer new to the show. He'd grown up in Glastonbury and several family members had come to see him. He was working with the elephants on the south side of the main tent when the fire started "near the area that the menagerie leaned against. I saw smoke. I suppose I saw it as early as anyone. There was a V of flame in the top of the tent. I thought, How are they going to get out of this. Someone yelled, 'Get the elephants out' [possibly George W. Smith, from the connection]. There was a great sense of urgency to get the animals out of the way and to keep them from charging the crowd."

The show elephants were in the backyard, getting ready for the spec. The bull men shouted "Tails! Tails!" and the herd formed the familiar trunk-to-tail queue, one attendant for every two animals, and lumbered around the south side, squeezing between the light plant and the victory gardens. When they hesitated, their handlers whacked them with their hands and prodded them with bull hooks.

In the tent the tops of the bleachers were crammed with people. Some had fallen through the boards and gotten caught; the crowd rolled over them, pressing for the edge. Not like lemmings but *against* instinct, people jumped. Some refused to, unsure where their children were. The surge from below pushed them over. It sent one teenaged girl toppling. She fell twelve feet to the ground, breaking her back.

Waiting for a little girl in front of her to jump, one woman witnessed man shove the child off from behind. She hadn't been going fast enough for him.

Some jumped and broke their ankles and then were unable to get up before others landed on them, knocking them out, hurting them worse. One girl remembered lighting beside a woman who couldn't move; she watched as the girl ran off. People jumped over the heads of the fallen, or climbed over them once they reached the ground. Another man recalled a lady in her thirties in a red dress whom he had to crawl over. She looked right at him, yet said nothing.

Don Cook finished his sprint across the top of the south grandstand and swung down over the railing at the end of section K. The sidewall here was loose and he slipped underneath and outside easily. People with seared faces ran choking into the underbrush. Unsure where his mother was, Don went around the east end of the tent where the biggest crowd was flowing out around the bandstand. He stood there watching everyone funnel past.

Another boy and his family ran. His father had the boy's little sister under one arm and the boy clinging to his belt. They jumped a shallow ravine where an elderly woman lay facedown in the muck. His father, never letting his sister go, reached down with one hand and pulled the old woman up and out by the back of her dress.

Another woman tore her dress going over the snow fence protecting the victory gardens. Just slats and wire, it was surprisingly strong. One young mother unable to scale the fence handed her daughter over to a man and told him to meet her on Barbour Street. "Yes," the man said, "of course I will." He ran, but once he reached the sidewalk he stopped and looked down at the girl in bewilderment. He'd been so intent on his goal that he didn't remember taking her.

And then a crowd broke out of the south side, roared across the scattered hay of the menagerie and hit the snow fence in force, bending and then flattening it, sweeping across the gardens, trampling the vegetables to mush.

Everywhere there were obstacles—wagons and stakes and crates, buckets and kegs and bales. A mother fleeing the east end tripped over a coil of rope and fell on the son she was carrying, bruising his forehead. There was chaos here with people careering out, tractors dragging wagons off, and the circus water trucks finally rolling up to fight the fire.

For people coming out the east end there was nowhere to go except down the road into the woods where there was a dump. A boy and his mother came across two older ladies sitting down, exhausted. "I wouldn't sit there," the mother said. "What if some of the animals got loose?" The ladies jumped up and took off, outstripping them.

In the confusion, rumors took on the weight of truth. The elephants were on a mad rampage. The state police had come with shotguns to hunt the lions down. Survivors pitied the animals that died in the fire; in actuality, there were none.

But, running, having just come from watching two full cages of jungle cats, naturally people assumed the worst. At this point, having escaped the tent, they were more afraid of the lions than the fire. When they finally stopped and took stock, they found they were bruised and burned and bleeding, the luckier ones just missing pocketbooks and shoes, perhaps a hat or a wristwatch. The woods were full of mothers searching for their children, the badly burned crying for help. Some didn't stop running until—blocks, neighborhoods, miles later—they made it home.

Don't look back

Sergeant Spellman ran out of the house and told an officer to move the cruiser on the lot by McGovern's out of the way, down the street. Spellman himself stayed on Barbour, herding the crowd away from the pavement. They needed to keep the road open for the fire trucks and ambulances.

Most people were out now, stunned, unsure what to do or where to go. They wandered around, watching the spectacle of the big top being consumed. One woman recalled: "I stood transfixed and saw one woman outside the tent. Before my very eyes a burning piece of canvas ignited her dress and then flame enveloped her. It all happened so fast. It was like a nightmare, unreal."

George W. Smith had caterpillars pulling menagerie wagons away from the southwest side of the tent so fire trucks could get in. Engine Company 16 was en route. The station was only a mile and three-tenths from the circus grounds. As they turned from Blue Hills Avenue onto

Tower, they saw the flames and smoke in the sky. The huge drift was so dark the men were convinced it was an oil tanker, maybe a gas station. They raced down Coventry Street and took the turn around Municipal Hospital onto Vine. Vine to Westland, Westland to Barbour—all the while glancing up, wondering, unable to make the connection.

A group of kids up on Blue Hills Avenue thought the smoke was coming from the dump, since there was always smoke coming from there. Then a pair of state police cars came roaring past, lights and sirens going, followed by two cruisers from Bloomfield.

John Stewart was walking down Barbour Street, headed back home to clean up after all his hard work, his six free passes from this morning in his pocket. He was hoping to go to the show that night. He saw the smoke and ran back toward the circus grounds.

Southeast of the tent, Spencer Torell had lost his friend Wally. He looked back at the big top, the fire licking up the centerpole toward the flag, and instinctively raised his viewfinder to his eye. Flames covered the top. The smoke billowing off it was eerily reminiscent of Pearl Harbor, the listing battleship *Arizona*.

Torell took the shot and backed off. Bits of burning canvas floated down around him like confetti, nothing but ash by the time they hit the ground. Women fainted from the shock and the heat, and people gave them first aid. Cageboys fastened the shutters of the animal wagons before the tractors dragged them off.

Outside the northeast bleachers, ring stock hands led their horses farther northeast, toward a grove of trees on Sponzo's property, then, afraid they were still in danger, down the dirt road toward Hampton Street, warning people out of the way. A boy stood there holding a plumed pony. The boy was crying. He said his uncle was one of the Wallendas; he didn't know if he'd gotten out.

At the back door, Dorothy Bocek waited for her sister Stella and her nephew Francis. They'd been right behind her at the chute. She had no way of getting home because they came by bus and Stella had all the money.

Inside, by the northeast bleachers, the crowd threw one boy to the ground. To escape the stampede of feet, he crawled beneath the bleachers. Under the boards, among the programs and smashed Coke bottles, sat a

The fire climbs the pole and catches the flag. As the flames sweep east, people inside and out panic. The boy in the foreground to the left with his hand covering his mouth is Donald Anderson. PHOTO BY SPENCER TORELL, COURTESY OF THE *HARTFORD COURANT*

baby. The boy picked it up and carried it outside. The father rushed over to him. Nearby, a barefoot woman was crying for her baby.

Two girls from Plainville jumped from the bleachers and ducked under the sidewall. Outside, they came upon a little girl who'd become separated from a neighbor. At first the child believed it was just a "play fire," then became frightened when people bolted from the tent. By luck, she'd been pushed to safety. After quieting her down, the girls found out her name and went off to call her parents.

Another boy and his mother and sister had been in the north grandstand and had gotten separated at May Kovar's chute. The boy found his way out using a big man in front of him like a blocking back. He waited outside the main entrance for them among hundreds of others. The family was Catholic, the boy in parochial school. He was wearing a scapular under his T-shirt and in the rush one end of it had come out. His mother recognized him by it. The story at Immaculate Conception was that the boy had been saved by wearing a scapular.

As one father herded his family out the east end, they came across a boy of nine. The boy was crying; he'd lost his mother. The man took him by the hand. "Come on, we'll try and find her." They searched the grounds, going from group to group, but no luck. He spotted a police lieutenant radioing from his cruiser and handed the boy over to him.

The lieutenant's car became a clearing house for children. After the first child, "a little boy of three was turned over to me by some unknown man. I put both in my cruiser. The little lad fell asleep. I told the older boy to stay with him."

Don Cook stood outside the back door, looking for Edward and Eleanor and their mother. A couple with two children noticed him and said he could stay with them until his family came out. And he could have missed them, there were so many people. They would stay with him and try to help find them.

A distracted father wandered aimlessly about the grounds, saying over and over that he thought he'd rescued his son but when he got outside he found he had a different child by the hand, one he'd never seen before. Police and circus hands restrained him from plunging back into the flames.

Children were calling for their mothers, mothers calling for their children. And still people ran past the raised bandstand on both sides, streaming out as the music played. Clowns and other circus folk urged people to keep going. "Don't look back," one was saying.

A four-year-old boy from Windsor Street had seen the circus train with its animals pass by the day before. Now he was running out of the tent with his grandmother. They'd stayed too long; the heat from above their section had burned his arms from the elbows down. "My hands and arms were like peanut butter." His grandmother suffered burns on her shoulders. She wanted to go back in because she'd lost a shoe, but the boy clung to her and she came to her senses.

Those coming out collided with others rushing back in to find loved ones. One woman spotted a little blonde girl trying to get back into the tent, crying for her grandmother. The woman held on to her. She was only four or five.

A Middletown man saved his children, but his wife was still inside. He set the children under a concession tent and ran back in. The children sat there in the shade until, minutes later, he returned with their mother.

"Keep moving!" Emmett Kelly was shouting. "You can't get back in there!"

But people could.

One woman emerged from the crush and didn't see her niece. She fought her way back through the people streaming out and inside again. Unbeknownst to her, the girl had already made it out. The woman didn't. Later her brother, a doctor, identified her at the State Armory.

A mother reached the fresh air and discovered her son and daughter weren't right behind her. She dashed back in and burned to death with her daughter. The son escaped untouched.

Caught in the confusion by the front door, William Epps could feel his grip on his cousin Muriel Goff slipping, but he had younger brother Richie in his other hand and couldn't let go to get a better hold of her. Bodies jostled them from all sides, hips and shoulders and elbows. And then his hand was empty and he only had Richie.

Mabel Epps jumped from the bleachers with no one to break her fall. She tried to turn in mid-air to protect the baby and landed hard. She dragged herself under the canvas and out, but something was wrong with her legs, they pained her with every step. Later the doctors would tell her she had a broken pelvis, but for now she just wanted to get away from the tent.

Her sister Maurice Goff made it out unscathed, but when she couldn't find Muriel, she became hysterical. "Where is my baby?" she screamed. "Where is my baby?" William and Richard were nowhere to be seen. Someone told her the child had run back into the tent—in all probability searching for her. Maurice Goff believed them and went in after her.

The Stars and Stripes Forever

The wind took the fire east, burning embers settling on the women's dressing top, treated with the same paraffin mixture. An aerialist climbed a rope hand over hand and someone passed him up a bucket to quench them.

Each performer had a wash bucket. Some of the bally girls were taking bucket baths when the fire broke out; a few ran out into the backyard stark naked. Troupers gathered their costumes, threw water on their trunks and slipped under the sidewalls. A bucket brigade formed—the wardrobe mistress, two midgets and a whiteface clown—and soon they had the situation under control.

John Stewart, the neighborhood boy who helped feed the elephants that morning, reached the grounds and saw the fire. His first reaction was to run away. He backed across the street and stood on someone's lawn. By E. B. McGurk's the neighbors had arranged a staging area for the burned. In the distance, sirens rose and fell, closing. People were draining out of the midway holding their heads, their clothes smoking. John Stewart felt overwhelmed by his inability to help them, paralyzed, and then—he couldn't explain why—he walked back across Barbour Street and began leading the injured to McGurk's.

In the big top, things seemingly hadn't changed. The band played, the people screamed. Emmett Kelly held the canvas aside so folks could get out at the east end. But the fire was closer now, the heat down on the crowd. The very air burned people's ears; women raced about with their hair afire.

A West Hartford man had his daughter and a neighbor's son with him. They were caught in the south grandstand behind a piled-up aisle.

The man had recently graduated from the army's survival school. When he saw the fire coming he pushed the children down, knelt on top of them and cupped his hands over their mouths. His daughter bit him so hard he would carry her teeth marks the rest of his life, but he never let go. "We were hit by a terrific wave of heat. I could smell my hair burning and the heat through my shirt. I got to my feet and by that time the grandstand was sufficiently emptied to see the seats and get down in the ring. The grandstand was starting to smoulder. We went straight off the grandstand and we went headfirst through the iron fence [the railing]. I have a bum leg so we went through headfirst. When we hit the ground, the grass in the ring was burning. The kids fought to get away from me. If one got away, I would never have gotten it back again. The only way for us to go was the whole length of the tent. I started to run and by that time the crowd was milling around in the ring. I did more or less [open] field running, and I went down on my knee but I got up and kept on going. I seemed to travel in a pocket, and the flame was right behind us. The heat was ahead of us. While I was running I could see the sky and see the flames going through. Also there were pieces of canvas coming down burning."

Barbara and Mary Kay Smith and their mother followed the same route, staying away from the animal cages. Barbara had lost her shoes; her mother prodded her along across the straw and matted grass. Somewhere near the east cage they saw Eva Norris, caught in the mob. "Eva," Mae Smith hollered, "we've got to get out of here." The girls were already burned, every inch of exposed skin roasted, their summer clothes no protection. The crowd surged and turned, taking the Norrises away.

The heat made people faint. They dropped, and the swarm stomped on them.

Bill Curlee, whose mother had told him he'd go home in a coffin, led his son David to the northeast chute. David was crying; his father told him to stop because it wouldn't do any good. "Go to the car," he said, "I'll meet you there," and tossed the boy across.

Curlee climbed onto the bars as if to follow him, but stopped. He saw another boy behind him and reached back and grasped his wrist and pulled. It worked. There were more hands, more kids, mothers holding toddlers up for him. Curlee stood atop the chute, throwing children to safety, one after the other. He was a big man, and young, a rarity in this audience. Dozens at the chute watched him in awe; later they'd relate their admiration to reporters, and his story made the front page. But, unlike Donald Anderson and May Kovar, Curlee would be a tragic hero. As he was lifting yet another child over, his foot slipped between the bars, he fell, and the crowd dragged him under.

The fire had spread down the sides now. One woman was in charge of a girl who refused to jump from the top of the grandstand even though the fire was right overhead. Her arms burned from shielding the child, she tossed her over the sidewall and followed.

Outside the northwest corner, Thomas Barber turned away from the cat wagons just in time to see two boys scramble through Donald Anderson's slit in the sidewall. He shouldered through the opening and carried some smaller children out near the wooden part of the chute. Farther in, he found a woman lying on her back with her clothes on fire. He took off his jacket and smothered the flames with it, helped her out by the arm and set her down by the tree line.

The flames were above section H, the centerpoles beginning to sway. The tent was almost gone, only the east end still standing, the flags on top burning. Great sheets of canvas rose in the smoke.

Mae Smith and her girls ran past the bandstand. The skin hung off Barbara's arms.

Pushed by the wind, spread by flaming scraps of canvas, the fire burns the top down to the sidewall. PHOTO BY SPENCER TORELL, COURTESY OF THE CONNECTICUT HISTORICAL SOCIETY

Inside, the northeast chute was a nightmare. Marion LeVasseur and her six-year-old Jerry waited as Officers Griffin and Kenefick lifted over the friends the LeVasseurs had come with. When it was their turn, Marion reached out her free hand. The officer on top of the bars leaned across to take it, but the crowd cut her legs out from under her and she fell, taking Jerry with her.

Stanley Kurneta threw his son Tony over the chute, then helped his mother and his niece Betsy up. When he turned back for his sister Mary and nephew Raymond Erickson, they were gone. He hauled himself over and ran.

Behind them came Elliott and Grace Smith, holding hands. The crowd was packed, and all Elliott could see were people's waists and backs. The Smiths weren't moving much, but the constant crush, the insistence of bodies, separated them. Jostled, lost, Elliott swung his fists, hitting people, trying to break clear. The crowd pushed him along. He had no idea where he was, he was just trying to keep his feet. People were screaming, he couldn't hear the band, and then someone knocked into him and he felt himself going over, those closest to him folding, falling on top of him, and he was flat on his stomach, his chin on the ground.

Somewhere behind Elliott Smith were the four Norrises, driven north between the animal cages in the tumult but sticking together.

Fire blazes in the rigging above the east end of the south grandstand. People are still inside. PHOTO BY SPENCER TORELL, COURTESY OF ART KIELY

On top of the chute, Officer Kenefick felt a gust of heat. "Run!" yelled Griffin, and Kenefick looked up to see the roof above them in flames. He dropped down on the far side and sprinted out the northeast exit by the cat wagons. One of the circus water trucks was there but having trouble getting pressure.

Everywhere around the tent there were last-second rescues. A clown dragged a ten-year-old boy to safety. A man picked up a thirteen-year-old girl and carried her out, the girl tearing madly at his face. She'd been trying to find her brother.

The last out were the worst burned. One woman's back was raw from her hips to the top of her head. Another man who was helped out was blackened from the waist up, his lips puffed to twice normal size.

People leaving couldn't help but look back at the less fortunate. As one man swung down a rope he saw bodies of victims trapped in the stands. Another on his way to Barbour Street said, "I hated to think of what went on behind me."

One older fan helped save a woman whose arms were burned to the shoulder, her skin hanging down like empty sleeves. She cried that her three children were lost. The fan and another man supported her out the performers' entrance.

About the grounds, survivors wandered barefoot, clothes in tatters, choking up sooty mucus. Some fainted. There was no water to splash on their faces, so rescuers used pink lemonade.

Stanley Kurneta made sure his mother and Betsy were far enough from the tent, then put Tony over a fence and told him to keep moving. Mary Kurneta and Raymond Erickson were still in the tent, and Stanley was responsible for them. He went back in the same way he'd come out. The heat seared his face and hands and he had to retreat, bleeding.

One young woman in costume ran into the tent three times, twice coming out with children. The third time she returned empty-handed and fell to the ground.

A New Britain man guided his wife and child down the sidepoles and then went back in to save a woman and two children who were lying on the ground and screaming. As he left he saw at least fifty people piled up at the northeast chute.

Commissioner Hickey witnessed it from the east end. "I saw people trying to climb over the chute cages in the track on the north side, and when I left the tent, owing to the heat and fire settling there were people piled alongside of this chute cage, and these folks were flaming and burning, and shrieking and hollering. On the ground at that point I saw a number of people who were afire and were rolling themselves on the ground. I saw from that point looking in, there were people still lying on the ground at the track at the east side whose clothing was afire, and under the stands I saw bodies on fire."

He ran to call for more help.

Ten more bars!

The band blasted it, sat there while the fire came straight at them, the crowd splitting like a river around the bandstand. The flames were above the end grandstand sections, not far to go. It was snowing fire. Hot cables were falling, cinders, embers.

The kettle drums exploded from the heat.

"Jump!" Merle Evans directed, and the band bailed—like true musicians, taking their instruments with them. A flaming quarterpole toppled, dropped onto the stand like a hammer.

Faces smudged, white uniforms scorched, they regrouped outside and serenaded the dazed crowd that stood there watching the drums and the organ burn.

A man leading two children straggled out. "By the time we got to the end of the tent we got out the door on the right of the bandstand. I do recall going outside of the tent, and the bandleader was standing there blowing his trumpet, and there were a couple of bandsmen around there. They were playing right at the entrance to the tent." Both children had third-degree burns all over, the man second degree burns on his lips.

By the southeast exit, a Coca-Cola top caught fire, flames enveloping tiers of empty deposit bottles in yellow wooden crates. The glass melted and pooled like water.

Inside, in the withering heat, a twelve-year-old boy and his mother reached the top of the stands. She dropped him down and told him to go. He did what she said.

The fallen top burns darkly, the lighter sidewall still untouched. Note the small Coca-Cola concession top to the left and the float in front of it. PHOTO BY RALPH EMERSON SR., COURTESY OF THE CIRCUS WORLD MUSEUM

Torell gets the Coca-Cola top in flames. PHOTO BY SPENCER TORELL, COURTESY OF MR. TORELL HIMSELF

The end of the top itself. Note that only part of the sidewall behind the south grandstand is gone. The grandstand would burn soon, the thickly painted chairs making a pyre.
PHOTO BY SPENCER TORELL, COURTESY OF THE CONNECTICUT HISTORICAL SOCIETY

The top falls on a section of the north grandstand. A small piece of sidewall still survives. PHOTO COURTESY OF THE HERTZBERG CIRCUS MUSEUM, SAN ANTONIO

In the smoke, some rigging still stands. Now that the paraffined roof has been consumed, the smoke is lighter.
PHOTO BY SPENCER TORELL, COURTESY OF THE CONNECTICUT HISTORICAL SOCIETY

High up, the guyropes parted, the rigging gave way, and the poles by the northeast corner slumped inward, then the center of the canvas. The tent sagged—slowly, not all at once, the flags on top bending almost horizontal—and then with a hissing, swishing sound, the big top collapsed on itself, the heavy centerpoles falling one after another, smashing the animal cages, crushing people. The quarters—thick as phone poles—banged into the grandstands, denting the railings.

Robert Onorato caught it on film, shooting from atop an embankment at the east end. Slowed down on video, the fire licks up the visible tip of the eastmost centerpole and wraps the flag. The flag catches and drops as if it's melting, falls, and immediately the tent collapses, softly, belling like a ball gown when its wearer curtsies, like a sail emptied of wind.

Around the south side, Spencer Torell got off shot after shot, the series showing the fire eating the tent's skin away, leaving the skeletal rigging, the quarterpoles still vainly linked by wires.

As the canvas fell it pushed the heat beneath out through the sidewalls. The blast of hot air almost knocked people down.

A woman burst from the back door, badly burned on her face and arms, crying "Find my child! Find my child!" A policeman hurried her to the doctor's tent. She kept asking about her son, where was he, was he all right.

Another mother crawled out from under the sidewall with her son, striking daylight just as the tent collapsed, a samaritan pulling them free.

The last dashed out with their arms and legs and bodies raw and bleeding, heads and necks grotesquely blistered. The smell of burned hair turned stomachs.

Not everyone escaped. The tent fell on those unlucky enough to be inside. A lot of people outside watching it fall had no idea where their loved ones were. Don Cook watched it fall, and Joan Smith, and Stanley Kurneta, and Barbara and Mary Kay Smith, and Mabel Epps.

The burning tent settled on top of those left, pinning them. Under the pile by the northeast chute, Elliott Smith could hear people above him moaning and praying. At the bottom of the mound on the track, Donald Gale thought his leg was broken. He tried to push himself up and discovered he couldn't budge.

The fire came crackling over the paraffined canvas, a soft rushing *whoosh* like the approach of wind.

The praying stopped, and then there was just screaming. People outside were stunned to hear women and children moaning and crying for their lives. Like howling, witnesses described it as. Terrible, eerie screeching.

Several survivors said the one thing they will never forget about the circus fire as long as they live is the sound of the animals as they burned alive. But there were no animals.

Death by fire

The ones on top burned. Trapped by their weight, flat on his stomach, Elliott Smith could hear them screaming. He could breathe all right, he wasn't suffocating. He could see the reflection of the fire on the ground directly in front of him. He spat at the sawdust, trying to put it out.

He felt short stabs of pain in his back, like being jabbed again and again with a knife. Above him, the screaming stopped.

Donald Gale gathered his strength and forced his hands free, and then his arms, his face—just as the fire roared over the track. He saw a flash of light and pulled back, trying to hide in the pile, but it was too late. The burns were like being pinched hard all over, like someone was sticking pins in his hands. The heat fused his knuckles into lumps, seared his arms up to his shoulders. After a minute he passed out.

The pile at the northeast chute only covered Jerry LeVasseur from the chest down. The fire tore at his head and hands and shoulders, turning his skin into fuel, then moved on.

In a typical structural fire smoke is the killer because it has no place to go—as in the Cocoanut Grove. Trapped victims fall unconscious, like Mildred and Edward Cook. They involuntarily breathe in superheated air which scorches the lungs, and poison gases. The body responds by dousing the lungs with fluid, and the victims either asphyxiate or drown in their own juices. In an overwhelming percentage of cases, fire victims die before the flames touch them. Here was the exception, and on a grand scale.

Those who'd jumped off the top rows of the grandstands and bleachers and broken their ankles or legs and couldn't run were helpless, trapped and tangled under the burning canvas. The fire ate their clothes and then their skin and then their tissues, the fat raging like gasoline.

The stands burned, the bibles and bleachers—everything. This part of the fire was probably the hottest. The circus painted their grandstand chairs with a dip method, hanging them on hooks and lowering them into a bath of that year's color. Over the seasons, the chairs built up thick layers, all of them volatile. Nearly fifty years later, when a Hartford detective touched a match to a paint chip taken from one lucky chair, it flared up like a chunk of Sterno.

The heat withered trees, sent people fleeing, afraid the woods might catch fire. Deacon Blanchfield directed his water trucks. "I started the trucks over to protect the wild-animal cages, and someone told me there were people in there burning, and I countermanded the order and put the trucks to work. . . . They told me there was a little boy burning in the exit, and when the trucks came to the exit, I stopped them at the exit, and had them play water onto these people."

The jacks and stringers and seats burn. In the foreground, left, sits a float from the Panto's Paradise spec, an ocean with a leaping dolphin at the front; foreground right stands #201, a prop wagon. PHOTO BY SPENCER TORELL, COURTESY OF ART KIELY

Torell moves west as a concession tent to his right goes up. We're on the other side of the dolphin float, prop wagon 201 still in frame. PHOTO BY SPENCER TORELL, COURTESY OF ART KIELY

The remaining sidewall on the south side burns. In the background, a centerpole still stands. PHOTO BY RALPH EMERSON SR., COURTESY OF THE CONNECTICUT HISTORICAL SOCIETY

Emerson backs off as the concession tent and sidewall smoke. Note the Coca-Cola truck just left of center. PHOTO BY RALPH EMERSON SR., COURTESY OF THE CONNECTICUT HISTORICAL SOCIETY

The wagons to the south side of the tent were burning, and some concession tops. A circus hand jumped in a Coca-Cola truck and backed it away from the tent.

The flames were dangerously close to the light plant and its generators, which were filled with diesel. In his Weary Willie costume—complete with huge shoes—Emmett Kelly came rushing over with a wash bucket full of water, his painted frown a perfect expression of dismay and helplessness.

Hands filled buckets from a canvas trough on wheels near where the menagerie had been. Gangs of roughnecks strained to push the light wagons away from the tent. Their tires were burning. Deacon Blanchfield had tractors come in and drag them out, water truck 133 spraying them as they rolled.

Engine Company 7 was the first unit to arrive. As they neared box 82 at Clark and Westland, they slowed. Two boys in the road pointed toward the circus, and they accelerated. The tent was down on the ground, the fire confined to the east end. At a glance, 7's captain saw that despite George W. Smith's efforts they couldn't fit the truck along the south side. They'd have to lay a line in. There was a hydrant right by the grounds, but still it would be a ton of hose. The captain called on the civilians standing there to lend a hand. Young John Stewart stepped forward and volunteered.

On his way out along the south side, Emerson stops to take this shot of Emmett Kelly lugging a bucket of water toward the light plants. Note prop wagon 201 in the background. PHOTO BY RALPH EMERSON SR., COURTESY OF THE *HARTFORD COURANT*

They laid nine hundred feet, then had to add another one hundred fifty. It stretched down to the southeast corner where the Coca-Cola top was now a puddle of glass and ashes. "That's not water," someone warned the firemen, and they detoured around it. By the time they reached the east end there was no tent left, only the bleachers burning, so they directed their attentions to the wagons.

Commissioner Hickey hustled down the midway and found a policeman. He asked the officer to see that all cars with stretchers went to the east end, and as soon as possible, even if they had to run over the hoses. He slid into cruiser number 8 where Chief Hallissey was sitting. After a brief conference, Hickey got on the radio and called Governor Baldwin, a friend and fellow Republican. They would need to mobilize all civilian defense forces within reach of the city. Immediately. Yes, it was that bad. Transportation was going to be a problem, and crowd control.

"Listen," Baldwin said, "I'll go on the air and tell them not to go out there when they hear of the fire but to communicate with this office."

Hickey agreed.

Mayor William Mortensen arrived minutes after the first fire crews. He saw the bodies at the chute and conferred with Hickey, then used the phone at McGovern's to call the State Armory. They would use the huge floor of the drill shed as a makeshift morgue.

The governor contacted the state police and asked the Connecticut State Guard to alert their reserves. Baldwin then enlisted all the doctors, nurses and medical supplies he could get from the Veterans' Home in Rocky Hill and the Veterans' Hospital in Newington. He mobilized a corps of state employees there at the Capitol to take care of the clerical duties at the armory, then set up his emergency broadcast with WTIC.

A popular governor, Baldwin had recently announced he would not seek reelection. State's Attorney H. Meade Alcorn and some other Republicans had drawn up a petition urging him to reconsider—for the good of the state, not just the party—but Baldwin was firm. He was supposed to be taking it easy, cruising through his last months in office. Now this.

He wasn't alone in his efforts. The state and the city were fully prepared for a disaster of this magnitude. After the flood of '36 and the great hurricane of '38 and the Charter Oak Bridge collapse in '41, both had de-

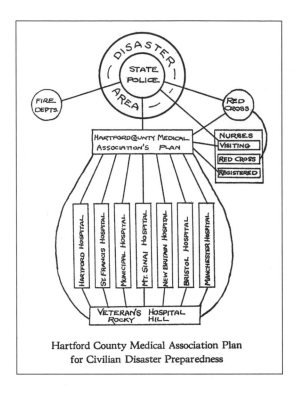

Hartford County Medical Association Plan
for Civilian Disaster Preparedness

vised wide-ranging organizations capable of responding to any catastrophe in a concerted manner. After Pearl Harbor, the State War Council added thousands of volunteers to the mix and a level of vigilance that would never be duplicated. On the heels of the Cocoanut Grove, Dr. Donald B. Wells of Hartford Hospital coordinated all these agencies with the state police, the Red Cross, and Hartford County's seven civilian hospitals.

A major air raid, a tornado, a munitions explosion—the plan and the equipment were in place, right down to dozens of department-store delivery trucks fitted with special racks to accommodate stretchers. Bandages. Blood plasma. The new wonder drug penicillin.

They would need all of it.

Alive, alive, alive

The elephants were just coming out onto Barbour Street as Engine Company 2 pulled in. Their handlers lined them up side by side by the far curb.

They trumpeted and swung their heads and tried to circle, making everyone nervous. 2 hooked a double-gated connection onto the hydrant across from McGovern's so the other units could use it, then laid in a thousand feet of line, snaking their way through the crowd, knocking into people, weaving around clumps of bystanders.

Engine Company 4 arrived right behind them, and Deputy Chief of Police Michael J. Godfrey in his cruiser. The elephants were blocking the street, and their handlers turned them south down Barbour, trunk to tail, past 345 and 337 and the city's Maternity Home and into a grassy lot at the corner of Charlotte and Barbour vacant except for a billboard. 4 fought its way up the midway, following 2's line, shouldering people aside.

Commissioner Hickey saw the difficulty the firemen were having maneuvering through the confusion. He gathered some policemen and formed a walking picket, herding the crowd back toward Barbour Street.

On Barbour Street, Emerson shoots past the sideshow top at the smoke from the seats and bleachers. Foreground right, handlers have their elephants turned away from the blaze. PHOTO BY RALPH EMERSON SR., COURTESY OF THE *HARTFORD COURANT*

*Firemen from Engine Co.
No. 4 put water on the
grandstand.* PHOTO BY
SPENCER TORELL,
COURTESY OF ART KIELY

On the south side of the lot, the fire from the grandstands was so hot that the light crew had to take cover. The wind was like a blowtorch. Stakes in the ground were burning, guyropes catching the dry grass. Wagons forty feet from the tent caught fire—two of them diesel plants. A circus water truck turned its hose on them, but a man ran up and wrestled the nozzle away, trying to get water on the still-burning canvas. The workers man-handled him, flinging him to the ground.

The man was a Hartford fireman on his day off. He'd attended the show with his wife and three children, and he knew there were still people inside. He later reported the incident and the city issued warrants for the men involved. The crews of all four water trucks reported for a lineup, but the man couldn't identify anyone.

Meanwhile, Chief John C. King and his driver piled out of his radio car and ran toward the smoke. King later said: "Truck crewmen attempted to rescue the panic-stricken women and children that were caught in the path of the onrushing flames. Several ran toward us with their clothing ablaze and they were writhing in pain. As I pulled one elderly woman from under the tent, the woman fought with me to allow her to go back and get her little boy. The firemen kept her on the outside as it meant another life saved. If she had returned under the tent she would never come out alive."

A cruiser stuffed with beat cops picked up on the way bumped across the lot. The men jumped out and headed for the tent. Among them was

Det. William Dineen, whose two children had been at the show with their uncle. He ran like the rest of them.

Engine Company 16 set up shop, tying into 2's double gate and laying their line with the help of civilians. They were stunned to see the tent already on the ground. It had only been minutes since they received the alarm. They turned their water on the seats and bleachers, mopping up.

On the north side, the cat wagons were scorched but not on fire. Lions roared as teams of workers muscled the cages away from the tent.

One circus performer recalled a doctor's assistant, his arms and hands raw, carrying a burned child out of the wreckage. The child looked up at the man and said, "You aren't my daddy."

"I know I'm not your daddy," the man replied, "but I'm going to take care of you." Just as he got her inside the doctor's tent, the child died.

At the east end, by the chute, flames snapped and danced over the pile of bodies. Thomas Barber and John Stewart watched as firemen played water on it.

William Cieri was working Truck 4 out of Engine Company 14, a hook and ladder. He was new. His primary job was rescue, and when they reached the grounds he jumped off, looking for someone to help. The first person he saw was a woman running with her dress on fire. She fell to the ground, the fabric burning off her back. He wanted to turn her over to smother the flames and went to pick her up by one of her biceps. Her flesh felt like putty; it had been cooked. She stiffened up right there in his hands.

The stands and chairs smolder.
PHOTO COURTESY OF THE
HARTFORD COURANT

Oh my God, Cieri thought, from now on I'm wearing gloves. He turned her over and discovered she was pregnant and a feeling of uselessness came over him. He kept moving.

Inside the tent—where the tent had been—he found a boy by May Kovar's ring. He was kneeling as if in prayer, his hands clasped in front of him, his head resting on the ring curb. He wasn't charred but the heat had cracked his skull like a boiled egg left too long in the pot, his brain sticking through the fissures. If Cieri hadn't been so anxious to help, he would have gotten sick.

He went on. The stages had hardly been touched, but on the ground nearby lay a woman, her arms and legs sticking up like a cartoon of a dead animal. Beyond her, in the center ring, lay a middle-aged man cut in half by a pole, one half here, one half there. Cieri kept walking.

Under the pile on the track, Donald Gale came to, cold water shocking his skin. It came fast, cascading down through the layers of bodies above him. Donald cupped a hand over his mouth and nose so he could breathe. He could feel people pulling the bodies off him, and then a pair of hands gripped him and lifted him up. A soldier in uniform took him in his arms and carried him to the chute and handed him across to another soldier on the far side.

The pile at the chute took longer to untangle. At the bottom, firemen found Jerry LeVasseur, badly burned but still alive, not even crying.

Elliott Smith never lost consciousness. After the screaming stopped he lay there waiting, the pain constant but dull. All he could see was the ground in front of him. Eventually he heard male voices and then the stream of water splashing over the bodies on top of him. Some of the water trickled down onto his back, cool and soothing.

"Hey, that's good," he said. "More!"

The firemen heard him and poured it on, but so much that the water pooled on the ground in front of him and began to rise. Elliott couldn't lift his chin out of the mud because of the weight pressing down. "Cut it out!" he yelled. "You're gonna drown me!"

They stopped and clawed the bodies off. The last body they lost their grip on and it fell back on top of Elliott. They reached down and grabbed it with their bare hands, but again the body slipped, thumping against him. The third time they dug their fingers in and hauled it off. A man with dark hair and a mustache picked Elliott up and cradled him in his arms. He wore a bright white button-down shirt. Elliott looked down and saw what had been on top of him.

The bodies on the ground were black and featureless, arms drawn up as if to protect their faces. Human in shape, missing hands and feet, they seemed to him like rag dolls.

The man with the mustache carried him away. Elliott was burned and wet and bleeding. In the man's arms, the pain a continuous presence, Elliott Smith thought: He's going to ruin his shirt.

Have you seen him?

There were bodies on top of the chute and back along the track, but those were mostly scattered and obviously charred, beyond help. Firemen and show folks dug at the main pile beside the chute—seven or eight deep, Thomas Barber said—hoping to find more people alive beneath it. The bodies on top were fused together like cooled lava; rescuers had to crack them apart to reach Jerry LeVasseur and Elliott Smith.

There were more. Firemen discovered four or five at the very bottom.

At the inquest, Deacon Blanchfield remembered: "There was two ladies on the bottom that was alive, and one of them only had a little hole burned in her stocking, and all the other bodies there wasn't a stitch of clothing on. I carried one of these ladies out."

They separated the living from the dead. Clowns in sooty greasepaint helped lift the injured over the chute. Men swore, shaking their heads. An officer carried out a horrifically burned girl in a blue pinafore. He was crying but the child was mute, too hurt for tears.

The rescuers improvised stretchers from wagon sides, ladders wrapped in blankets and large squares of canvas, hauling the few injured still living out the back door. The hero Bill Curlee was among them, crushed under a quarterpole, badly burned yet miraculously still alive. They rushed him outside.

The rest were dead, sixty or seventy matted at the chute, some burned so severely that longtime firemen couldn't determine what sex they were.

Officers Griffin and Kenefick returned to help carry out those they'd failed to save. Thomas Barber pitched in, lugging out eighteen bodies by his own count. It was a mess; they were all baked. Another detective had two nephews in the tent and didn't know if they made it out. He knew they wore brown shoes. He saw his partners carrying out kids with brown shoes, but the children were so badly burned he couldn't tell if it was them or not.

John Stewart had heard the screams from the street; now he stood by the pile and saw what fire could do to a person. Around him, firemen were overhauling the bleachers and seats. The ground was hot; a doctor called to the scene from nearby Municipal Hospital had rubber-soled shoes on, and they melted. The smell of cooked flesh was heavy.

Farther in, charred bodies lay beneath the rear of the grandstands and under the bleachers—people who'd fallen through or passed out. A fireman from Norwich had come to the circus, and naturally he helped afterward. Kneeling by the sidewall, he reached for the hands of a little girl lying under a fold of canvas. For some reason the body was stuck. He raised the canvas and discovered why. The child was clasped in the arms of her mother.

The rescuers moved the bodies from the chute to a plot of ground outside, covering them with several panels from the sidewall of the dressing tent. Commissioner Hickey made sure no one removed the dead to the armory until Medical Examiner Dr. Walter Weissenborn—already on his way—had a chance to inspect them.

Headquarters had called not only Weissenborn, the Red Cross and the state's attorney's office (whose three prosecutors were en route), but also nearby St. Michael's Rectory. With so many dead and dying, he figured they would need priests.

The first to arrive was the young Reverend Joseph G. Murphy of St. Justin's, a five-minute ride away. Father Murphy had only been ordained in May. As a seminary student, he spent his summer vacations overseeing neighborhood playgrounds in Waterbury. St. Justin's was his first parish; he'd been named curate just a month before. He came upon the rescue efforts at the chute as they were breaking the bodies apart. The first victim he approached seemed to have died in a terrible struggle. The remains hardly resembled a human form. There was no chance of performing the full last rites on the corpse, anointing all five senses; there were no eyes or ears or hands. And, truthfully, who knew what faith this person held in life?

The dead on stretchers. Notice the pugilistic posture of the corpse behind the sailor's leg.
PHOTO COURTESY OF THE HARTFORD COLLECTION, THE HARTFORD PUBLIC LIBRARY

Surely though, in the end, they must have been contrite and desired absolution from their sins. He could safely say that at least.

Father Murphy took a vial of oil from his pocket. "By this anointing may the Lord forgive you in whatsoever you have failed," he recited in Latin, and rubbed some of the oil on the victim's forehead. And then the next soul, and then the next. He would be on the grounds for five hours.

The Reverend Thomas Looney of St. Michael's dashed out of the rectory there and hailed a passing car. The driver took him straight to the circus grounds. As they pulled up, Father Looney saw a woman lying on a stretcher in the middle of the street, her arms stripped of skin. He knelt by her side, absolving and anointing her before a pair of MPs just arrived from Bradley Field hustled her off. The army had sent three truckloads of soldiers to help with the dead and wounded. Inside the charred ring of seats, Father Looney went to the pile on the track and began anointing all he could reach. Somewhere among them lay Hulda Grant, dead, her jaw broken.

"I shall not describe the physical condition of these bodies," the Father later wrote. "That is something I am trying to erase from my mind."

Downtown, a Hartford County deputy sheriff sat in a lawyer's office, wrapping up some business. The way the government was structured then, lawyers paid the sheriff and his deputies piecemeal for serving writs, five dollars a summons. As he was about to leave, the lawyer's phone rang. He made to excuse himself, but the lawyer said, "Wait a minute." The circus was on fire, he said; it didn't look good. There would probably be a fair amount of work coming his way the next few days.

A Wallingford man was parking his car in the business district and noticed the column of smoke to the north. He'd just dropped off his mother-in-law and his two children at the circus. Ambulances and fire trucks screamed through the streets. He asked a traffic cop where the fire was. The circus, the cop said. The man hopped in his car and followed the sirens, blowing through red lights, oblivious of the other traffic.

Regular ambulance service at this time in Hartford was just starting. Usually undertakers picked up victims in a method informally known as "bag 'em and drag 'em" because the drivers would wrap the injured in blankets, put them in hearses and drop them off at one of the hospitals. Pearl Harbor changed that. The State War Council put in place an emergency transportation plan in case the Germans bombed Colt's or United Aircraft. Alarms would go off at G. Fox, Sage-Allen, Brown Thomson—all the large department stores—who would then scramble their delivery vans. The council and the Red Cross ran drills to make sure the plan would work if it was ever necessary. After the success of the Normandy invasion, it appeared they would never have to use it.

One seventeen-year-old boy was working in the shipping room at Brown Thomson, delivering furniture. The phone rang on his boss's desk; they were supposed to go to the circus grounds and help remove bodies to the armory.

His boss drove. Their truck was brown and had sidebars in back to take stretchers. The police had cordoned off Main Street so emergency vehicles could get there faster. The teenager hardly saw any traffic on the way up. He knew the tent had burned and that people had been killed, but beyond that he didn't know what to expect.

Far ahead of them, a *Courant* photographer raced north in the paper's '41 Ford. He had his 4 × 5 Speedgraphic and a woman reporter with him. A twenty-year-old summer intern, he'd gotten the nod from the people upstairs and he was making the most of it. The night before, the two of them

(Top) Looking north up Barbour. The elephants have left their business in the street and moved to the corner of Charlotte and Barbour. The sideshow tent stands untouched. (Above) Hoses run straight up the midway. The marquee still stands, and the sideshow banners, but the big top is gone. Note the Circus Diner lunch counter to the left, and the ticket wagons beyond it. PHOTOS BY SPENCER TORELL, COURTESY OF ART KIELY

had gone to Bristol to do a puff piece on a local aerialist and her family. Now they had an actual story. Army trucks with sirens in their grilles tore up North Main. Mail trucks, milk trucks, an armored car. They all converged on Barbour Street.

Outside the tent, people ran around frantically; others stood dully, as if hypnotized, their hands laid open from sliding down the sidepoles and ropes. The photographer and the reporter hurried up the midway, high stepping over the hoses. All that was left of the big top was the marquee, strangely untouched, still promising THE GREATEST SHOW ON EARTH.

Inside, Engine Company 16 were on the west stage, soaking down the last stubborn flames. The ground was muddy from the water. On the track was a small pile of bodies, still stuck together from the heat. A crowd surrounded them—police and firemen and circus workers. One fireman was busy pulling the mound apart. The *Courant* photographer came up behind two workmen, framed the shot and nailed it.

The mix of rescue workers is typical of the fire, all the men pitching in yet helpless before the dead. The firemen are from Engine Company 5; the priest in the background is Father Hewitt—like Father Murphy, also from St. Justin's. At the bottom of the frame a charred quarterpole rests heavily on the grandstand railing, bending it nearly perpendicular; after a heavier post, the railing continues, outlined against the slacks of the policeman, proving this isn't the chute, as the picture is usually captioned, though close to it.

Looking west across the center ring from the east stage (the sideshow top and the house on Barbour in the left background). On the fallen main poles, note the bale rings. Once the canvas lost tension, these steel doughnuts dropped to the foot of the poles. The third and fourth main poles straddling the center ring fell directly westward, toward the main entrance, while the other four (outside) main poles folded eastward toward the bandstand. The quarterpoles mostly fell outward, leaning east. PHOTO BY PAUL R. SHAFER, COURTESY OF MR. SHAFER HIMSELF

As soon as the photographer got his shot, the roughnecks were on him, spinning him around, pushing him away. Son of a bitch, they said. They threatened him with clubs, and then when he didn't move fast enough, gave him a few whacks. Afraid they'd break his camera, he handed it off to the reporter. Get out of here, they said, go on, and they weren't kidding. He retreated but not far enough; they chased him back out the front door.

He took one more shot, two of the convalescent soldiers from Bradley Field standing by the rear of the circus bus, before returning to the *Courant's* offices on State Street. When the shots were developed, his editor liked them. But they couldn't run the one with the bodies—too gruesome.

Back inside, rescue efforts continued. Sideshow performers and concessionaires worked shoulder to shoulder with MPs and civilians, doctors and nurses and Red Cross volunteers. Girls from the aerial ballet lugged pails of water to the gangs who labored under the hot sun. Mr. and Mrs. Fischer, the giants, were crying. The Wallendas had all made it out okay, though Karl didn't know how. His leotard was scorched, his face black with ash. "This will mean the end of the big top," he predicted. "And a good thing too."

The less badly burned lay dazed in the grass, knees skinned, hair and clothes singed. One boy separated from his family could only recall his first name, saying it over and over.

A woman asked Dorothy Bocek if she was waiting for someone. Dorothy told her about losing her sister Stella and her nephew at the chute. The woman asked if she had a way to get home, and Dorothy said no. The woman had a car, she'd take Dorothy home. Maybe her sister would be there.

Joan Smith couldn't find Elliott or their mother so she climbed a slight rise on the north side of the tent to get a better view. There were just too many people roaming around. Some neighbors from Vernon happened to see her standing there and took her back to their car. They would stop by her father's office and let him know what the situation was.

Another girl was crying because she'd dropped a handkerchief her mother had given her that morning with strict instructions not to lose it. She was frightened by the animals, and her father had to carry her across the street.

Neighbors had set aside a space on the lawn of the Maternity Home for missing children and directed frantic parents to it. In yards up and down Barbour Street, people waited by their cars, searching the crowd for familiar faces.

Janet Moore Sapolis, seven, had gone to the circus with her aunt, her grandmother, her five-year-old cousin and some friends. Separated during their escape, she came across a friend who remembered where their car was parked. When her aunt and cousin finally showed up, her aunt told Janet that her grandmother had been burned and was on the way to the hospital.

One young woman found a little blond girl, four or five years old. The woman's father combed the grounds for the little girl's parents but no one claimed her. They would stop at a police station and give them her description, he said, then take her home with them.

The police had arrived in force now, patrol wagons swinging up in front of the grounds, squads of officers hopping down out of the back. Hickey had them clear the midway and set up ropes to keep people out.

Inside the ropes there was just as much confusion. One distraught woman walked around holding her arms outstretched. She kept saying over and over again, "He's only this big—have you seen him?" She peeked under scraps of canvas, repeating her plea.

Another woman knelt down in prayer with a man. In minutes the woman's two children, faces smudged and clothes torn, emerged from the crowd and sprinted into her arms.

One bally girl had rescued several children during the fire. Now she tended to the wounded, tearing off strips of her slip to bandage the arm of a woman whose hair was burned to a cinder. Next she tried to help a father carrying his badly burned son. The man was hysterical, laughing and crying at the same time.

People keened and prayed out loud. Women roamed the grounds, shoeless, stockings ripped, weeping and calling for their children. Terrified children flitted about blindly, crying for their mothers.

Don Cook stood outside the east end with the couple and their two children, waiting, until it was clear no one else was coming out. Then he walked back with them to their car.

David Curlee had made it to their car. The metal was hot in the sun, and there were people everywhere. Finally his uncle showed up, leading the other children.

"Where's your dad?" he asked.

David pointed back toward the big top. "He's in there."

Bringing out the dead

The man with the mustache carried Elliott Smith outside and lifted him into the back of an army truck. A G.I. was kneeling there, tending two other wounded. The man with the mustache banged on the side of the truck and shouted, "Go, go!" and the six-by-six rolled over the grounds. Every bump hurt.

Another soldier helped Donald Gale onto the white circus bus, filling with burned survivors. The bus had a bad spring, and leaned, higher on one side. The soldier held him all the way to Municipal Hospital.

A cab full of mothers and children took Jerry LeVasseur. They were all crying except Jerry. He felt it wouldn't do any good.

Mae Smith found a man to drive her girls, the three of them in his backseat.

Another man drove Mildred and Edward Cook to Municipal. Edward whimpered from his burns. In bad shape herself, Mildred had him on her lap, trying to soothe him. When she touched him, his skin came off in her hands. He moaned and moaned. With the traffic and all that had happened, the driver snapped, "Can't you keep him quiet?"

Stanley Kurneta discovered his nephew Raymond Erickson among the injured, lying on a board in the shade of a circus wagon. Raymond's face and neck were burned brown and his clothes were soaked; he'd been in the pile against the chute. He was sobbing quietly, his eyes rolling from side to side. His uncle gently picked him up and carried him to an army truck filled with victims. He climbed in after him, and they were off.

The Red Cross Motor Corps cars in which the convalescent soldiers from Bradley had come were pressed into service. A few of the men had suffered minor injuries escaping from the big top, but even those who were unhurt weren't allowed to help. They were patients. They stood there in the middle of all the chaos, frustrated.

The emergency plan worked. On Barbour Street, trucks from Pratt &   *127*

Hands load the dead into an Army truck pulled up beside the cloud float for the Panto's Paradise spec.
PHOTO COURTESY OF
AP/WIDE WORLD PHOTOS

Whitney and Colt's waited for the cars and six-bys to leave so they could bring in their loads of stretchers and blankets. All war industries had their own plant protection squads and medical departments—some with ambulances fashioned from station wagons—and these arrived in force, the doctors, nurses and guards spreading throughout the grounds.

The Connecticut Company offered its buses to the police and the Red Cross. There were enough trucks for the dead and wounded here, but the hospitals would need extra help. The War Council sent the buses to Trinity College to pick up one hundred fifty naval cadets trained in first aid.

At the east end, outside the back door, casualties overflowed the circus doctor's medical tent and lay strewn about the ground. There was no room so he set up an emergency hospital in the partly burned dressing top. Hands brought in four victims on a wide board—two men, a woman and a child. The men were dead, the child tucked in a fetal position, its face bloated with fluid. The woman moaned, her skin a rusty brown, eyes thin slits. A man who witnessed this found his way out to Barbour Street where his family was waiting at their car, completely unharmed. He walked by them, looking all around as if they were lost. "We're right here," his wife called.

One woman had worn plastic combs in her hair. They melted, blistering patches of her scalp.

On the sidewalk a mother holding an infant to her chest was crying.

A man went over to help her. He took the baby from her and saw her chest and the baby's stomach were burned raw.

Another mother came up to a man on the sidewalk with a terribly burned child in her arms and asked him what she should do. The man directed her to a house up the street where they were taking in victims. The man knew at a glance yet couldn't bear to tell the woman that her child was dead.

Back at the east end, Thomas Barber and his partners were still bringing out the bodies. A Wethersfield woman saw them carry out a stretcher with what she thought was an animal, because its paws were sticking up in the air. They put it in the trunk of a police car and closed the lid. Then she realized it wasn't an animal. It was a person.

"They looked like gelatin being carried out," another woman recalled. "All gush. All I could think of was they looked like black Jell-O."

The worst resembled dried relics or lumps of coal, charred logs, chunks of black pumice. Rescuers covered them with horse blankets from the ring stock top and some others with Pratt & Whitney stencilled on them.

As they turned onto Barbour, the teenager from Brown Thomson and his boss could smell the fire. They drove their truck over the sidewalk and right up onto the grounds. My God, this can't be real, he thought. There were bodies everywhere and people walking all over. The ruins were still smoking, and the smell of the dead was inescapable, stronger than rotten eggs.

They jumped down from the truck. People were picking up bodies. Some lay on stretchers, uncovered, frozen in grotesque positions. One woman, colored a golden brown, lay naked on her back, rigid as a statue; her bladder let loose and a stream of urine arced straight up from her.

One man told the teenager that he'd tried to pick up a body and his hands had gone through the flesh right down to the bone. The bone was hot and he'd burned his hand, jerking back as if he'd touched a hot stove.

The teenager and his boss were anxious to get out of there. He held his breath and swallowed a couple of times. He didn't want to do this, but it had to be done; it was what they'd gone up there to do, to help where they could. They lifted one blackened body very carefully, set it on a stretcher and placed it in the truck. They did another one, and one more after that. Then they got back in the truck and headed downtown for Broad Street and the armory, trying not to think of what was bumping in the back on every turn.

Another man from Hartford brought a truck from Colt's. The bodies he had to deal with were hidden under a big piece of canvas, probably the sidewall of the dressing tent. The stench was like burned chicken. At one point he went off into the woods and vomited. The firemen and cops pulled the canvas back; underneath were sixty or seventy of the dead. Their clothes were gone, and their hair. The heat had dehydrated their tissues so their skin split apart, their organs boiled hard and protruding. They all looked like they were nine months pregnant—men, women and children.

A young woman was running the Aetna Florist Shop for two uncles away in the navy. They'd fitted their delivery truck for emergencies, and the woman ferried the injured to hospitals and families to the morgue in search of loved ones. "You saw people burned so bad it was sickening," she recalled. "I couldn't eat for days."

A mortician from the O'Brien Funeral Home in Bristol had his ambulance on the scene early and took five bodies to the armory. Very plainly, the undertaker said they were in the worst shape he'd ever seen.

In the middle of this, mothers and fathers stalked the grounds, searching for their children. One man's three-year-old son had become separated from him as they left the tent, and he feared the child had been trampled. The father finally found him in a yard on Barbour Street, every stitch of clothing torn from his body, including his shoes.

Commissioner Hickey's nieces and nephews were safe back at Aunt Isabel's house down the block—all but one, who for some reason chose to walk home. The boys had gone over the snow fence into the victory gardens and cut through a yard to Barbour Street. Aunt Isabel took care of little Billy and the girls. When they had everyone together, Adolph Pastore fit them all into the Cadillac and drove up to the grounds to let the commissioner know everything was okay.

In the backseat with the other boys, one of the nephews wasn't sure everything was okay. In the scramble his shirt had somehow fallen out of his back pocket. His mother was not going to be pleased.

Girls lost their hair ribbons, women lost their purses. One older gentleman lost his upper denture.

A child of five was upset because he'd lost his program. A woman came up to him and said, "Here, little boy, you can have mine." Her arms were burned from her wrists to her shoulders, but she handed him the program as if nothing was wrong.

The police collected lost children, sitting them in their cars for the time being.

The man from Wallingford who'd seen the smoke downtown screeched up and ran for the midway. He'd had three miles to imagine the worst, but the scene was beyond his comprehension. The police at the ropes wouldn't let him in to look for his children and mother-in-law. They restrained him like anyone else. One cop finally convinced him to wait, that there was nothing he could do here. He padded back to Barbour Street, his mind still flying, only to find his mother-in-law and the two kids waiting for him. His daughter had recognized their car.

Another woman spotted her missing daughter on the street and made her way through the crowd, eyes locked on the girl, afraid she'd disappear again. A fire engine swung between them, nearly hitting the mother.

The grounds were a maze of bystanders, cars and fire equipment. Through it snaked an endless procession of trucks and buses and makeshift ambulances filled with burned survivors. The trucks bumped over the dirt laid across the sidewalk and turned onto Barbour, headed west to Municipal or south to Hartford Hospital. Behind them came a convoy of the dead, slower, though their sirens were just as insistent, spreading across the city like an invading army.

Triage

At 2:45, as soon as they heard from Sergeant Spellman that the big top was on fire, police headquarters called Municipal Hospital and asked them to send doctors to the grounds. The call also served as an alert. Municipal was only a few minutes from Barbour Street. They'd see the brunt of the casualties.

Also known as Hartford City Hospital, Municipal would never be mistaken for their much larger, private cousin, Hartford Hospital.

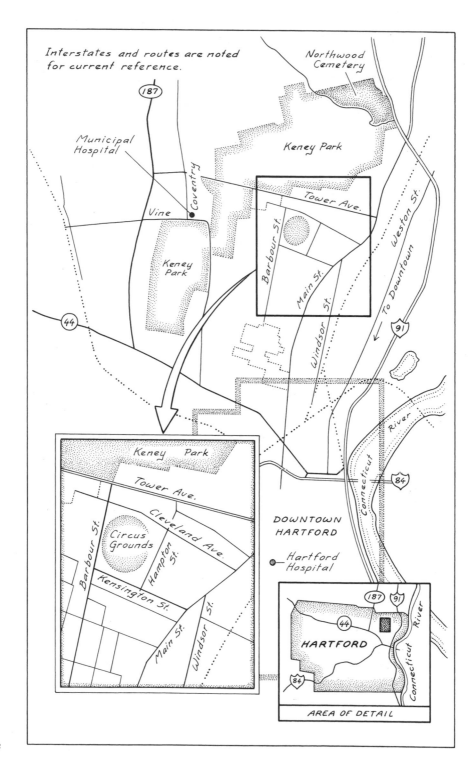

Interstates and routes are noted for current reference.

187

Northwood Cemetery

Municipal Hospital

Coventry

Vine

187

Keney Park

Keney Park

Tower Ave.

Barbour St.

Main St.

Windsor St.

Weston St.

To Downtown

44

Keney Park

91

Connecticut River

84

Keney Park

Tower Ave.

Cleveland Ave.

Barbour St.

Circus Grounds

Hampton St.

Kensington St.

Main St.

Windsor St.

DOWNTOWN HARTFORD

Hartford Hospital

187 91

44

HARTFORD

84

Connecticut River

AREA OF DETAIL

Municipal was the charity hospital, the place you went when you couldn't pay. Its clients were the poor and indigent, and in the last decade the hospital had come to resemble its patients. "It was a dog," said one nurse who worked at both Municipal and Hartford. There was no money for upkeep. The equipment was old and there were holes in the floors. It was a place no one wanted to be, and now everyone was coming here.

As the ambulances rolled, Municipal scrambled. Each floor sent their spare nurses downstairs to admitting. The switchboard called back all off-duty personnel and requested extra internes from Hartford and St. Francis Hospitals. Nurses prepped the four operating rooms. The staff gathered morphine and plasma and bandages and rushed them downstairs. Janitors set up extra cots and mattresses in the wards and halls.

Downtown, Hartford Hospital had a few more minutes to prepare. The chief of staff put all personnel on alert, addressing them over the PA system. After Pearl Harbor, the hospital had drafted an emergency plan for civilian disasters. They'd run a drill the previous fall so everyone knew their battle stations. They'd also designed a large triage room on the ground floor of their brand-new South Building capable of handling one hundred patients, outfitting it with lockers full of equipment and laying in direct oxygen, suction and electrical lines. An overflow maternity ward happened to be empty, and by chance a large surgical ward had recently been cleared for painting. Minutes after the call, Hartford Hospital knew where their wounded were going to go.

In addition, Dr. Donald B. Wells, who coordinated the county's emergency plan, was the resident expert on burns. After the Cocoanut Grove fire, he'd taken a team of Hartford doctors up to Mass General to study their new emergency treatment procedures. When he returned he established a special burns committee and drew up guidelines for a similar disaster in Hartford. This would be the first time they used them.

Up on Westland, the truck carrying Elliott Smith weaved through traffic, blowing its horn.

"It hurts to lie on my back," Elliott told the soldier with him.

"Roll over on your stomach."

The pain was dull, just something that was there, steady. Then Elliott passed out.

At Municipal, the first car to pull up was a police cruiser. Right behind it came the circus bus, the Red Cross cars, the army trucks, the private ambulances—filling the yard, parking on the grass. Like the rest of the country, the hospital was shorthanded because of the war; it had no paid orderlies, so janitors helped carry the injured in.

The corridors smelled of roasted flesh. The rescuers had brought everyone, so even before triage the doctors had to first separate the dead. "Some of the children were just plain black, their skin was seared so badly," said a driver for the Red Cross Motor Corps. "Some couldn't even be described as human beings."

The halls were lined with stretchers. One girl lay on her stomach, her back burned from her derriere up to her shoulders. Some of the injured were screaming, others mute, off in shock. Children jumped up and down with pain.

A doctor knelt beside Donald Gale and calmly talked with him. Donald gave him his name and address. The doctor said, "Lie still," but Donald was uncomfortable on his back. He went to roll over and noticed the pillow he was lying on was black with ash. He lay down on his back again.

He knew he was burned, but didn't know how bad exactly. His arms looked like they'd been sunburned. The skin was already peeling in sheets, the tissue beneath weeping fluid. From the end of his right index finger poked a bone. He wasn't scared so much as stunned, dumbfounded. He wasn't quite sure what was going on.

Two nurses came with scissors to cut away his clothes. He remembered his chameleon then; suddenly he was concerned about it. He looked down at his shirt. It was still there on its string leash, but stiff, motionless, its lifeless eye peering up at him.

Elliott Smith came to in a room with a few other survivors on cots. A nurse's aide was going around handing out tiny paper cups of orange juice. Elliott took one. It tasted so good he begged her for more, please, but the woman only had so much, and everyone was asking her for more. He passed out again. When he returned they were cutting his clothes off.

Jerry LeVasseur woke up inside an oxygen tent, separated from the world by a wall of canvas and plastic panels. Someone asked him his name and he gave it. Another person faraway said, "He may not make it."

When Stanley Kurneta carried Raymond Erickson inside, someone told him to go to the fourth floor. He took the elevator with Raymond in his arms. Another person up there told him to lay his nephew on a mattress by the side of the hall. Standing there in a straw hat was a tall, stocky priest. He had a ruddy face.

"This is Raymond Erickson," Stanley told him. "Give him the last rites."

"All right," the Father said. He removed his hat and began to read a prayer from a book.

Stanley left. He needed to find his sister Mary and the rest of the family. Dazed, he couldn't find the elevator, so he walked down the stairs and out through the crowd and back along Vine Street toward the circus.

Downstairs, Mae Smith settled her girls in the hallway. She located a pay phone, hoping to let her husband in Middletown know what had happened, but her fingers were so swollen she couldn't dial the number.

Bill Curlee was here, though there was nothing they could do for him, and Mildred and Edward Cook. She could barely remember the ride. Now they came and took Edward from her, spirited him away to be treated.

First they gave the victims morphine to ease their pain, then administered plasma to replace lost blood volume, rehydrating patients so they wouldn't go into shock. (For years afterward, this was standard practice; now plasma is discouraged as it leaks into the lungs.) Because most had badly burned limbs, nurses had to search for veins, especially on small children, occasionally cutting them down to get the big needles in. Nurses snipped their clothes off and covered the injured with sterile sheets. Following Mass General's procedures after the Cocoanut Grove, they didn't debride the burned areas but left the blebs alone. Dressing teams wrapped patients with Vaseline-impregnated gauze and covered this with light plaster casts for even pressure. Tetanus shots and sulfa drugs would fight any infections.

Not all the people coming in were burned. Some had broken ankles and wrists or bad lacerations, others just rope burns or bruises from being stepped on. A twenty-two-year-old woman had a bad combination of both: two broken ankles and burns over most of her body. She'd taken her niece as a birthday present and tried to protect her when the flames rolled over them. The niece was here too, also in grave shape. And unknown to Elliott or Joan Smith, their mother had come in, her scalp and shoulders seared.

A young doctor stood at the front desk, shunting the less severely injured to the outpatient clinic, and still there were too many. The operating rooms were full, the dying backed up into the halls. He called the Red Cross for more doctors and nurse's aides. They promised to have the radio stations broadcast his request, but it would take time to mobilize people. Everyone seemed to be on vacation.

All the while, relatives of the dead and missing mobbed the lobby, trying to find their loved ones, demanding answers, crying and wailing, standing around and getting in the way. The place was bedlam. Outside, the injured and bereaved sat in the grass. A man who drove up with his wife took one look at the jammed entrance and turned around.

Hartford Hospital, with more room and adequate staff, fared better, but the scene was essentially the same—people brought in with skin hanging off their charred arms, the peeled patches a raw red. Broken limbs, victims passed out on cots, moaning. A nurse there said, "Those that weren't as bad could talk to you, and you tried to tell them it would be okay." Anxious parents moved from patient to patient, searching.

As the ambulances dropped off the injured, doctors and nurses set them out on stretchers in the hallways and did triage in the receiving rooms, then shipped the stable patients up to the wards. One interne devised a quicker method of delivering plasma to children by skipping the extremities and using the more protected femoral vein in the groin, eliminating the need for any cut downs. They followed the Cocoanut Grove procedures of no debridement and Vaselined gauze. Instead of the binding plaster casts used at Municipal, they substituted rolled newspaper splints and sterile-sheet wadding wrapped with Ace bandages. In addition to sulfa drugs, Hartford Hospital had access to penicillin and used it liberally. (As with the use of plasma to combat shock, penicillin is now discouraged in burn cases since it travels in the bloodstream while infection gathers in the burned, dead tissues; modern hospitals rely on antibiotic salves.)

Despite their emergency plan and its execution, the hospital was still a war zone, with all of war's horrors. A boy and his grandmother were here, both burned, the boy with a possible skull fracture, his grandmother burned on her face. A great number of adults were burned on the top of the head. The smell in South Building was like a roast left in the oven.

Though the number of dead was much smaller here, the heartbreak was the same. One mother asked a nurse to check on her son, but when the nurse walked into his ward the child had just died. By hospital policy she had to report the death to a doctor; the doctor would inform the mother. The nurse was relieved. She didn't have the stomach to tell the woman.

Another young woman was unburned but had miscarried. The strain of escaping aggravated an older man's heart condition. Fractured pelvises, broken backs. After having seen the people downstairs, they were glad to be alive.

St. Francis, the city's large Catholic hospital, didn't see its first patient until 3:25, well after the fire, but eventually treated nearly sixty people, using the more old-fashioned boric acid ointment on their burns. Among them was Mabel Epps, hysterical, worried for her unborn child and her two boys, her sister and her niece—all still missing. She wasn't burned, so the examining doctor assigned her to the maternity floor. The nurses there didn't know what to do. The woman would not stop crying.

Mt. Sinai, the small Jewish hospital downtown, hardly saw any casualties. A plastic surgeon there knew his wife had planned on taking their daughter to the matinee. When he called home there was no answer. The doctor's specialties were burns and skin grafting, so he was in charge of an ER team. With every stretcher he held his breath.

Unexpected guests

WTHT, an affiliate of the Mutual Broadcasting System, was carrying their "Game of the Day," the Red Sox and Tigers live from Fenway Park. The Sox were tarring Detroit behind Bobby Doerr's 4-for-4, Tex Houston cruising to his thirteenth win, when the station's news staff heard about the fire from the *Times'* city desk. Their studios on the upper floors of the American Industrial Building downtown overlooked the North End; from their windows they could see the smoke. They were debating interrupting the network feed when the Mutual news broke in with a bulletin.

In New Britain, fans listening to the game noticed ambulances going by, screaming north for Hartford. When the announcer cut in, it suddenly made sense.

Governor Baldwin addressed the public at 3:00 P.M. Before he went on the air, "I was trying to keep calm myself. That's one thing that was going through my mind. I had been in hot spots before. I was in the navy in the First World War and had been in many hot spots and I know that to get excited, to do things hastily, was to confuse the efforts."

He came on and gave the basic facts, then asked everyone to please stay away from the grounds and let the rescue workers do their jobs. "I urge you all to be calm. Just remember this: Hysteria will only add to the confusion. It will only prevent us from doing everything that we can do to take care of the injured and identify those who are missing."

People who'd made it out of the tent easily were shocked to hear that others had been killed. Though they'd been involved, they hadn't realized the seriousness of the fire until they heard it on the radio.

Word spread throughout town. At the Palace and the Strand and the Allyn, announcements over loudspeakers asked all volunteers and nurse's

The aftermath on Barbour Street, a hook-and-ladder parked beside the sideshow top. The elephants are gone, replaced by police cars.
PHOTO BY RALPH EMERSON SR., COURTESY OF THE *HARTFORD COURANT*

aides to report to the box office. The manager of the State Theater stopped *Snow White and the Seven Dwarfs* in mid-reel, the screen suddenly blinding white. At Loew's Poli, ushers alerted the rows; at the Lenox, police went up and down the aisles.

Downtown, shoppers at G. Fox listened to the call-out for medical personnel every ten minutes. Report to the office and a truck will take you up to the grounds.

One father was working first shift at Pratt & Whitney in East Hartford when the announcement came over the intercom. He immediately punched out and drove to Shepherd Tobacco on Windsor Street to pick up his wife. Like so many parents, the two of them would search for hours.

Back on Barbour Street, as soldiers loaded bodies into the slat-sided army trucks, two small boys without a scratch on them stepped up to the white ticket wagon. Seeing as they didn't get to watch the whole show, they figured they ought to at least get a refund.

The sideshow top was untouched. The wind had pushed the flames east, away from the menagerie. Not a single animal was hurt. Camels and donkeys stood in the shade in neighbors' yards, tethered to tree trunks. Safe on the lot at the corner of Barbour and Charlotte, the elephants were still spooked by the fire, trumpeting with fright. Their handlers had to whack them to keep them quiet.

A cub reporter for the *Times* remarked on their eerie blasts as he made for the grounds. The sidewalks teemed with people, the firehoses solid as concrete underfoot.

Survivors straggled back to their cars only to discover they'd left their keys in their jackets and their jackets in the tent. Two women from Bolton returned to the yard where they'd parked to find their Pontiac gone. They'd left the keys in the car so the attendant could move it if necessary. Someone must have taken it to use as an ambulance, they concluded. They reported the incident to the police, trusting the car would be returned to them.

Families on Barbour Street opened their homes to the victims. One elderly woman served milk and ice water to children separated from their families. Stands that an hour ago sold lemonade at inflated prices now passed it out for free. A woman sewed a button back on for a little girl; her mother was so grateful she wrote a letter to the editor.

The house at 378 Barbour, the first one north of the grounds, was inundated, the porch a field hospital. Delivery trucks veered to the curb and dumped their loads so they could take victims. The sidewalk was covered with dry cleaning and fresh bread.

Up and down the street, mothers rummaged through medicine chests for ointments to soothe the more superficial burns. Some fell back on trusted home remedies. One mother sent her children to fetch as many sacks of potatoes as they could get. She laid raw slices on the burned until the sacks were empty. Another mother put on a pot of coffee and started tearing up the family's sheets and towels for bandages. Later they had to buy all new linens.

People needed to phone home and let their loved ones know they were okay. They waited in lines that stretched outside, stood there in the heat while the homeowners came out and gave them water. Pay phones at the time cost a nickel. On Barbour, some charged a dime, some a dollar. One woman asked for five dollars a call and got it. Others were glad to help and asked for nothing, flatly refusing to take callers' money.

Many couldn't get through to the outer towns because the circuits were jammed. One woman couldn't reach her mother in New Britain. Her friend called his wife, and his wife called the mother. "It's okay," the wife said, "they're safe." At first the mother didn't know what she was talking about; she didn't have the radio on. The woman's brother was a navy pilot who'd been killed the previous January. The mother didn't need any more bad news.

In line, people were crying. One woman was so shook up that when it was finally her turn to call she forgot where her husband worked.

Others focused on more practical matters. One woman with two children in hand shook her head at her ruined dress. On top of that she'd lost her purse. Stop worrying about the money, her husband said. Just thank God the kids are safe.

The staging area at E. B. McGurk's that John Stewart had helped the wounded to was overflowing. While employees gave the injured first aid, two secretaries calmed the children.

Next door at 353 Barbour, a homeowner stood on his porch, talking with a male aerialist from the circus and looking out over the grounds. The performer said the fire started at the end of the animal act, just after a spotlight had been turned off. Someone turned the light off or away as the cats went into their chutes.

Meanwhile, in the victory gardens and the backyards along Barbour, the injured lay, fallen in the rush to get away from the flames. A policeman found a man sprawled in the grass off Kensington Street, raving. Nothing could be done with him. He lay on the ground facedown, moaning about how they burned, those poor kids. He didn't struggle when the officer helped him up. All the police could get out of the man was that his name was Joe and he lived on Barbour Street. They arranged for him to be taken to Municipal. One block south, on Earle Street, a burned woman stumbled into someone's house and asked them to call an ambulance.

Jaivin's Drugstore at the corner of Barbour and Westland had a pay phone. A line formed early. While people waited, Mr. Jaivin gave the children free ice cream and treated their burns with salve at the soda fountain's marble counter. Molly Garofolo came over from her beauty shop next door where she was watching some lost children. She'd tried to soothe them by washing their faces and putting Band-Aids on their cuts; maybe ice cream would prove to be a more effective medicine.

A young mother and her son wandered down Barbour and stopped across from Jaivin's. They sat down on the curb to take stock of the situation. The woman was badly burned, her leg bruised, her hair singed. She noticed the crowd in Jaivin's and had her son stand up.

They didn't have a phone at home, so she called a neighbor. She reached the neighbor's five-year-old. The child haltingly took the message, then ran outside to the husband—on a ladder, painting their house—and screamed, "Your wife is in the circus fire!"

Another woman took her girl past Jaivin's and farther down Barbour to a Jewish grocery—Levine's Fruit Market or Fleishman's Meats or Weinbaum's Delicatessen—where a lady put ice on her arm.

Some of the burned walked the mile to Municipal Hospital. They looked fine when they came through the door, but when the nurses touched them they screamed in pain. The superheated air, though below the flashpoint of their clothes, had baked their skin.

Along with the emergency workers, prosecutors were on their way to Barbour Street. Their office downtown dispatched a messenger to McGovern's with twenty-five freshly issued subpoenas, all of them summoning Mr. John Doe. They also ordered to McGovern's the clerk of the police court, to take Messrs. Does' statements. Commissioner Hickey sent a police officer to McCoy's Music on Asylum (where Hickey himself had purchased his tickets) to see if they had a seating chart. In minutes the officer called back: No, there was none.

Right about now, canvas boss Leonard Aylesworth and his crew returned from Springfield. They hadn't expected to be gone so long, but the stake truck had gotten lost on the way up and they had to wait; then they ate a long lunch in the dining room of a good hotel. As they neared the circus grounds they heard the sirens, growing stronger each block. They pulled up to find the big top had vanished, the yards filled with parents and children.

There were so many children missing that parents who asked bystanders if they'd seen a boy this size or a girl wearing a blue sunsuit were sent off on wild goose chases. The easiest way to be found is to stay in one place, but that requires a patience the survivors didn't have. Adults and children, they ranged up and down the street, in and out of the grounds, hoping to bump into loved ones.

Sometimes they were lucky. A six-year-old boy wandered north to the entrance of Keney Park. He stood there as if trying to decide whether to go in. A soldier approached.

"Will you take me home, mister?"

"Sure, sonny," the soldier said. "What's your name and where do you live?"

The soldier walked him to a bus stop and got on with him. As they approached Wolcott Avenue, the boy recognized his street. He hopped off and ran home to his parents, leaving the soldier on the bus. The parents were disappointed; they wanted to thank the man personally.

William Epps didn't know where his mother or his aunt or his cousin Muriel were. They were from Bellevue Square; this part of the North End was foreign territory to him, absolutely new. With Richie in hand, he followed Barbour north to Tower Avenue, moving with the crowds. Across the busy intersection stretched the green fields and woods of Keney Park like a great forest. He waited for the light to change, then hustled his brother along.

A girl asked a policewoman to help her find her mother and her aunt.

The officer advised the girl to go wait by their car. In a few minutes the aunt came along and told her that the mother had been taken to a hospital, she didn't know which one. The policewoman suggested they try Municipal first. While they were searching the hospital for the mother, she was scouring the grounds for the girl and would soon report her missing.

The police rounded up all the lost children and moved them east through the woods to a line of cruisers parked on Hampton Street. In the front yard of the circus grounds Commissioner Hickey's men set up a sound car with speakers on its roof and asked anyone with unattached children to please bring them to Hampton Street. Officers would escort them to police headquarters.

Downtown, headquarters assigned a team of policemen and -women to establish a clearinghouse in the juvenile division. They would take the names and addresses of the children as they came in, then try to contact the parents.

Back on the grounds, Stanley Kurneta searched for his sister Mary. He couldn't find her. He couldn't find Tony, his mother—nobody. His head and neck and arms were burned, his clothes a shambles from carrying his nephew Raymond Erickson. Police noticed Stanley's condition and convinced him he needed treatment. They packed him into an ambulance and sent him off to Hartford Hospital, still unsure just what had happened to his family.

Extra, extra

Officially, the situation was under control. The fire was out, the most severely injured being tended to. The dead were in no hurry. Now the panic and confusion moved from the circus grounds out into the city at large, heralded by sirens. On Barbour Street, the authorities and their many volunteers started mopping up. Trucks rolled in empty and rolled out full.

The strangest injury of the day came after police had sealed off the lot. A policeman was working crowd control, keeping rubberneckers behind a temporary fence, when a bee stung him in the neck. His throat swelled up—classic anaphylactic shock. Another officer drove him to Municipal, where they had to wait while the overworked doctors handled more pressing cases.

The head of the War Council was on the grounds now, directing his men. Mayor Mortensen had attracted an entourage of reporters hoping for a quote, though he was only there to help and lend moral support. Thomas Barber and his fellow detectives followed the mayor's party around, running errands for them until higher-ups arrived to accompany him more formally. The mayor would stay for two hours, pitching in, making sure everything was taken care of.

There were no phones on the lot, so Southern New England Telephone ran in four lines for police and firemen to use. Linemen mounted the phones on short poles stuck in the ground.

On orders from Prosecutor Burr S. Leikind, police stopped circus personnel from removing debris and cleared the interior of the tent of everyone except army guards. The wife of a Willimantic police officer went around picking up loose pocketbooks, her arms full of them; one recovered by the northeast chute proved to be Mary Kurneta's. About one hundred fifty MPs and troops from the antiaircraft unit formed a perimeter around the site. On Woodland Street, neighbors watched as truck after truck passed carrying soldiers holding shovels.

South of town, Motorcycle Troop A of the State Guard roared in from Niantic, escorting the 10th Battalion Ambulance Corps. They'd been at Camp Baldwin, playing softball, when they received word. They changed, hopped on their bikes and peeled off. As they took the first curve, one man laid his down. Legend is, he was killed; actually he was just bruised—and pretty damned embarrassed. He got back on. Reportedly they made the fifty miles in thirty-three minutes.

The Office of Civilian Defense scrambled its air raid wardens, sending half to Barbour Street and half to the armory.

The manager of the Coca-Cola bottling plant in East Hartford escaped the tent with his children and immediately called the office. Seven Coca-Cola trucks rolled, filled with emergency first aid supplies.

And still the makeshift ambulances pulled up from Sage-Allen and Max Sanders and Underwood Elliott Fisher, weaving their way through the blistered circus wagons, the people sitting in the grass and staring vaguely into

space.

On Garden Street, the quickest route to the armory, a young mother and her two-year-old daughter sat on their front steps and watched the trucks pass with their odd cargo of bodies. They'd planned to go to the circus that day but never made it.

Sirens crisscrossed the city. In neighborhoods all over Hartford, people spilled out into the streets to see what was happening. They stood at their porch rails and on their front walks, looking up into the air. From the west, the smoke could easily be misconstrued as coming from East Hartford. Some thought the Germans had bombed Pratt & Whitney. Others imagined a plane crash, maybe a B-25 out of Bradley Field.

WTIC had the first radio crew on the scene. As they crossed the grounds and saw the carnage and confusion, they realized a live broadcast would just add to the panic. They decided to quell the wilder rumors already circulating (such as the lions running amok) and focus on what they knew to be true. During the '36 flood, TIC had cooperated with the authorities, broadcasting missing persons reports. Now they canceled their regular programming and opened their studios to the Red Cross, the fire and police departments and other relief agencies.

Gathering effects at the northeast chute.
PHOTO BY WESLEY MASON, COURTESY OF ART KIELY

Up on Blue Hills Avenue, the neighborhood kids were watching the cops wail past when a lady ran out on her porch and screamed that the circus was on fire and people were dying. Of course, the children all knew friends who'd gone that afternoon, but there was no way to find out about them.

Adults could. People drove straight to the circus grounds—or as close as possible, owing to traffic. They abandoned their cars and continued on foot, only to be stopped by the police cordon.

One brother would not be denied. He decked a policeman and bulled past the line and inside, where, miraculously, he found his sisters, one slightly burned, the other fine.

For the first time in its history, the *Hartford Times* city desk sent a flash by wire to the Associated Press. Their first Extra hit the presses minutes later. FIRE SWEEPS CIRCUS, the headline read. The story ran without pictures, and there wasn't time for editorial to check all the facts. The *Times* didn't commit to a particular number of casualties, but a prominent subhead mentioned that three performers had died. According to the story, Municipal Hospital received calls for ambulances, with reports that "quite a few" people were injured. The Silver Spur Riding Club, whose stables and show ring were on Barbour, confirmed that the big top collapsed about 2:45.

The details were sketchy, even contradictory. "One eyewitness said he thought that everyone must have escaped before the tent collapsed because the fire spread so slowly." But then, in the next paragraph: "It appeared that a considerable number of persons died in the flames or in the rush to leave the tent."

The story went out over the AP wire, making papers across the country. The *New Britain Herald* printed the very same copy. Directly beside it—as if to put it in context—ran an article headlined: HAMBURG DEATH TOLL REVEALED AS 41,385. While the firebombing of the city had taken place the summer before, the German press chief had just released the figures— he conceded—to counter Churchill's outrage at their use of V-2 rockets against civilian targets.

In Bristol, people crowded the Press office, relying on the speed of the AP wire to bring them news of their families. They scanned the teletype for casualty lists.

When word reached Sarasota, the home of the circus, the city virtually stopped. The *Herald Tribune* was overrun with friends and relatives of the circus employees. They'd heard that three performers had been killed. Like the people of Bristol, they were waiting for names.

The news crossed the world by teletype. One woman's brother, in New Guinea with the Army Air Corps, heard the report and had the feeling someone in his family was at the fire. He stopped what he was doing, went back to his quarters and prayed the rosary.

Downtown, Spencer Torell walked into the State Street offices of the *Courant,* sweaty after his long trek. He had some pictures of the fire they might like, he said. A man in the photography department said they'd have to develop them and take a look. Fine, Torell said; he'd wait if that was okay.

While he was sitting in the lobby, a couple of reporters came back from the grounds. Since he was an eyewitness, one of them interviewed him. While they were talking, Torell asked if anybody had been hurt. The man's answer shocked him. He and Wally had been sitting so far down in K, away from the fire, so low and close to the exit that all they had to do was stand up and turn the corner and they were safe. He'd just assumed that everyone else had gotten out.

The photographer came back from the lab with the prints. These were the best shots he'd seen so far; maybe they'd use them tomorrow if nothing better came in. The *Courant* paid Torell $25. He left feeling lucky—unhurt, with some extra spending money in his pocket. He walked across the street to the Isle of Safety to catch the bus back to New Britain. For him the day was just beginning. He still had to go to work.

We can't reach you, Hartford

Half an hour after the fire, hundreds of relatives crowded Municipal Hospital's lobby, searching for loved ones. The odds of finding anyone at this point were slim, since admitting had not had time to compile a list. One grandfather, after checking everywhere, discovered his granddaughter standing outside on the walk, still clutching her circus program.

A force of thirty auxiliary police from New Britain moved in to clear the area. Along with a clutch of Bradley Field MPs, they stood guard on the front steps and the lawn while air raid wardens directed inessential traffic up Coventry and down Holcomb.

Inside, the burned and injured filled the wards and lined the hallways. Empty, Municipal had a maximum capacity of 145 beds. That afternoon they saw 143 patients, many of them critical.

An anaesthesiologist from Hartford Hospital visited Municipal. "People were dying in the corridors," he said. "The staff was overwhelmed. No one seemed to know who was in charge, and those in charge didn't seem to be sure they were."

One nurse also worked at Hartford Hospital but ended up helping out at Municipal. The place was chaos, all the crying. Some children didn't know their own names. A doctor asked her if she had any operating room training; she said yes, she'd been a scrub nurse once. It was good enough for him. She walked into the operating room. On the table was a girl with dark hair, about fifteen, lying on her side. The woman recognized her—it was a neighbor of hers. The doctors pulled a sheet over her. They rolled her out and brought in the next one.

The janitors were so busy carting stretchers they didn't have time to clean up the mess. In a corner of the lobby sat a heap of torn paper cartons labeled: Plasma—For Human Use. Down the hall a priest with a purple stole around his neck bent over a bed and quietly recited the last rites. A nurse waited until he was done, then asked, "Can you come up to the fifth floor, Father? There's a woman."

The hospital assigned a nurse's aide to every patient. One aide drew a badly burned woman. "The woman said, 'I had a permanent and they cut all my hair off.' And I said, 'Oh, that's all right. When it comes back it'll come back naturally curly.' She was so sick. She threw up all over me."

The aide had to take a gurney down to the morgue. "When the elevator doors opened in the basement and I went to push the stretcher out, there were a lot of men down there. There were bandages all over the floor. They didn't let me in, I just stayed on the elevator. I didn't want to go in there anyway. I just handed them the stretcher and went back upstairs."

The men she saw were soldiers. The trucks that had brought Elliott Smith and Raymond Erickson now shuttled the newly dead downtown to the armory on Broad Street. Five came in DOA. Another six succumbed within the first hour.

By now the alarm broadcast over the radio had mobilized an army of nurse's aides. Bluebirds, they were called, after their blue uniforms. They streamed in from the surrounding towns and went to work setting up extra beds, taking patients from admitting up to the wards, passing out cups of orange juice, rolling bandages, applying dressings, administering plasma—anything they were asked to do. Sometimes they were more of a comfort to the injured than anything, sitting with children and holding their hands so they wouldn't be alone.

Hartford Hospital saw fifty-one patients, nineteen of whom they treated as outpatients and released. The others they stabilized with fluids, swathed in gauze bandages and sent up to their respective wards.

A brother and sister sat in the lobby of the old Brownstone Building, waiting for their parents. Both were staff doctors, their father a urologist, their mother a pediatrician. They'd taken the day off and gone to the circus, only to wind up back at work. Across the courtyard, in South Building, they were seeing victims with black eyes and broken ribs from the struggle at the chute. The children would be here for hours.

While Hartford Hospital had far fewer casualties and much more room, they still had to deal with the same flood of relatives Municipal was seeing. The chief of staff had to go on the radio and make the following statement: "The public are urgently requested not to visit or make telephone inquiries about disaster victims in the Hartford Hospital. Not more than two members of the immediate family may visit disaster victims during the next twenty-four hours, and this visit will be limited to ten minutes. Patients in critical condition may be visited by the immediate family at any time."

This might have worked if people knew where their relatives were or whether they were in critical condition. As it was, all that many knew was that their loved ones had gone to the circus and not come home.

At St. Francis, nurses cut clothing off the victims and gently peeled the fabric from their skin, then soaked the open burns in tannic acid baths. They dipped their surgical masks in wintergreen oil to camouflage the stench.

An elderly doctor from Meriden and his female companion were burned on the head, arms and hands, but chose not to go to Municipal or Hartford or St. Francis or even tiny Mt. Sinai. Realizing that casualties would overtax the city's hospitals, the doctor decided to drive them home to Meriden.

As word spread, the preparations Connecticut had made for the war started to pay off. The county blood bank that opened weeks after Pearl Harbor was fully stocked with frozen plasma. For years now women's church groups had gathered monthly to fold bandages, proud of reaching their quotas; because of them, all the hospitals had an ample supply on hand. Plants sent stretcher crews trained for air raids. The War Council stoked up its Rolling Kitchen and headed for the armory.

The country was in a state of general readiness, and after the Normandy invasion morale was high. The ideals of shared toil and sacrifice were almost second nature by this time. On hearing of the fire, many people left work early to help out, unasked. Donors overran the Red Cross blood center on Pearl Street.

From New York, Mayor LaGuardia pledged the full support of his resources. In Boston, Mayor Tobin dispatched the team of experts that had successfully identified all 492 victims of the Cocoanut Grove in just four days.

Also catching the first flight out of Boston was the national chaplain of the Circus Fans Association of America. He'd just left Barbour Street at noon. One of the circus girls had been run over by a truck during their Boston Garden stand, and the troupe had collected $300 to help with her medical expenses. The Father had just delivered it to her in a Boston hospital when he heard the news. "It's terrible," he said, and then, reacting, it seems, to early reports that three performers had died: "They were all my friends."

In Waterbury a machinist heard at work. His supervisor told him that his wife and three-year-old daughter were unhurt but that his mother-in-law was still missing. He jumped in his car and tore for Hartford.

It was futile to call. All long-distance connections had to be made through an operator. Coming in, going out—the switchboards were jammed. At Southern New England Telephone's headquarters on Trumbull Street, operators watched their boards light up solid. They jabbed their jacks at the open holes. Operators from out of town broke in and scolded, "We can't reach you, Hartford."

"That place was lit up like Merry Christmas," one operator said. "The sirens were screaming around the building. Some of the girls on the board got upset because of the tension. One girl broke down crying; they had to relieve her."

Neighborhood exchanges were especially busy. Around town, company switchboards were clogged with outbound calls. Between 3:00 and 5:00 P.M., incoming and outgoing calls were impossible at the State Capitol and the State Office Building; eventually they cut their trunk lines to lighten the burden. The *Courant* and *Times* didn't waste their circuits; they greeted all incoming calls with busy signals.

For sheer volume, it was the greatest number of calls since the '38 hurricane. SNET reeled in as many extra operators as they could, even calling people back from vacation. By Thursday night they had two hundred fifty instead of their regular one hundred fifty. For supper the company gave each one half an hour and a voucher for the cafeteria.

People from outlying towns unable to break through called their local papers, desperate for news. In Winsted families tried the offices of the *Citizen,* in Willimantic the *Daily Chronicle.* So far no one had a list of the dead.

On Blue Hills Avenue, getting information was simpler. Groups of children waited at the bus stops. When a boy who'd been to the circus got off, they asked him a million questions, then shut up to hear what happened. "All of us kids cried," said a ten-year-old.

In West Hartford, the boys of Linbrook Road were playing ball in the middle of the street when one of their friends wandered up, disoriented and covered with soot. He couldn't find his mother, and his father was working, so a neighbor took him in.

The mother who was eight months pregnant and couldn't celebrate her daughter's birthday with her at the circus heard the news on the radio and called her husband. He was waiting at the stop when the bus pulled up with the girl. He lifted her into his arms and carried her all the way home.

Dorothy Bocek got home and asked her mother if she'd heard from her sister Stella yet. She hadn't.

The family who'd found the little blond girl drove her back to their house. The daughter washed the girl's face, then took her outside and read to her while her father called all the police stations in Connecticut. In the end it turned out the girl was from Springfield, Massachusetts. Later that night her family drove down to pick her up.

In Southampton, Massachusetts, the woman renting half a house from Mildred Cook's sister Emily Gill heard a bulletin over the radio. The woman knew the children were at the circus. She ran across the hall and found Emily. "Did you hear what happened?" she asked.

Emily Gill went straight to her brother-in-law Ted Parsons's place. Marion Parsons was off in the eastern part of the state. There was no time to wait for her, so they left together for Hartford.

The *Times* Wall Street edition came out, promising "Complete Stocks." The new headline read: CIRCUS FIRE KILLS SCORES. "An indeterminate number of persons were killed," the story began. It quoted a county detective estimating the number of dead as "at least 100," and said, "the State Police announced an hour after the disaster that the State Armory would be opened as an emergency hospital, because the scope of the disaster was beyond the capacity of local hospitals." Also that: "In the pandemonium, the crowd surged forward against police lines as each body was carried out, vainly trying to learn the victim's identity." And still no list.

Afraid their relatives would worry, troupers gave more than seventy telegrams to a local member of the Circus Fans of America to take to the Hartford Western Union office for them.

At police headquarters, officers gathered the missing children on the main floor, then led them upstairs to a courtroom. One by one a policewoman took their names, addresses and telephone numbers. Volunteers from the American Legion tried to keep them all amused. Another officer returned from the circus grounds with a carload of mothers hoping to find their children, which they did, tearfully.

At the armory the teenager and his boss rolled up in their Brown Thomson ambulance. They had to wait while some other trucks backed up to the west entrance, then got out and unloaded their bodies. The place was crowded with help. Bodies on cots lined the back wall of the cavernous drill shed; another row ran down the center. It smelled like hell.

Done, they hopped into the truck. "You want to go back?" his boss said.

"No," the teenager said, "I don't."

"I'm glad you said that, because I don't either."

His boss stopped outside a local gin mill by Bushnell Park. The teenager was underage and didn't want to get him in trouble.

"Come on," his boss said, "you're old enough."

They went in and sat down at the bar. The bartender looked hard at the teenager.

"Give the kid a drink," his boss said. "He needs it."

There were no questions. They had a couple of whiskeys and returned to the store by quitting time. Then they went home.

A G.I. party

At 3:50 police dispatchers sent all available cruisers to the lot. Officers coming in from Barbour Street drove over the hoses, then bottled up on the midway and behind the sideshow top. Headquarters instructed all units to use the dirt road off Hampton Street. They inched through the woods on Sponzo's property, pulling off to the side to let the trucks and ambulances by.

Cops on Tower and Main set the stoplights on caution and did traffic by hand. The luckier survivors squeezed into what buses were left, but many ended up hoofing it, some of them shoeless. One man found a shoe store and bought his wife a pair and the two of them kept on walking.

One girl had gone to the circus with her best friend. As they turned onto their street, they noticed their neighbors lining the sidewalk in front of their houses. A cry went up, "The kids are coming."

"Run home quick," someone said to the friend, "your mother's hysterical," so she crossed the street and ran.

Farther down the street, the other girl's parents saw the first girl running by herself and thought their own daughter had been killed. When they saw their daughter, they hugged each other and cried.

The girl was surprised they knew about the fire. Her mother explained: An uncle in St. Louis had heard it on the radio and called them. She took the girl into the kitchen and gave her ice cream and listened to her story.

Ice cream was a common welcome-home treat. One girl's parents were so grateful they served her five bowls.

Anna Cote and her sister Iva had been calm for the entire ordeal. When they finally dragged themselves through the front door, their father asked how come they were home so early. Anna burst into tears. Neither her father or Iva could get her to stop.

Other survivors were fine, then broke down when they heard over the radio how many had died. Most got home okay, maybe a little bruised, a little dirty, but basically unharmed. Mothers insisted children take baths before supper. One father had the entire family kneel down on the carpet and thank God. Only in a few rare cases did husbands come home to empty houses, neighbors debating who should go over and tell them.

The missing children were about to move. The phones were so overtaxed at police headquarters that parents couldn't get through. Headquarters put a lieutenant in charge of the operation, at this point rather small; at 4:30 the officers only had ten children in the courtroom. But as the crowd on Barbour Street dissipated, rescuers found more and more. Soon several cruisers full were en route.

The lieutenant had the numbers of some of the ten already there, but the circuits were so deluged with incoming calls that he had to walk up Market Street to Weiner Fruit and Produce and use their phone. The rumor had somehow gone out that the missing children would be at the armory; it was soon mobbed with frantic parents. To alleviate both problems, headquarters ordered the children taken to the nearby Brown School.

The officers walked the children up Market Street. Two workers at the nursery school opened the main hall, three classrooms and the playground, giving the kids something to do. Volunteers from the Red Cross, the American Legion and the Blood Donors League helped set up a checkpoint to take names and addresses. From now on this would be the clearinghouse for any missing persons. Dispatch ordered all cruisers to drop children off at the Talcott Street entrance.

Among the police ordered to the grounds was Det. Sgt. Edward Lowe. He arrived by radio car at 4:30. The prosecutors' office had already begun investigating the cause of the blaze. Lowe was supposed to keep watch over the officers and department heads of the circus so they couldn't get together on a story.

Marine James Kinsella had come from Bradley Field to help police the bodies. The army lieutenant in charge of the detail said, "We are going to have a G.I. party." Kinsella had no idea what that meant because it was an army term and he was a Marine. He soon learned. It meant Graves Identification. It meant hauling bodies in the hot sun.

Reports circulated that victims had run flaming into the woods on the north side of the tent—human torches setting the underbrush afire. An officer and a squad of MPs searched the area, lifting branches and poking under shrubs with their nightsticks. They found nothing and no one.

The G.I. party lasted until 4:45. At the east end, Medical Examiner Dr. Walter Weissenborn released the last of the dead, then he and Commissioner Hickey left for the armory, following the procession of trucks downtown. James Kinsella went back to Bradley, got drunk and threw up.

Outside on Barbour, a police sound car eased through the crowds, asking them to please clear the area, advising them that the armory would be used as a morgue, and the Brown School for missing children. Transportation would be provided, they said, for those who wished to go to the armory. But many onlookers refused to leave. They lined the ropes and temporary fences holding them back, gawking at the remains of the big top.

Strangely, the southwest bleachers where the fire had begun were the least damaged. The entire south grandstand had burned to cinders; the

The crowd on the south side of the lot, behind a section of the victory garden fence still standing. PHOTO COURTESY OF THE HARTFORD COLLECTION, THE HARTFORD PUBLIC LIBRARY

Looking east from the untouched southwest blues, May Kovar's west cage in the left foreground. PHOTO COURTESY OF THE *HARTFORD COURANT*

skeleton of the north still stood. Between them lay a herringbone pattern of quarterpoles fallen to the east, the outer poles reaching over the railings and into the seats. The centerpoles had come down plumb, neatly bisecting the stages and rings and bent animal cages—in which, amazingly, most of May Kovar's and Joseph Walsh's perches still stood in formation, untouched. A quarterpole leaned against the bandstand with its metal chairs askew; on the top tier stood the burned-out shells of the kettle drums and the organ.

The Wallendas' platforms now rested on the ground with their bicycles, as did the heavy rigging from the aerial acts. One of the first props to burn was the cardboard house the clown firemen saved twice daily, and blistered among the wreckage tilted the squashed box of a clown's hot dog machine, the secret compartment of which turned his live dachshund into a string of prop wieners. Near the bandstand sat an aerialist's wash bucket, forgotten during the rescue efforts.

While camels and donkeys hitched to trees munched at the grass, police and MPs scoured the area, hunched over like beachcombers, filling pails and steel garbage cans and cardboard boxes with articles. At the railings they found a number of pocketbooks, some just metal frames clasped shut, their contents in small charred piles: compacts and lipsticks and cigarette cases, coins warped and colored from the heat, bills burned to worthlessness. One officer discovered a half dollar curled like a dry leaf.

By the northeast chute sat a pile of shoes large enough to fill a bushel basket—women's high heels, children's sneakers and sandals. Shredded clothing stuck to the iron bars. A smashed umbrella anchored a swath of flotsam. In the debris police found a tiny silver cross on a chain, probably clawed off in the struggle, and under a layer of shoes and pocketbooks, shiny with flies, the skin from a pair of hands.

The fire was so intense it burned the hands and feet off people. Chief Hallissey discovered some and put them in a bag. Another officer found a small hand. Sergeant Spellman, who reported the fire, picked up a variety of parts.

Another policeman returned to the lot after taking the bee-stung officer home and driving some nurses to a hospital. He came back at just the wrong time. "Chief Hallissey told me he had a job for me. He told me to take a bag to the State Armory for the Medical Examiner which contained pieces of arms, legs and parts of skulls of small children. I drove to the State Armory and gave the bag to the Medical Examiner."

Police gathered all the pails and bags and boxes of salvaged articles in the superintendent's office at E. B. McGurk's, then took them downtown to the property room in the basement of headquarters, hoping they might aid in the identification process.

In the backyard, barred from the tent, show folks were taking care of their own. The doctor treated band members and some workers whose hands and arms had been burned while helping people out. Casualties were light—a fact the papers would make much of, implicitly accusing circus employees of saving their own skins and leaving their customers to die. But the shock and strain on troupers couldn't be overstated; the big top was their home. Without the next show to prepare for, they sat around in a daze. One bally girl collapsed hours after the fire and had to be taken to Municipal Hospital.

Another circus employee was already there, Harry Lakin of the lighting department, suffering from what he thought was a broken leg. Lakin was new, just signed on in Portland a week ago. As the stretcher bearers brought him in, he called over a Red Cross volunteer. "You, come here.

Will you take hold of my hand?" The woman thought he was hysterical or drunk and decided to humor him.

He said he was an electrician and worked with the spotlights. "I'm not squealing," he said, and started crying. "I'm not yellow, but I'm not going to talk."

The woman told him to buck up, that there were lots of people hurt worse than he was.

He asked after the bally girls, then said, "You will never get another girl like Lydia."

The woman could only agree with him.

"I never knew it would be like this," Lakin said. "I don't know if I can take it."

Two volunteers lifted the stretcher and took him off to X-ray, leaving the volunteer confused and suspicious.

Back at the grounds, one concessionaire told police he saw a drunken circus employee exit the men's toilet and totter toward Barbour Street as the fire started. Hailed by the concessionaire, the man said, "Get the hell out of here. This place is going up in a blaze in a minute." He ran down the street as the flames ate the big top.

Police arrested drunk roughneck Ernest Westgate after witnesses claimed he said, "Okay, let it burn down, I know all about it," as the tent went up.

The crowd still pressed against the fences, but it was different now, mostly curiosity seekers. The survivors were on their way home.

"But I've got to get through!" one father pleaded. "My child was there!"

"Now take it easy," a patrolman said. "There's nobody there now, they're all gone."

A sound car crawled by, booming out news from the Brown School: "If the guardian of Danny Dawson is in the neighborhood, will he please call for the boy immediately."

Across Barbour, a handmade sign in a tenement window advertised "There is a phone on the third floor," but the lines had vanished.

Engine Company 16 finished overhauling the last batch of embers and rolled up its hoses. The city police shifted their personnel, leaving the state troopers and MPs to watch the site. Thomas Barber and Edward Lowe drew morgue duty at the armory. They would report at 5:30 to assist Dr. Weissenborn at the checkout desk.

It was enough time for Barber to get home and take a bath and change clothes. He came in soaking wet from the heat and the hoses. Once the front door closed behind him, he broke down. It was the first time his daughter Gloria had seen her father cry.

The *Hartford Times* published another Extra, headlined CIRCUS BLAZE KILLS 200, with a photo of the smoking bleachers. The number was an unofficial estimate—by whom was never said. Authorities were taking the bodies to the State Armory. Otherwise the text itself changed little: The detective still gave his figure of "at least 100"; the three performers were still said to be among the dead. The cause was undetermined so far, though there were rumors a cigarette had been dropped on the canvas. And still no list.

This would change quickly. Missing a nephew himself, Mayor Mortensen sent a cruiser to each of the three major hospitals with instructions to bring back rosters of the dead and injured—complete, partial, whatever they had.

In the next Extra, Governor Baldwin gave a telephone number for people with missing persons inquiries to call. SNET had set up a battery of twenty-four phones in a conference room overlooking the drill floor of the armory. Those dialing Hartford 7-0181 reached the headquarters of the State War Council, staffed by women volunteers who took down the names and addresses of both the missing and the complainant.

Even volunteers weren't immune to the tragedy. One man was supposed to be part of Connecticut Mutual Life's Emergency Medical Assistant Corps, but received word that his brother's family was missing and went off in search of them.

A Rockville woman had taken her nine-year-old daughter and a friend to the circus. The friend was the first out, but in escaping, the daughter hurt her back; while her mother tended to her, the friend got lost in the crowd. The woman accompanied her daughter to Hartford Hospital, then headed for the Red Cross to check on the friend, armed with a description. The child was wearing a yellow print dress, yellow hair ribbon and black shoes.

A Plainville woman left the grounds believing her son had died in the fire. She'd searched and searched, then come home on the bus. There she received a phone call from his grandmother in Bristol who told her a stranger had brought the boy to her. According to her son, the man helped him out of the tent. When they couldn't locate his mother, the boy gave the man his name and address. The man took him to Plainville by car but found no one at home. Instead of becoming frightened, the child gave the man his grandmother's address. The grandmother never learned the man's name.

At Municipal Hospital, a Middletown woman waited for the outpatient clinic to take her. She'd been carrying her four-year-old daughter toward the bandstand when someone knocked into her and she fell, dropping the child. A man reached down and helped her to her feet and out of the tent. She was burned, and the crowd was so large and moving so fast that she never saw what happened to her daughter, whether anyone rescued her or not. Now she didn't know how she would find her. But she would.

The names of the dead

Workers in the buildings downtown could see the olive drab army stake trucks coming south on Main, escorted by motorcycles. The convoy turned right onto Asylum. The odor of the charred bodies was so strong, people could smell it four floors up.

A line had already formed at the front door of the armory. As the trucks rolled by the massive granite and limestone facade, relatives of the missing grimly tracked them. A patrol of soldiers and city police had cleared Broad Street of all civilians below the west entrance and all the way to Capitol Avenue. A truck slowly backed over the bridge to the west archway, an officer waving it in; it stopped and the tailgate banged down.

Used for indoor formations, the drill floor of the armory stretched 185 by 200 feet. The roof loomed sixty feet above, a giant peaked skylight, the windows around the cream-over-forest-green brick walls merely slits, gunports befitting a fortress. The floor was varnished wood, as in a gym. It was actually the second floor of the building; the area beneath contained both a pistol and a rifle range and a complete supply depot.

As the bodies arrived, State Trooper William Menser wired green casualty tags to their wrists or ankles, where possible. Thomas Barber and Ed Lowe helped segregate the bodies by sex and age, laying them out on narrow army cots. The majority were women and older girls; seventy-five of them took up the northeast corner, close by the east archway. The children were set up in three rows by the west entrance, the ten men in the middle. Many were faceless, missing limbs. Since the relatives would cross the long armory floor from the south, Barber and Lowe put the ones in better shape in the front rows; the fewer dead they saw, the better.

Menser went cot to cot with Dr. Weissenborn and Dr. Edgar Butler, a dentist, filling in the tags with the bodies' probable sex and age. He made a sheet for each victim, taking down the height, weight and build, noting clothing and dental work and any identifying marks like scars or tattoos or jewelry. These sheets filled a looseleaf notebook they could consult when trying to guide a searcher.

One of the saddest cases was a woman in her fifties with no eyes and no right forearm, the fragments of a pink corset still clinging to her. A three-year-old girl she'd been carrying had fused to her stomach. This was the pair the Norwalk fireman had discovered under the folds of the tent. As if to comfort himself, Menser wrote of the child: "fear absent."

Clothing was mostly absent as well in the worst burned. Occasionally he'd find the rear segment of a waistband, part of a collar at the nape of a neck, but little else.

The size of the room diffused the smell somewhat, but morticians from the Newkirk and Whitney Funeral Home went around spraying the corpses to make it easier on everyone.

Soldiers draped olive drab blankets over the dead, but in many cases they weren't large enough. The fire caused the bodies to take on what is called the pugilistic posture. Heat makes the muscles contract; the larger the muscle, the greater the contraction. The heavy muscles like the biceps and quadriceps win the tug of war, so the knees pull up toward the body, the arms raise as if to protect the face. Soldiers tented blankets over the dead as best they could, but some lay with their shoes poking out at the bottom.

The governor was there, and the heads of the War Council and the State Guard, but it was Commissioner Hickey who took charge, standing

From left: State trooper in pith helmet, State Police Commissioner Edward J. Hickey, Governor Raymond Baldwin, State Adjutant General Reginald B. DeLacour, State War Council administrator Henry B. Mosle. PHOTO COURTESY OF THE *HARTFORD COURANT*

on a dais in the middle of the makeshift morgue, surrounded by a crowd of state guardsmen, nurses, and Red Cross volunteers. He was in his shirt-sleeves, the knee of his trousers torn; he hadn't changed since leaving Barbour Street and he reeked of ashes.

Here's how it would work, Hickey said. Relatives would sign in down-stairs and give a description of the person they were looking for. A dozen at a time would come up, each accompanied by a state trooper and a nurse. Depending on the age and sex of the missing person, the relative would look in one of the three areas—or, in the case of someone searching for more than one person, several of the three areas. There would be three first-aid stations in case they were overcome. Nurses would carry smelling salts as well. If a relative could not identify their loved ones after a full pass, they would certainly be allowed to try again. The process would start at 5:45. People were already waiting outside.

In the lobby downstairs, soldiers set up four long tables for the clerks and nurses to work at and made space for the Red Cross canteen and a first aid station. Upstairs, in the War Council's offices, secretaries ran off mimeographed forms to record the searchers' information. The conference room with its twenty-four lines was a beehive.

Dr. Weissenborn was joined by Dr. Henry Onderdonk. The two established a checkout desk by the east entrance with a complement of women at typewriters to fill in death certificates. All bodies would have to pass through here before they were released to funeral parlors. The five in

Edward Lowe (in hat) and another detective sit on a cot by the checkout desk. PHOTO COURTESY OF JUDITH LOWE

pristine condition waited here to be claimed. Thomas Barber and Ed Lowe sat on an empty cot, Barber imagining his son Harry under a blanket across the room. Thank God for Uncle Boots—typically, he had forgotten his promise to take Harry to the show.

Before the crowd was allowed in, six priests arrived. They went from cot to cot, lifting the blankets and anointing the dead's blistered skin.

Downstairs, the tall doors were open to let a breeze in, but a heavy wire grate held the people at bay while clerks readied the tables.

Outside, the line stretched from the arched doorway and along the walk and around the corner of the building. Early on it was predominantly fathers, a few mothers, even in one case a little girl. Another sound car with a big speaker aimed at them delivered the newest lists of injured and found. A few relieved parents left the line, but most remained, arms crossed, tight-lipped. The heat was wearing people down; many had just come from work. A nurse stood by, and the Rolling Kitchen was handing out cups of milk and lemonade and ginger ale. For those who could eat, they offered sandwiches and coffee, and cookies for dessert. Across Capitol Avenue, a crowd of onlookers had formed, pointing every time another truck went by.

Upstairs, a police sound car rolled in the west entrance, drifted to the middle of the drill floor by the men's section and stopped. They would use it as a PA system. Now, with everything in place, Hickey gave the sign for the doors to be opened.

A state guardsman unlocked the grate and the lobby filled with the first wave. For the amount of time they'd waited, and what they were waiting for, there was little pushing, and little noise. Everyone tried to be polite. The clerks registered the missing and then the first dozen went up the twin switchbacked staircases, led by their escorts.

Jennie Heiser was supervising the clerks downstairs when a former neighbor from Storrs came in looking for his wife and daughter. "Jennie," he said, "will you help me find Betty and Mary?" She accompanied him up.

The drill floor was so large that the morgue only took up a small portion along the north wall. As they crossed the polished wood, their footsteps echoed dully, swallowed up in the vast space above. The air was hot and still.

She took her friend to the corner with the women's bodies. A pair of legs stuck from a blanket, one shoe off and one shoe on. Another victim was

The line outside. Many have come straight from work.
PHOTO BY WESLEY MASON, COURTESY OF THE *HARTFORD COURANT*

covered, her blocky pair of white flats neatly arranged at the bottom. Jennie Heiser started at the front row, hoping it would be quick. The ones in decent shape had been caught in the pile at the track or the northeast chute. Like Jerry LeVasseur, every part not covered by others was burned, the rest of them mostly untouched. They still had some of their clothes, even their rayon stockings.

Jennie Heiser knew the man's wife; she checked the tags until she came to a likely candidate. When she lifted the blanket, she could see it wasn't her. They tried another one—not her. Throughout, the husband was silent, overcome by what he was seeing.

The farther back into the section, the harder it got. The worst were like abstract statues. They'd lost their clothes, their features, even their pubic hair. With each body, the man grew more discouraged. Jennie Heiser

An overview of the drill floor from the balcony, the checkout desk to the right. Note the state police car to the left midground. The banner beneath the clock commemorates Connecticut's war dead and those currently in service. PHOTO COURTESY OF THE LIBRARY OF CONGRESS

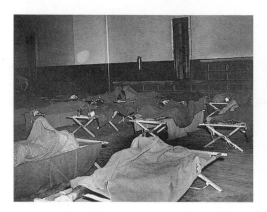

(Left) The women's section, northeast corner of the drill shed floor. PHOTO COURTESY OF THE *HARTFORD COURANT. (Right) Police remove an identified body to the checkout desk.* PHOTO COURTESY OF AP/WIDE WORLD PHOTOS

didn't want to show him the few they couldn't determine the sex of—bloated, their abdomens broken open by the heat, their teeth bright against their blackened lips—unless she had to.

She had to, and even then they came up empty.

They went through the women again, this time skipping the better preserved ones, pausing longer at those they couldn't absolutely rule out. Nothing.

Next they tried to find his daughter, going through the rows of little girls the same way. The man couldn't be sure. They were in such bad shape.

Around them fell a reverent silence broken only by the scuff of footsteps, the buzz of an announcement from the sound car. The damage stunned people, yet hardly anyone went into hysterics—possibly because the corpses didn't seem human. The fire had robbed them not only of life but of identity, reducing them to objects to be feared or pitied. Faceless, they were the same, and provoked the same reaction over and over until, numb, relatives abandoned their searches. The man thanked Jennie Heiser and went home, defeated.

For some, the corpses were too much. One young woman felt positive her mother and father were here, but after four bodies she turned and hurried downstairs again.

Det. Sgt. William Dineen hadn't been able to locate his son Billy or his daughter Marion at the grounds or any of the hospitals. He listed them missing at the Brown School, then climbed the stairs to the drill floor like so many others. In the children's section he found an eight-year-old who fit Billy's description. He knelt and inspected the boy's teeth and then his toenails. Yes, it was him, he was positive. The trooper took down his information and revised the green casualty tag. It was 6:20. The first identification had taken thirty-five minutes. Dineen watched the soldiers lift the cot and haul it to the checkout desk where Barber and Lowe waited, then went to see if he could find Marion.

The work proceeded slowly, for many reasons. Children rarely carry identification. The fire had burned the flimsy summer dresses from the girls, and the women had lost their pocketbooks. In the rush to flee, people stepped on each other's feet, knocking their shoes off. The transient population of Hartford with its war plants also contributed to the uncertainty, and likewise the impermanent, even casual status of the lowest rung of circus workers. "I did hear that one of our ticket sellers was killed," a hand said, "but I think he showed up."

And there was the intensity of the fire itself, and the tent's unique structure. Unlike the Cocoanut Grove, in which most of the victims suffocated or were poisoned by the by-products of the burning interior of the nightclub, most of the victims in the circus fire suffered little if any smoke inhalation. There was no roof to force it back down on them. They burned to death; a few were trampled but Dr. Weissenborn noted not one single case of asphyxiation. The death certificates read either fourth-degree burns, trauma to head and torso, or a combination of the two. The doctor was sure that a good third of the bodies would never be identified.

Still, nurses folded the blankets back, state troopers shone their flashlights on the charred faces of the dead. Dentists bent over them with tongue depressors, prying jaws open, marking charts. And still, searchers reached the ends of the rows and asked, "Are you sure this is all of them?"

One man identified his wife and son and then his mother-in-law and niece.

A prominent Unionville doctor identified his wife and daughter. His friend Governor Baldwin had run out to take care of business and missed him by minutes.

The boyfriend who'd taken Donald Gale identified Hulda Grant. (Her ex-husband came the next day to double-check.)

One father identified a daughter by a tiny gold locket. A second daughter would die that night at Municipal Hospital, where her mother and brother were in critical condition. A third girl somehow escaped unharmed. "It was to be a party for them," an aunt said. "Regina's birthday was the first and Joan's the third. They had their first permanents and went to their first circus. Regina died in the hospital, but Joan never got out of the tent alive. She never would push anyone for fear of being rude."

Worried about his wife's health, the father hadn't told her yet—or the surviving girl, in case she might say something.

Downstairs, the line moved through, each searcher cataloguing the last clothing the missing person wore. The clerks wanted unique features. "Was there a wide space between his front teeth?" they asked over their typewriters. "Did he have any identifying scars? Were those gold or porcelain fillings?"

Jennie Heiser's husband stood guard outside by the line. He was part of the troop who'd ridden their motorcycles up. Another friend from Storrs waited in line, a professor of music; he was looking for his wife and children. Carl Heiser commiserated with him briefly, then went back to his post. Now the names of the man's family blared from the sound car—they'd been found. Carl Heiser went over to the professor, expecting him to be overjoyed. The man stood there blankly. He was in such a daze he hadn't heard the names.

At the west entrance two trucks from Mercer & Dunbar pulled up and unloaded their cargo—eight unidentified bodies from Municipal Hospital, bringing the total number of dead to be cleared through the armory to 135. The hero Bill Curlee was among them, though no one knew. He received a green tag, then two guardsmen set him on a cot, draped a scratchy blanket over him and trundled him to the men's section.

One of the new arrivals was a young girl barely touched by the flames, just the left side of her neck and that cheek blackened. She wore the scraps of a white, flowered dress and brown shoes. On her tag, Dr. Weissenborn estimated her age as five. "I placed her in the front row of the children's section," William Menser said, "feeling that she was going to be the first one to go out."

She was impossible to miss, and so easy to show. With her face in such good shape, there was actually a chance someone might recognize her. But again and again, people shook their heads, almost sorry the answer was no.

"I saw that little girl many times," Jennie Heiser said. "She was a beautiful little girl. The others were mutilated, but she was so easily identifiable."

In their rounds, Thomas Barber and Ed Lowe noted her. "It was that face that caught my attention," Barber remembered. "She was a pretty little thing. She looked almost like she was asleep." She was nearly the same age as Harry.

Searchers wandered solemnly through the cots, handkerchiefs and ammonia-soaked gauze clutched to their noses. State troopers in pith helmets and uniformed nurses bracketed them, ready to step in. The sound car droned out the names of people wanted in different parts of the armory; otherwise the huge room was so unnaturally quiet that the occasional sob traveled across it like a shock wave, chilling the skin, freezing the heart like a close call.

All it took was a blackened bit of jewelry, a missing incisor, an appendectomy scar. One little girl had cut her palm that morning, and her father had fixed it with a Band-Aid. Her clenched fist still cupped the bandage. Otherwise she was almost unrecognizable, her clothing burned away except for her black patent leather shoes. Another girl had been wearing a sunsuit. There was just enough material left between her legs to make out the color—proof to her family that this was indeed her.

Sometimes the escorts didn't need to uncover the face, just a hand with a ring, a wrist with a bracelet, a foot with a sneaker. Occasionally they'd show the whole body; this method proved especially worthwhile in the case of husbands looking for wives and wives looking for husbands.

Though no one fainted and there wasn't a trace of panic, it was not all calm. A grief-stricken woman screamed as she identified the body of her son. She beat her forehead and wailed as her nurse led her away. A soldier pulled the blanket back over the boy's face. Some turned and walked away swiftly, in tears; some stood with a hand clapped over their mouths; some clutched their heads.

After identifying his wife Anna, Salvatore DiMartino had to be supported by his escorts. They gripped his hands and biceps, leading him away between them to the checkout desk like a prisoner. The DiMartinos had eight children. They lived on Barbour Street. Anna didn't even like the circus; she preferred going to the Princess Theater where she collected free dishes for her kitchen, one a show. She'd only gone with a cousin because

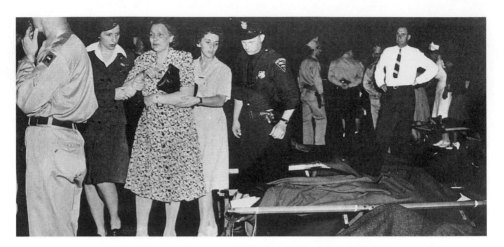

A nurse or nurse's aide and a policeman accompany each searcher.
PHOTO COURTESY OF ART KIELY

Mr. DiMartino, a cabinetmaker, received free tickets from the owner of a furniture store he'd done some work for. Compounding Mr. DiMartino's grief was the hard fact that he knew he didn't have money for a proper funeral.

Dr. Weissenborn made out her death certificate right in front of him: "Burns by fire, 4th degree (Conflagration)." She'd been born in Beila Blanca, Argentina, and had only come to Hartford in 1923.

A close reading of the death certificates showed the heavy first- and second-generation European immigrant population of the city at that time. The nationalities listed included Lithuanian, Russian, Romanian, Polish, Swedish, Greek, Hungarian, Austrian, and of course Italian, over and over again.

Some of the dead were from outlying towns, a few from far-flung spots like Brooklyn and Pittsburgh. A line on the form that read "In this community" attempted to ascertain just how long people had been residents of the city. For two Rockville natives, the answer was: "1 day."

Like many of the Italian dead, Anna DiMartino was released to the Laraia-Sagarino Funeral Home on Washington Street. A white-coated mortuary attendant zipped her into a bag on a wheeled cart and took her out of the east archway to a waiting hearse. The crowd of onlookers tracked it as it turned onto Capitol.

Salvatore DiMartino left for Barbour Street to tell his children. The oldest was eighteen; the youngest, only one, would never understand.

Only one identification was made with paper. By the northeast chute, rescuers had found a handbag under the body now tagged #4540. The woman was horribly burned, missing her hands and even a piece of her chest. Her body had protected the bag; inside was a ration book with her name on it. Authorities contacted the Glastonbury Chief of Police, who had an officer call the home.

The woman's husband answered. Gently, the policeman broke the news to him.

"Oh no," the man said, "she's right here with me."

The policeman had seen grief and denial before. He patiently asked the man to just come down and take a look at the body.

"She's right here," the man insisted.

And she was. They'd been in the middle of the grandstand with their son when the fire broke out. Twice the crowd knocked the woman down, but she managed to escape. Her son was safe and she didn't care that she'd lost her purse.

Still, the police needed the husband to come down—to officially take her name off the body. He went to the armory and looked at 4540 for just a second. Of course it wasn't her. His wife did get her bag back though. The next day she was listed in the *Courant* among the dead.

More trustworthy were wedding bands and dental charts. The melting point of gold is 1,945 degrees Fahrenheit, and dental gold's is even higher, being an alloy. Silver fillings survive even complete cremation of the body. Rings and watches held inscriptions. As evening settled, Dr. Butler began receiving charts. He moved through the rows with a clipboard, squatting down to peer deep into the mouths of the dead, noting posts and crowns and bridges.

Downstairs, Emily Gill gave the clerks her information. No, she didn't know what the Cook children were wearing. When she and Ted Parsons had first arrived at her sister's apartment at 4 Marshall Street, they couldn't find any of the Cooks. She left Ted there to man the phone in case anyone called and headed out to the Brown School. A list there said Mildred was a patient at Municipal Hospital. Emily registered all three children as missing, got in her car and drove. She found Mildred and also Edward at

Municipal, both of them in critical condition, drifting in and out of con-sciousness. Edward's face had been burned; he was wrapped like a mummy. Mildred didn't know what had happened to Donald or Eleanor.

The escorts took Emily up the stairs and through the doors and onto the drill floor. The nurse handed her a gauze mask to hold over her nose. She gladly accepted it.

They took her to the children's corner, to the girls. The well-preserved girl who'd just come in—#1565—seemed to fit Eleanor's description. The escort checked the tag, then folded the nap of the blanket back.

Her hair was the right color, light brown, but seemed a little curly, un-brushed, too wild for Eleanor's. The crowd had stepped on her, and her forehead had swelled up like a pumpkin. And her teeth were wrong, the only two permanent teeth the lower ones in front. Eleanor had at least eight permanent upper teeth—or so Emily Gill thought. Eleanor didn't live with her. Maybe Marion should take a look at the girl.

No, Emily told them, it's not her.

One girl's father identified her mother by the soles of her feet, where he sandpapered her calluses. The girl's brother was never totally identified. Her father just picked a size and shape.

Some IDs were simpler. A Canton man recognized his mother im-mediately. He expressed his belief that she died from a heart attack, as she was burned only slightly. It was a blow, he said; he'd just lost his father the previous July 7th.

The one thing that struck the workers at the armory as odd was how few people were identified early that first evening. Hundreds of searchers came looking, but only a score or so bodies left through the checkout.

After the Cocoanut Grove, one state trooper had escorted a local cou-ple to Boston's South Morgue to view their daughter. Now he saw the same hesitation in the searchers at the armory; their reluctance to approach the rows of cots was plain in how slowly they walked the floor. And naturally, relatives had qualms with identifying their loved ones when the bodies of-fered no longer resembled anyone. People were hoping they *wouldn't* find the person they were looking for. Some of the searchers acted like they didn't understand a word their escorts said. They were numb.

Others were still in denial, unable to accept that this tragedy had ac-tually happened, and happened to them. Mrs. Grace Fifield had gone to the circus with her sixteen-year-old son. The boy thought his mother was in front of him when they came out of the exit, then couldn't find her. Her husband visited the hospitals and finally the armory. Failing to locate her, he decided she must have been stricken with amnesia and wandered off. The family was from Newport, Vermont; Mr. Fifield allowed as she might have taken a train to Montreal.

Like all other major stages of the circus fire, the armory spawned lots of tales. One volunteer was helping a family search for their boy. They stopped in front of a cot. The family couldn't bring themselves to pull the blanket away from the victim's face, so the escort did it for them. The dead boy was the escort's son; the man had no idea he'd even been to the circus.

John Cleary, Grace Fifield's stepson-in-law and a reporter for the *Times,* remembered leaving the drill shed to use a phone on a landing. A man stumbled out and half collapsed on the stairs.

"Are you all right?" Cleary asked.

"Yes," the man said softly, "I'm all right. I found my wife and three children in there." He put his face in his hands and sat very still.

Yet, according to the records, there was no man who identified a wife and three children at the armory.

One tale that may or may not be true is the rather common one of morticians breaking the brittle arms and legs of victims to fit the bodies into rubberized bags—but right there in front of people? Similarly (in)credible is John Cleary's assertion that someone bumped a cot and a charred foot fell to the floor.

Though there was no need to overstate the sensational here—as with the fire itself—people couldn't resist. The event engendered such overpowering feelings, such awe and incomprehension, that any means of relaying the waste and horror of it was fair game. The tallest tales could not be worse than what actually happened.

But the armory wasn't a story. It didn't end neatly with a gruesome twist or a heartbreaking minor chord. It just ground on, minute by minute, hour by hour. There were still a hundred bodies waiting to be claimed.

Those who'd found their loved ones could leave. After the checkout desk, they went with a police officer, who drove them past the crowds and through the dusky streets and home. No one said much. The policeman dropped them off, then came back for more. He would be doing this all night. There was still a line outside, and more arriving all the time. In a quiet corner of the drill floor, nurses were bolting down their dinner of coffee and doughnuts, speaking in whispers. Upstairs, behind the glass door of the conference room, the phones were ringing off the hook.

Bad face

For parents missing children, the optimistic route started with the circus grounds, police headquarters, and the Brown School, followed by inquiries at Municipal, Hartford, and then St. Francis Hospital, and ended with the armory. The pessimistic went straight to the armory, enduring a kind of purgatory for their lack of faith, then raced off to the hospitals.

By six o'clock, three hours after the fire, all the children who'd been at headquarters were now at the Brown School, sliding down the slides on the playground, or inside, under the watchful eyes of the policewomen. The radio stations had announced that parents should call for them there, and a line formed outside, smaller than the one at the armory yet just as desperate.

A father of two had rescued one child and left him with a stranger while he went back into the tent for the other. When they came out safely, the stranger and the first child were gone.

The registration of names was on a much smaller scale. The War Council had sent a stenographer, and the American Legion and Red Cross volunteers manned a table, but to the parents in line they were painfully slow. They compiled the names and addresses and ages of the missing and compared it to their single sheet of found children.

In their initial circuit around town, worried relatives and friends left the names of Barbara and Mary Kay Smith, Jerry LeVasseur, and Grace Fifield, among others. Of the thirty-five mothers and children on this early list, sixteen were already dead.

Beyond the table in the entryway, on the playground and in the classrooms, the children waited, thirty of them, unsure what had happened to their parents and brothers and sisters and cousins.

A Hartford couple gave the names of their three-year-old and his teenaged cousin. A volunteer checked the lists—they had a match. In a minute a policewoman reunited the four of them. During the panic, they'd been separated. The teenager had pushed his cousin over the northeast chute, and the crowd swallowed him. It took him several hours roaming the grounds to find the toddler again, but he had.

After touring the armory and St. Francis Hospital, another couple found their seven-year-old son at the Brown School. They'd been sitting in the east bleachers. When the fire broke out, the father dropped his son and then his wife down between the boards and squeezed through after them. By the time he got outside, the child was gone. A woman took him to a store, the boy explained. She called the police and stayed with him until a cruiser could come and take him to the school.

But for every happy ending, there were ten disappointments. The line was long, and there were only so many children. Some who came away empty had run out of places to look. They headed back to the armory to check the children's section once more, or off to Municipal Hospital to ask at the front desk again. A few stood on the sidewalk by Market Street, unsure just what to do.

A police captain conferred with Commissioner Hickey at the armory to make sure there were no lost children still there, then drove up Barbour Street. He cruised the blocks around the grounds, keeping an eye out for any children by themselves. He pulled his car up by the lot, got out and swept the backyards and parking areas on foot. From Kensington all the way to Cleveland he canvassed the houses and tenements, going door to door, floor to floor.

Another officer had had a long day. He'd started before noon, doing traffic on Barbour for the big crowd coming in. Now he drew duty at the Brown School, becoming the officer in charge. Three adults approached him. "Where do we get our refunds for our circus tickets?" they asked.

The man was so nonplused he didn't even laugh at them. "I'm sorry," he said, "I don't know. We're not taking care of that here."

The line kept steady. The Red Cross Canteen Corps furnished dinner for the staff and the remaining children.

Communications were still all snarled. They needed to get through to police headquarters to verify the name of a patient but couldn't raise them. Finally the officer in charge detailed a policewoman to Municipal Hospital to get a list of the injured.

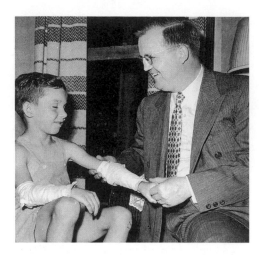

Mayor William Mortensen visits David Fitzgerald, who was only slightly burned. His younger brother James died at Municipal Hospital. His mother was badly burned but eventually recovered. PHOTO COURTESY OF AP/WIDE WORLD PHOTOS

Mayor Mortensen was already there, visiting the wards while Mrs. Mortensen, a volunteer, worked with the burned children. By now the radio broadcasts had brought in scores of nurse's aides; two took the train all the way from New York. The trouble now was space. Patients wrapped head to foot in bandages lay on cots along the hallways. Nurses walked about in masks—not from the danger of infection but because of the smell. Tall fans had been set up by windows to blow fresh air in, but it was still hot and there were far too many people. The children on the cots looked up, suffering. The mayor paused to offer a comforting word, then went on. In a room, two little girls—apparently unhurt—were playing. They were the only ambulatory children he saw.

His entourage got on an elevator. Before the doors closed, a nurse rolled a gurney in with a boy on it, his face swathed in gauze. Only his lips showed, puffed to twice normal size. His breath came in uneven, shallow gasps.

"He's going to be operated on now," an aide explained.

The doors rolled open and they took him away. The mayor's party stayed on.

Upstairs, just as he entered a room to cheer the injured there, one of the children in it died. A little girl—unidentified, said the hospital superintendent. They hadn't been able to locate her parents. It's likely from the girl's age, sex and time of death that this was the girl who came to be known as Little Miss 1565.

Municipal was not only running out of room but out of basic supplies. They had to call New Britain General to request more cots and stretchers, more sheet wadding and cast plaster. New Britain got a shipment on a truck immediately.

The overcrowding was pitiful. Nurses helped Jerry LeVasseur out of his oxygen tent and laid him in the same bed with a five-year-old boy, also critically burned. The boy had a pillow and Jerry didn't. He asked for one but they were all out. (A hundred were on the way, donated by the Veterans' Hospital in Newington; doctors needed them to elevate the arms and legs of patients.)

On the same floor, Barbara and Mary Kay Smith shared a bed. They were both burned on the arms, legs and back. Agnes Norris was on the floor above them, though they didn't know it. Down the hall, their mother was recovering. She hadn't been able to catch their father; he'd heard about the fire from their aunt and come up from Middletown to look for them, checking first at St. Francis, then Hartford Hospital and finally the armory. Because he didn't know the city, he'd never heard of Municipal.

Dr. Alfred Burgdorf, the city's health officer, ran into Mayor Mortensen in the hall. The overcrowding concerned him. He suggested a redistribution of the injured among the city's hospitals, since St. Francis and especially Hartford were nowhere near capacity. The mayor agreed— once the patients were stabilized.

Municipal was doing the best it could, considering. Volunteers had filled the gaps at every turn, and state, nonprofit and even private organizations stepped forward. The Red Cross Mobile Canteen established a stand on every floor to supply cold water and fruit juice to the workers as well as the injured. G. Fox, at owner Mrs. Beatrice Auerbach's bidding, sent five hundred sandwiches and twenty-five gallons of coffee to keep people moving. She heard there was a shortage of bedding and nightclothes, so she sent over a truckload. Nurses opened the linen cabinets to find brand-new sheets and pajamas, the G. Fox price tags still attached.

As the mayor left (for now; he'd be back, and Mrs. Mortensen would be here all night), the hospital superintendent called to a group of volunteer nurses going on break, "Please, all of you, all of you who can come back tonight, please do. I think we're going to need everybody we can get."

"We'll be back," most of them said.

The superintendent wouldn't get a break. Governor Baldwin was due soon.

The list of injured—still incomplete, not yet ready to be released—grew as people reached home and discovered they were hurt. The litany of outpatient injuries ranged from sprained backs, concussions and dislocated thumbs to "abrasions of both elbow flexures," "rope burns of the thoracic area" and "marked nervous shock." Some older folks were simply black and blue, their shins dented and bloody from stumbling through the grandstand chairs.

Friction burns were the most common injury, all the people who'd gone down the ropes and poles. Crush and trample injuries came next. One woman had sprained her ankle and suffered bruises to her head, shoulders and legs. Someone had stepped on another woman's foot and broken the second metatarsal. One boy showed up with burns from the elbow to the hand on both arms; though they hurt, he was more concerned about his mother, still missing.

The list of those recovering upstairs was more dire, and not for public consumption. Of ten-year-old Edith Budrick, it said: "bad face, legs, arms."

Of Mildred Cook, her age strangely estimated as twenty: serious. Mrs. Emily Gill, sister E. Hampton. Call Clarence Colson.

Edward Cook, room 505: legs, arms, face.

Agnes Norris, fifth floor: critical.

Marion Dineen, age fifteen: not serious.

Gerald LeVasseur, fourth floor: face, arms, head, buttocks.

But the first list of Municipal's injured given out to the police and newspapers and radio stations had entries even more upsetting. One patient was listed as "John, 5"—nothing else. A number were listed by a single name (Logan, 11), or names that would later prove garbled versions of their real names (Freddie Bryarz and Freddie Bryant turned out to be Freddie Boyajian). Their estimated ages, like Mildred Cook's, were way off. Relatives hearing this list over the radio would only grow more confused and anxious. And what could be made of "Unidentified Boy of 8 or 10"?

Downstairs in the lobby, the Red Cross and the hospital's social workers were busy taking missing persons reports, running through the same

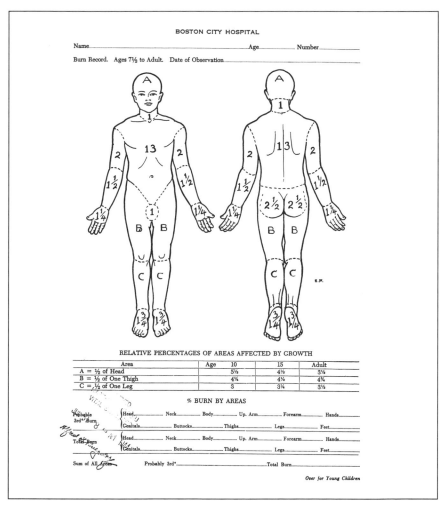

BOSTON CITY HOSPITAL

Name..Age.................... Number..................

Burn Record. Ages 7½ to Adult. Date of Observation...

RELATIVE PERCENTAGES OF AREAS AFFECTED BY GROWTH

Area	Age	10	15	Adult
A = ½ of Head		5½	4½	3½
B = ½ of One Thigh		4¼	4½	4¾
C = ½ of One Leg		3	3¼	3½

% BURN BY AREAS

Probable
3rd Burn { Head............ Neck............ Body............ Up. Arm............ Forearm............ Hands............
{ Genitals............ Buttocks............ Thighs............ Legs............ Feet............

Total Burn { Head............ Neck............ Body............ Up. Arm............ Forearm............ Hands............
{ Genitals............ Buttocks............ Thighs............ Legs............ Feet............

Sum of All Areas........... Probably 3rd*..Total Burn..................

Over for Young Children

A contemporary hospital chart used to compute what percent of a patient's body had been burned. Shirley Snelgrove, for example, was burned over 50% of her body, Jerry LeVasseur 25%, Mildred Cook 20%, Stanley Kurneta 5%.

routine as their counterparts at the armory and the Brown School, with similar results.

All these efforts were a first step at getting reorganized after the raw chaos of the fire. Downtown at police headquarters they were restoring order in a different way. In the basement, in the property room, two sergeants headed a detail that tagged and catalogued every item recovered from the Barbour Street lot—the shoes and pocketbooks and eyeglasses and earrings, the marbles and coins and buttons, the bankbooks and ration stamps. Outside, a clutch of onlookers huddled around a barred window well to see what they'd found. They placed all the valuables in the vault on the main floor. Above the clamor of the front desk, a voice on the radio slowly intoned the names of the dead.

The vice president of the circus, James Haley, could not escape the broadcast; it was on all the stations, constant. He left the lot and drove to the Hotel Bond on Asylum, where he and some of the star performers were staying. Haley had been an accountant in Florida, dabbling in real estate; he'd been politic enough to be appointed the state's representative of the John Ringling estate, then married into the business after falling for Aubrey Ringling. He was a money man, at best a local politician, not circus folk. A veteran, he'd seen his share of hell in World War I, but this was something else.

He parked the car and walked into the plush lobby, through the plants and brass ashtrays. The bar was already busy. Even here the excitement of the fire seemed to have stirred people up. He took the elevator, feeling the upward rush in his legs, then waited for the doors to open. He slipped his key in the lock.

In Evanston, Illinois, who knew what Robert Ringling was doing. He must know by now, Haley figured; somebody from the inner circle would have heard the news. All the more reason to call.

Finally he got the operator. He gave her the number, then waited for someone to pick up.

Evidence

Back on the lot, a detective accompanied a *Times* photographer as he slowly captured the scorched interior section by section. As part of the city's investigation, Prosecutor Burr Leikind had commissioned him to take shots from all angles. He wanted complete coverage, and the photographer was happy to oblige. Like any professional, he was taking forever.

The big top had become a crime scene, but the thousands of survivors and rescue workers had obliterated any traces of evidence except the most gross. That's what the photographer focused on: the hulks of the north grandstands, the fallen rows of poles. The crowd was gone now, the smashed and flattened chairs fallen off the back of the grandstand, one upset fire bucket beneath it. The cageboys had moved the menagerie wagons and pulled their canvas covers over the bars: on the sides, a stencilled message read:

Wild Animals

DANGER

Do Not Touch

The men's latrine still held the buckets from its toilets and the sectioned urinal trough and a large barrel containing waste, but everything else was gone. Behind the barrel, some of the jacks backing the southwest bleachers were charred, others surprisingly pristine. The photographer stepped to the west and caught another shot of the whole thing—jacks, men's room, menagerie cages. Not much of a picture, but they weren't paying him for art, just solid documentation.

Around the stages and chutes and railings the cleanup continued, MPs poking through the dust with their billy clubs. Standing perimeter

The remains of the men's room behind the southwest blues, the probable point of origin. PHOTO COURTESY OF THE *HARTFORD COURANT*

guard around them was Gloria Barber's fiancé Orville Vieth, brought by truck from Bradley. People were still finding things. A civilian and an auxiliary policeman reported to one officer that they'd picked up a child's leg, some money and other personal belongings. They had them in a bag. Rather than handle the bag himself, the officer chose to take the civilian to the armory and let him personally hand it over to the medical examiner.

On the north side of the lot, investigators noticed a curious effect. Some patches of grass within a few feet of the tent were untouched while trees fifty to sixty feet away had withered leaves and scorched trunks.

Along Barbour Street, groups of men and women chatted on porches, drinking beer and ice water and fanning themselves. The neighborhood kids sat on the curb like a defeated team. All the sacks of hot dog buns and bags of peanuts and gallons of orangeade weren't going to be sold this year, and everyone was glum.

At St. Michael's, a few blocks away on Clark, an exhausted Father Looney heard the phone ringing in the rectory. It was a fellow priest calling from the armory. He had bad news. Little Billy Dineen had died in the fire. Father Looney knew the Dineens well; they belonged to the parish, and Billy's sister Marion went to the parochial school.

The phones at the armory were a problem, the other priest explained, and Mr. Dineen hadn't found Marion yet. The detective had asked him if Father Looney would let Mrs. Dineen know.

Of course, Father Looney said.

On the lot, Burr Leikind led a posse of Hartford fire, police and building inspectors on a tour of the big top, stopping often to examine the damage. The men were in their shirtsleeves and still sweating. They found two full pails of water under the stands, one beneath the southeast bleachers and one near the center exit of the north grandstand. Leikind and the fire officials were especially interested in the four water trucks; they could only locate two, way at the far east end of the lot. According to workers they questioned, the circus carried their own fire extinguishers. Leikind ordered a squad of policemen to round up any fire buckets or extinguishers they could find and bring them to the office of McGovern's. The formal investigation had begun.

At the armory, Commissioner Hickey was too busy to get away, so he deputized a state police captain to act as fire marshal in his stead. Two other

An officer stands guard over pieces of the northeast chute to be used as evidence.
PHOTO BY PAUL R. SHAFER, COURTESY OF MR. SHAFER HIMSELF

troopers would accompany him to McGovern's and help the prosecutors interrogate circus officials.

They arrived in time to join Leikind inside the perimeter as his team measured the exits. In the middle of the southwest exit they found a heavy stake, still erect, unbudged, which split the path in half. One man commented on how it must have stacked up the people fleeing.

Next they went to the center break on the south side and inspected the electrical cables that ran in from the light plant. The cables took up much of the exit, leaving a useful width at the sidewall of less than five feet. At the light plant itself they found three water-type extinguishers, two of which were unused.

State's Attorney Meade Alcorn caught the tail end of the tour, just before they adjourned to McGovern's, leaving the photographer popping away at the bleachers. Working from observation, hearsay and years of experience, Alcorn and Leikind made up a list of twenty people they wanted to question—ushers and seatmen, Herbert DuVal, circus police chief John Brice. They had enough John Doe subpoenas to back the list up, so they sent a committee to the office wagon in the front yard.

Circus vice president James Haley was there, returned from the Bond, still smarting from a decidedly unpleasant conversation with Robert Ringling. The committee told him they wanted these people on the list

The south grandstand, looking east from the southwest blues.
PHOTO BY ROBERT D. GOOD, COURTESY OF THE CIRCUS WORLD MUSEUM

kept available for questioning. Haley said he'd try to comply in every way possible.

Meade Alcorn turned McGovern's office into a courtroom, complete with a stenographer. Prosecutor Leikind did the questioning. The witnesses—at first, mostly John Carson's ushers—waited outside in the custody of police so they couldn't compare their statements. Some of the more important witnesses they couldn't find, like general manager George W. Smith. The one department head they did locate was Edward "Whitey" Versteeg, of the light gang.

Because his department was in charge of the diesel generators, Whitey Versteeg also controlled most of the show's fire extinguishers. At Alcorn's request, the trooper acting as fire marshal questioned him.

Versteeg stressed how shorthanded they were, thirty men doing the work of fifty. They had extinguishers, yes; he listed the different kinds and where they were located—all outside, near his equipment, which, he implied, was right where they were supposed to be. "As far as I know there are no fire extinguishers in the big top."

Everything was operating normally, he said, until someone yelled fire. His engineer cut the power and his men grabbed the extinguishers.

The water trucks, he said, were Mr. Blanchfield's responsibility; it took them four or five minutes to get over to the south side and put water on the canvas. (In fact, they never did. The tent was too far gone to be saved at that point. They quenched the flaming tires and wetted down the light plants; that was their sole reason for being there.)

"I don't know how many men were on the trucks today," Versteeg said. "I believe that they are usually spotted about the big top." His diction here was a dead giveaway, a hint. *Usually* the trucks were positioned with their engines turning in case of a fire; today, for some unknown reason, they weren't—a charge Deacon Blanchfield would have to respond to later.

Asked about the top itself, Versteeg answered honestly: "In winter quarters the canvas was treated with a solution of paraffin and gasoline and brushed on with brooms. This was done by the canvas department, and I saw them doing this work."

Again, it was another department's problem; his had performed honorably. As for exit signs, he didn't remember seeing any. The ushers and seatmen? He couldn't say to the best of his knowledge whether they had been at their posts or not. But his lights were fine, all the plugs and switches checked before and after the fire. The lights were on inside the tent, and the big diesels were running outside, but he'd never detected any sparks from any of his machines.

Versteeg's confirmation of the top's waterproofing immediately added several names to the list of witnesses, including canvas boss Leonard Aylesworth and James Haley. Deacon Blanchfield made it because of the trucks. Detectives armed with John Doe subpoenas spread out over the grounds.

Publicly, Herbert DuVal was telling the press the circus had used nothing combustible, but the papers also mentioned that Hartford fire investigators were looking into a report that the top had been treated with inflammable weatherproofing. Ringling officials denied this, saying that the material had been treated by its manufacturer, not to make it fireproof but fire resistant.

Outside, the blank gravestones threw long shadows in the grass. The lights of the midway clicked on. As the sky colored, the photographer learned that he had to leave. The *Times* needed him to cover something else. A police captain took over, quickly going around the exterior, making sure he got it all before dark.

The police found Leonard Aylesworth, but when they checked the of-

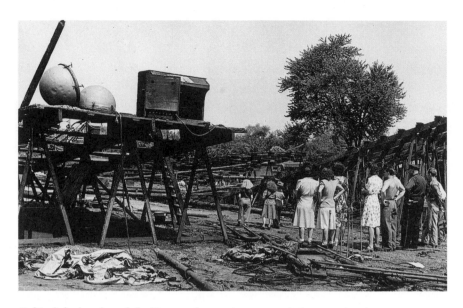

*Behind the bandstand, looking northwest. A quarterpole leans against it.
Legend has it a main pole crashed into the bandstand seconds after Merle
Evans jumped. A good story but untrue; the sixth main pole fell to the left
and just short of it.* PHOTO COURTESY OF THE *HARTFORD COURANT*

fice wagon, James Haley was gone. They combed the grounds and still
couldn't turn him up. A pair of detectives with a subpoena hopped in their
car and drove downtown to the Bond Hotel. They asked at the desk, official business.

Oh, the clerk said, I'm afraid the gentleman just left.

In the evening, sun is going down

Abdominal scars turn purple as the epidermis burns. A medical examiner
from Boston who'd worked on the Cocoanut Grove dead was taking
William Menser to school. Look close, and even through the black crust
you could tell if a woman had had a caesarean section, a man an appendectomy. Here was a ruptured navel, there a breast removed. The body was
a map, a diary, a sign.

Leaning over the rows, parents suddenly realized how intimately they knew their children's teeth—the missing incisors, the six-year molars just coming in. What a relief it was to see this girl had a gap, this one a canine that overlapped. It meant they could keep looking, that they might not find her here.

Soldiers moved the bodies who'd been identified to the checkout desk, past Thomas Barber and Ed Lowe, helpless as an honor guard. Here Dr. Weissenborn or Onderdonk removed all personal effects—some of which provided the only means of identification—and boxed them for the coroner to hand over to the next of kin. Clerks from the War Council kept a record, tapping at their Underwoods.

The phones upstairs had processed over three thousand calls, some from as far away as Iowa and Indiana—an oddity for the time, long distance being a luxury few used. Outside, the crowd on Capitol hadn't dwindled, stood vigilant as if they too awaited news. The whole city did.

A policeman led the civilian with the child's leg in a bag up the stairs and over to Dr. Weissenborn, who added it to the parts he'd already collected. Later, another officer also delivered a sack of fragments. In they went. Officially, the mix was named Unidentified #1. No one looked at it.

A sergeant who'd helped sort the effects salvaged from the grounds identified his niece and grandniece. The niece's husband had been a dentist but was now an army captain serving in the South Pacific. The girl had been their only child. The Red Cross would have to tell him.

A Hartford man worked downtown for the state health department. His younger brother and sister had gone to the circus on free passes given to their father. When their father heard of the fire, he was stricken.

"I kept calling home," the man remembered, "only to be told that they hadn't returned yet."

He drove to the armory and went through the boys' section, ultimately discovering his brother. He tried the girls over and over, lifting sheets, staring at the planes of faces. His sister, only thirteen, had been tall for her age. She was in with the young women. The man identified her by their mother's Hartford High class ring.

But these IDs were exceptions. By 9:30, when Mayor Mortensen returned to the drill floor, only twenty-five bodies had been identified.

Dentists had begun to accompany parents up the stairs. Dr. Butler directed them to the most likely cots.

Charles Coughlan of Bristol searched for his daughter Hortense Murphy and her young family. They'd all gone except baby Jimmy. Coughlan had located his four-year-old granddaughter Patty on the fourth floor of Municipal Hospital, badly burned on the arms and legs, but his daughter, son-in-law and four-year-old grandson Charles were still missing. Shortly before ten, he discovered his namesake in with the other boys. He still had a long night ahead of him.

Dr. Paul de la Vergne, who didn't mind sitting up high, identified his wife Elizabeth by a ring she wore. She'd been trampled and then burned.

Go to sleep

At 10:15, Mayor Mortensen went on the air to brief the public on the status of the missing and injured and to praise the city and state disaster organizations for their prompt response. WDRC and WTHT carried the address live. He'd already made the same speech once, at 9:00, right after he visited Municipal. The first time, his voice had caught on the words, and people listening at home or in their cars, in barrooms or on the shop floor, heard what seemed to be the mayor breaking down.

Now he steeled himself and leaned into the mike. He thanked the Red Cross and the War Council, the Salvation Army and the hospitals. He singled out Commissioner Hickey and Deputy Chief of Police Michael J. Godfrey for their work.

It was a bland performance, all compliments, unless you knew what the mayor wasn't saying. Noticeably absent from his list was his chief of police, Charles Hallissey. Like his circus counterpart John Brice, Hallissey was in his dotage, playing out the string. Mortensen, a reform mayor supported by the immigrant minorities of the North End, had inherited him from the previous, big-machine administration. He'd considered him inattentive to his duties before the fire, at best perfunctory. Now, secretly, he'd made up his mind to drum him into retirement. Political scribes for the *Courant* and the *Times* noted that today he'd named Godfrey his liaison in charge of all facets of the police response. Hallissey, there on the lot at the time of the fire, suddenly disappeared, eclipsed by the dynamic Bull Hickey.

The mayor's speech was brief, with good reason. The people listening weren't tuning in for him. They were waiting for the new lists. First he read the names of the few children still waiting at the Brown School. Then he read the lists given to his office by the four hospitals, in descending order of patient load: Municipal, Hartford, St. Francis, and finally Mt. Sinai. Then he read the names of the dead. Slowly. Clearly. He was surprised how many he knew, and how many—strangers at the beginning of the day— now seemed familiar to him, and precious. This time he didn't break down.

At police headquarters, the property room finished sorting the last batch of items that had come from the lot. The officer in charge boxed them up and fit them in the vault with the others, shut the door and turned the key. There would be more tomorrow, he figured, and people looking for their things.

At Municipal Hospital the rush had finally died down. Nurse's aides and janitors policed the lobby and the first-floor corridors, sweeping skeins of sloughed skin from the linoleum. The more stubborn bits they had to get down on their knees and scrub with brushes.

One bluebird was intimidated by the injuries of the patients but gamely carrying on. She had plans of becoming a nurse one day. Apparently a colleague could read the strain in her face. "We don't need anybody faint- ing," the person warned her.

Municipal's staff put into action the mayor and Dr. Burgdorf's plan to alleviate the crowding. They chose twenty-three patients, most with less serious injuries, and a few because Hartford or St. Francis had specialists who could take better care of them. Among those transferred by ambulance was Jerry LeVasseur. Finally he would have his own bed.

Donald Gale's parents finally found him at Municipal. They didn't own a phone. Hulda Grant's boyfriend had told them Donald was dead; other neighbors said he made it out and ran into the woods. Fearing the worst, the Gales drove straight to the armory. Only Donald's father went in. When he came up empty, they tried the hospitals. The Gales were new to the area, there for the war work; they didn't know Municipal existed.

When Donald regained consciousness, he gave a nurse the number of their next-door neighbor. By the time the volunteers downstairs called, it was far too late to catch his parents. They were driving around town in a panic. They blew through a red light, and a motorcycle cop stopped them. Donald's father explained the situation.

"Have you tried Municipal?" the cop asked.

Instead of giving them directions, he escorted them to the door. Mrs. Gale was afraid to come up, so she stayed in the car in the parking lot.

His father talked with Donald. There were three other boys in room 509 with him. By morning two of them would be dead. Donald himself was optimistic. Despite his injuries, he assured his father that he was okay. He imagined he'd be home in a day or two.

Father Murphy from St. Justin's was at Municipal too, anointing the dying as he had on the lot. A young husband asked him to bless his son. The boy died soon after. Father Murphy stayed with the father. The man was torn but clung to his faith; to the Father his strength typified the goodness and courage shown by all those he'd ministered to today.

In 502, in his oxygen tent, Elliott Smith drifted in and out of consciousness, his body packed in cracked ice. He still didn't know about his mother, but his mother knew about him. Downstairs, Grace Smith had been lying in a hallway on a gurney beside an elevator when the doors opened. She had a sudden compulsion to raise herself up and look. There, being wheeled out on another gurney, was her son.

In Vernon, the Smith family knew the two were in Municipal, but only after some confusion. Earlier, the hospital had called to say Mrs. Smith was all right but that she hadn't been able to locate Joan. Joan had answered; she said she was fine, then gave the phone over to her grandmother. Only much later did they figure out the call had been misdirected. Somehow the volunteers at the hospital had transposed the number supplied by Elliott and Joan's mother Grace Smith and the number of the Edward Smith family in Bloomfield. Their daughter Joan-Lee Smith was still missing.

Mr. Smith, like Mr. Gale, had gone to the armory and found no one. When he called home, Joan told him her mother was in Municipal. He went there and found Elliott listed as well.

In Middletown, Sophie Kurneta Erickson was trying to find out what happened to her son Raymond and her sister Mary. She'd missed the circus, taking care of baby Joann. Her mother, her younger sister Betsy and her nephew Tony had all made it home. Her brother Stanley was in Hartford Hospital. He hadn't seen Mary since the fire, but Raymond he'd taken to Municipal Hospital. He told Sophie the whole story over the phone—

bringing him up to the fourth floor, leaving him on the mattress with the priest—but when she called the hospital they had no record of a Raymond Erickson. Yes, they were sure. They'd checked and double-checked their lists. No one by that name had been admitted.

So, hours after the fire, unsure just what was going on, Sophie Erickson reported her son missing. Raymond Sr. was in the navy, stationed at Gulfport, Mississippi. She needed him here now.

The staff at Municipal had hoped to move Mildred Cook to Hartford Hospital with the other transfers. She was only in fair shape but stable enough to go. The trouble was Edward. "Child can't be moved," a note beside Mildred's name read. For now they would stay.

Emily Gill had already found Mildred; now Marion and Ted Parsons visited, bringing along Donald. He'd eaten supper with the family that had taken him home, then given them the address of his mother's apartment. Uncle Ted was waiting for him, also Aunt Marion and the family's minister, the Reverend James Yee, who'd accompanied her down from Southampton.

Mildred was not completely there. Her head was a ball of gauze, only her eyes and a hole for her mouth showing. The visit was quick.

Edward was registered on the fifth floor. They took the elevator up, watching the numbers turn. The room he was in had three other boys in it. The lighting was low so they could sleep. Outside, cars rolled by on Vine, accelerating through the turn by Keney Park, spinning off into the night. Donald could barely see. Edward's bed was tucked into a dark corner, his bandaged arms white lines on the blanket. Weakly, he asked what had happened to Eleanor.

Across the room, in his own dark corner, Donald Gale slept.

Downstairs, there was a crisis. Nurses noticed that the plaster casts they'd fitted some of the patients with were digging into their skin. Typically, the burned tissues had filled with edema and were now grossly swollen. The rigid casts pinched off circulation; people's hands and feet were turning purple. The staff began cutting the casts off, but soon it was clear there were too many for them to handle, and they had to call Hartford Hospital and ask for a fresh set of internes. There weren't any; they'd been working hard all night. They went anyway. "By that time we were exhausted," one doctor remembered. "We had to guzzle a few cups of coffee for energy and start cutting."

Mayor Mortensen returned to Municipal with the secretary of the Bushnell. She'd given her mother the tickets to take her daughter and a boarder. Now she was finding them, one by one.

The boarder was on the third floor. Charles Tomalonis was Lithuanian, and had only recently come to America; he didn't speak English. Municipal's lists never had his name the same way twice— Kamelonis, Tabolcoks. On top of the language barrier, Charles Tomalonis was in extreme pain, his face, like Mildred Cook's, lost under yards of cotton. The secretary spoke Lithuanian. She leaned close to the slit for his lips.

"Is Mrs. V. all right?" he asked, meaning her mother.

They knew she was dead because they'd just come from the armory, where her husband had identified her. But they didn't want to tell him bad news, not in his state. They said she was okay.

"Oh," he said, relieved. "Now I can die."

In the four operating rooms on the first floor, surgeons worked on the worst cases. On one table lay the woman who burned while huddled over her niece, both of them unable to run because their ankles were broken. The doctors would try to patch the sieve of her skin for hours, watching her blood pressure fluctuate, her pulse dwindle, finally, to nothing.

One volunteer nurse from New Britain spoke of a doctor toiling over the dead and dying all night even though he'd lost a child in the fire. At Hartford Hospital, the building staff set up cots for the exhausted nurses to catnap on. No one was going home.

At home, one woman's son couldn't get to sleep. All he'd gotten was a blister on his ear. He closed his eyes but it was no use, so she stayed up with him.

In Middletown, ten-year-old Betsy Kurneta couldn't sleep either. She had minor burns on her right arm, but that wasn't what was keeping her up. It would be days before she could sleep.

Joan Smith's father said she could sleep in his bed tonight. She had no idea why. It never crossed her mind that she'd have bad dreams.

Meade Alcorn and Burr Leikind weren't planning on getting to bed in the near future. Their investigation at McGovern's was slowly progressing with each new witness. The detectives who had failed to serve Haley returned, added two state troopers to their retinue and headed for the Windsor Street railyards. They went from car to car, stirring up the berths, and still they couldn't find him. They came back to Barbour Street again. Herbert DuVal—no great fan of Haley's, from his testimony—suggested he might go along as a kind of guide. They checked the railyard again. This time they found him easily.

In the meantime, Commissioner Hickey had made his way to McGovern's and caught up on what he'd missed. When the detectives brought in Haley, all the principals were in place. Hickey needed to hear very little testimony before he decided to move the entire procedure downtown. Unraveling exactly what happened would take some time. State police headquarters had a hearing room perfect for the job. For now, the admission that the canvas had been treated with the paraffin and gas mixture was tantamount to pleading guilty to criminal negligence. Prosecutors drew up arrest warrants on the spot for acting head of the circus James Haley, general manager George W. Smith, canvas boss Leonard Aylesworth, light gang boss Whitey Versteeg, superintendent of trucks Deacon Blanchfield, circus police chief Brice, and head usher John Carson.

They adjourned, Leikind leaving a detective in charge of interviewing the other circus workers they'd summoned. The detective was to take their statements and then release them, with the promise that they wouldn't skip town. Leikind went in one car with Haley; two policemen rode in another with Aylesworth, Blanchfield and Smith. The streets were deserted. They didn't need sirens.

Meanwhile, in a larger arena, Ringling's publicity machine fielded questions from the press. Roland Butler reassured America that the circus was far from done in. They still had last year's big top. The centerpoles were charred but structurally solid. The performers were fine, the menagerie untouched. They would probably retreat to Sarasota, retool and go back on the road.

Hal Olver, an assistant in the publicity department, said that absolutely no credence was being given to any theory of incendiarism or sabotage. He couldn't know that as he spoke J. Edgar Hoover's FBI was seriously examining that very possibility. After all, it was wartime.

At the armory, Marion and Ted Parsons were concerned with simpler questions. They had Donald stay at the car. James Yee went in with them.

Marion was a powerful woman, sure of herself. She'd taken on her sister-in-law's children without a second thought and loved them as her own.

Edward had come to live with her and Ted before he was a year old. Every day they were apart, Eleanor wrote to her. In many ways she knew the children better than their mother ever could.

The escort took the Parsons straight to 1565, in the front row of the girls' section. Marion knew at a glance that the body was not Eleanor's. 1565's hair was shoulder length; her niece's was cut short. The clothes weren't hers either—a white dress hardly touched by the fire. Eleanor had been wearing a red playsuit. She knew all of Eleanor's clothes, and she didn't have a dress like this. The brown shoes weren't hers either. Closer inspection made it certain: 1565 had all baby teeth; Eleanor had eight permanent teeth, four upper and four lower. No, she was sure this wasn't her.

Ted said no, and the Reverend.

The others were nothing like Eleanor, and they retreated to Marshall Street. Emily Gill was there. They compared notes, agreeing the girl they'd seen wasn't Eleanor. Marion and Ted decided they should take Donald and Reverend Yee back to Southampton. Emily was going to stay the night in the apartment and visit Mildred and Edward in the morning, then keep searching for Eleanor. She said good night to them and watched their car away.

On Broad Street, Governor Baldwin returned to the armory, shocked to find among the dead some of the patients he'd talked to this afternoon.

About now, Mayor Mortensen's office received a call from Salvatore DiMartino. He explained his situation. His wife had died, and he had eight children. He wasn't sure what to do about the funeral. "I have no money," he said. Could the city pay the expenses?

The mayor promised to do all he could.

Shortly before 11:00, the Brown School sent its last child home with its parents. They'd taken 113 names of missing persons, including Billy Dineen and Muriel and Maurice Goff. The officer in charge turned the list over to the night desk and checked the duty roster. His shift wasn't over yet.

At Municipal, graveyard came on, with extra nurses and nurse's aides. One nurse went home and had bad nightmares. She couldn't get the smell out of her uniform or her hair.

On Barbour Street, two doors north of the lot, Mrs. Dewey Howrigan noticed there were still three cars parked in her backyard. She went out to investigate. The air smelled of wet ashes and fresh hay and elephant dung.

It was still hot, the air thick. Nose in against the garden rested two Chevys, one a sedan, one a Suburban; on the far side, in the el that abutted the circus lot, sat a black Buick backed up to the trees. She peered through the Buick's windows and saw a blanket and an umbrella on the backseat. The door was open; she decided to take them into the house for safekeeping.

A block north, in Keney Park, William Epps slept on the soft ground beside his brother Richie. No blanket, no night-light. The boys weren't scared though. It was a warm night, and the stars were out.

Bad news

Of Hartford's two main dailies, the *Courant* was the paper of record. Continuously in print since 1764, it was known as "The Old Gray Lady of State Street" for its Brahminic independence, and was often so thorough as to be unreadable. The *Times* had a leaner, grittier style befitting its earthier subjects, and powerful allies in the state's Democratic party. Both were solid big-city newspapers, and both were totally overwhelmed by the circus fire.

At no time in American history was the delivery of accurate news more important than during World War II. Censorship and self-censorship were issues that concerned not just journalists but average citizens. To impress this on war workers, both papers ran little fillers at the bottom of their columns. "Don't be a rumor-monger," the *Times* reminded. "Watch your speech in public," the *Courant* advised. The same rules applied to their writers. Hearsay and scuttlebutt were useless. Even eyewitnesses were suspect; the era of firsthand reporting—sometimes live—had begun, and stories had to be both right and on time, often an impossible combination.

The *Times,* being an afternoon paper, had a much harder job with the fire than the *Courant.* Its initial reports were sketchy at best, and wrong about some very important points. No show people died in the fire, yet for several hours the AP wire ran the subhead: Three Performers Killed. Forty years later, while researching a radio documentary on the tragedy, a local radio journalist spoke with the reporter responsible for the gaffe. The man had seen three bodies whose lips were grossly oversized, their cheeks bright red, and had just assumed. An honest mistake, compounded by later writers who gussied up the bare facts with sentences like "Three performers were carried out dead, the bright makeup on their faces darkened by smoke."

Some reporters opened the show with a grand parade or spec complete with horses and elephants; others had Alfred Court performing with his big cats in the center ring (he was in his room at the Bond Hotel at the time). One journalist said several ringmasters and ushers had tried to lead the crowd in a sing-along of "Old Black Joe" to calm them. The Wallendas, it was written, had performed seven minutes of their twenty-minute act.

Not one but two witnesses recalled a member of the Wallendas falling to the ground: "The most awesome sight was seeing the guy jump from the trapeze. And when he landed on the ground—there was no net—one leg was askew at a strange angle in front of him and one ankle was behind him. I watched him all the way down. He was screaming for help." And later, a different man: "While we were waiting on the street, a dump truck went by with the high-wire person in it. He was lying flat, like a sack of grain." Both episodes were apocryphal; of the five, only Helen was hurt, stepped on in the rush for the exits.

The gravest falsehoods, predictably, came when discussing the most serious issues. "Almost all of the dead were believed to have died in the panic of suffocation, of shock induced by acute fright, and of being knocked down and stomped under the feet of thousands stampeding for the exits." (No. At least one hundred showed no crush injuries, none died of asphyxiation, and death by shock was just wild conjecture.) Many papers said the majority of the dead were children; the *Waterbury American* went so far as to say two-thirds. For years, papers have reprinted these figures as if they were true. They weren't. Of the 167 victims, only 67 were children below the age of fifteen.

Yet in a way the need for both falsehoods is understandable. In their gross overstatements, they deliver two important truths; they tell the reader who wasn't there two very important things. First, there was no way you could imagine the panic inside of that tent. And second, a hell of a lot of kids died.

The prose that reporters chose to work with was melodramatic and overheated—possibly, again, because they felt there was no way to overemphasize the actual happenings. A sampling: "The flames shot up to the top like slivers of lightning." "Then screams and moans and frenzied shouts laden with lunacy induced by panic burst upward like an explosion." "The band's tunes were drowned out by the screaming throng." "Afterward, they couldn't find a piece of canvas more than three inches square." "It was like looking at a giant skeleton stripped of all flesh."

One writer whose articles for United Press bear little resemblance to actual events had Gargantua and M'Toto pathetically in tears in their air-conditioned cages.

And there were rumors and tall tales galore that never made the paper, or did so only years later. They became part of the lore of the circus fire, unverifiable, strange. The one most widely reported as being true was that there was an infant who died in the fire and then went unidentified and was cremated in the incinerator of Hartford Hospital. The Incinerated Baby. In reality, that was the fate of Unidentified #1, the grab bag of parts Dr. Weissenborn didn't show to anyone checking at the armory. Officials made the mistake of including #1 in the initial tally of the dead, as if the parts constituted one whole person. They didn't, so the number of 168 (eerily the same as the Oklahoma City bombing) is wrong. The real number of people who died in the circus fire is 167.

Another famous story is that of the fake doctor at Municipal Hospital. In the commotion an unbalanced woman who'd always wanted to be a doctor volunteered at Municipal, bringing a little black bag with her. No one questioned her skills. She set up shop in a hallway, setting broken limbs. Later, after she'd disappeared, nurses discovered her amateur handiwork. The people she'd worked on had to have their arms and legs amputated. Perhaps this is a sideways and sexist reading of the plaster cast fiasco, the results of which could have been just as dire.

Despite all the schlock and misinformation, and the twenty-seven hundred people reported missing in the first twenty-four hours after the fire, the papers and state officials combined to provide near flawless casualty lists. They were a comfort to the public, a quick way of comprehending what had happened. Readers were used to them from war coverage. Here were the dead, the wounded, the internees, the missing. Along with the pictures of the circus fire dead ran posed portraits of local boys killed in service—"PFC J. A. Longo, 20, Killed in France."

Less accurate and comforting were the answers given by Ringling executives in Sarasota concerning the big top. The circus now claimed the tent had been treated to resist fire, but, being canvas, could not be made fireproof. Robert Ringling, reached in Evanston, Illinois, said: "Every test we put that through showed that it would resist fire. A fire might endanger some of the equipment but would never endanger human life."

Later the circus would fall back to a position that maintained they had tried to find fireproofing chemicals for some time but that with the war the army had priority.

Even this didn't wash. Since the Cocoanut Grove, every decoration in city restaurants and nightclubs had to be fireproof. New York City's acting deputy fire chief in charge of places of public assembly said a blowtorch test was applied to all canvas trappings before they were permitted to be used in public gatherings. The fire department had sanctioned several types of chemicals to be sprayed on canvas, and tested the treated material at least four times a year with four hundred degrees of heat from a blowtorch to prove it remained fireproof.

In addition, the Clyde Beatty and Russell Bros. Circus, playing in Portland, Oregon, advertised that all their tents were fireproof. They hauled hundreds of gallons of flameproofing in their wagons, spraying their canvas every four weeks in case the chemicals wore off during setup and teardown. Most of their personnel were former Ringling employees who said the Big Show's claims that they couldn't get priority were spurious.

The argument at this point was legal, and useless after the fact. The dead were dead, the dying were dying. At Municipal and Hartford Hospitals the operating rooms and corridors were still busy—as were the basements and halls of the Weinstein Funeral Home, and Dillon's, and Farley's, and O'Brien's.

As Barbour Street shut down for the night, Mayor Mortensen made his last public announcement of the day. He let the criminals of the city know that he'd asked Deputy Chief Godfrey to assign a dozen policemen to watch cars in parking lots and on the street near the site of the fire. He asked that the license plate numbers be taken and the owners identified. He asked that the police guard against the stripping of these automobiles.

Were you in Cleveland?

Commissioner Hickey began his hearing at state police headquarters on Washington Street by interrogating the highest-ranking Ringling official in custody, Vice President James Haley.

To keep the witnesses' testimonies separate, he detailed police to the hallway to stand guard over Smith, Aylesworth, Blanchfield, Versteeg, Brice, and the ushers and seatmen who'd responded to their summonses until Hickey called for them. Of the seven accused, only head usher John Carson was missing.

Inside, Haley faced not just Hickey but State's Attorney Alcorn and Prosecutor Leikind.

Commissioner Hickey did the questioning. The first fact he ascertained was that Aylesworth was responsible for treating and maintaining the canvas. He verified that John Carson assigned the ushers to their respective sections, though Haley couldn't say if he kept a record of it. Haley estimated the capacity of the top as approximately nine to ten thousand— six thousand in the grandstands and three to four thousand on the blues— but as Hickey asked him to describe the precise layout of the lettered sections, Haley turned vague. He wasn't familiar with their firefighting equipment; Smith would know that. And while he believed their public liability insurance was spread among several carriers, he himself couldn't name them; his secretary could. There were nine exits, though, he was certain of that.

Haley admitted that he'd called Robert Ringling from the Bond. Hickey didn't press him for details of the conversation. He did, however, request and receive Ringling's address in Evanston. When asked of his plans for the next few days, Haley said he would be on his car at the Windsor Street yards. Hickey told him to let the court know if he planned to leave town. And would he have any objection to Hickey communicating with Mr. Ringling? Of course not, Haley said.

The interview was through. Hickey reminded him that he was under subpoena to attend the coroner's inquest, yet to be scheduled. He officially

referred the matter of Haley's arrest to Leikind with the recommendation
that a bond be set with respect to whatever charges the prosecutor felt appropriate. Meanwhile, Haley could wait outside.

Second was George W. Smith, who knew the daily schedule of the Big
Show better than anyone. Smith was circus through and through. He'd
started the hard way, as a busboy in the cookhouse of the old Forepaugh-
Sells unit, and through the years worked himself up to general manager of
the Greatest Show on Earth.

Smith confirmed that Carson had charge of the ushers but said
Aylesworth ran the seatmen. There were eight seatmen in all, one under
every bleacher section and one under each of the four long grandstands.
Aylesworth's men had the responsibility of filling the fire buckets and setting them beneath the planks—twenty-four under the grandstands, any ex-
tras under the blues.

The extinguishers were Whitey Versteeg's lookout. There were
twenty-four in all, charged and inspected every year by the Sarasota Fire
Department.

Two of Blanchfield's drivers manned each of the four water trucks,
though Smith admitted they'd never been trained to fight fires. The trucks
were used primarily to water the animals and the cookhouse.

Smith also described the Barbour Street grounds as being "a tight lot,"
with just enough room for wagons to pass outside of the stake line.

"Were you in Cleveland?" Hickey asked.

"I wasn't with the show," Smith answered. "I had the Army War Show
all during that year."

Hickey turned to the issue of fireproofing, getting Smith to say
straight out what the circus publicly could not.

Q. Is there any process at all applied to the canvas for fireproofing?

A. No.

Q. None whatever?

A. No. As far as we could determine in trying to find that out, there's
    nothing that would fireproof it and waterproof it at the same time,
    and this year it was impossible to buy what you'd call fireproof
    equipment.

Two detectives with a section taken from the burned sidewall.
PHOTO COURTESY OF THE
HARTFORD COURANT

They discussed the paraffin treatment, how brushing it on sealed the pores of the canvas. Then Hickey went right back to the fireproofing.

> *Q.* Did I understand you to say that this year you were not able to get the materials for fireproof purposes?
> *A.* That's right.
> *Q.* Was the canvas top for the previous years fireproof?
> *A.* No sir.
> *Q.* How long since you have been fireproofing?
> *A.* We never fireproofed.

Smith mentioned a firm in Baltimore, the Hooper Manufacturing Company, with which they'd had some correspondence, even going so far as to try samples of their product, but, "We couldn't put it on the canvas so it would remain fireproof."

From this testimony it would seem they'd made an effort, but Hickey wasn't satisfied.

> *Q.* Now I understood that in 1943 you were not able to fireproof the top or the canvas?
> *A.* That's right.
> *Q.* In 1942?
> *A.* That's right.

Q. 1941?

A. That's right.

Q. How long since you had a fireproof—

A. Well, Commissioner, I have been around the show since 1910, and we never fireproofed the top.

Q. You never fireproofed the top?

A. Never.

Asked why they'd even looked into the possibility, Smith said it had been the idea of their new president, Robert Ringling. He also testified that the hose on the water wagons was two and a half inches, which would be compatible with the city's fire hydrants. He estimated capacity at 9,048— 6,048 in the grandstands, 3,000 on the blues. It was this number that Hickey indiscriminately combined with Haley's for his own total of 10,048.

Hickey now turned to the chutes, asking if the one pair of stairs over each had been taken away before the cats went out. No, Smith said, the stairs were there.

Hickey asked Smith to wait outside and not discuss his testimony with the others. Smith assured him that he wouldn't.

Next up was Leonard Aylesworth, the canvas boss. Hickey didn't waste any time, establishing that he'd been in Cleveland. Aylesworth had witnessed that fire but not the one today, he claimed—as if that might absolve him—because he'd gone to Springfield. But he was in charge of treating the big top, Hickey reminded him.

Q. Who determined the mixture that was to be applied to it?

A. Why, that's just been handed down.

Because Aylesworth was in charge of the seatmen, Hickey worked on their role in the origin of the fire. John Carson and his ushers, it seemed, were blameless in this. Outside, William Caley waited in the hall.

Q. Have you had any fires at all start on the sidewalls anywhere else which were immediately put out?

A. Yes. We've had people throw cigarettes, such things as that. My seatmen are usually on the alert for those things. We find little holes from time to time in there.

Hickey discovered that Aylesworth did a walkaround before every performance to make sure his men were in position. His assistant William Dwyer did it when he was out of town, but Dwyer had been called away because of a death in the family, and Aylesworth had failed to designate a replacement.

Hickey produced a list of the canvas crew and asked Aylesworth to mark the names of the eight seatmen. Aylesworth named Caley as one of the men under the southwest bleachers. The other, John Cook, had been missing since the fire.

Aylesworth said his thirty buckets were under the stands, presumably filled.

> *Q.* What other firefighting equipment of any kind is placed under these seats?
> *A.* The electrical department puts fire extinguishers under there.
> *Q.* There were fire extinguishers under there?
> *A.* They're supposed to be put under there.
> *Q.* Did you see them there last night?
> *A.* No, I didn't.
> *Q.* Did you see them there yesterday?
> *A.* I saw them unloaded yesterday but I didn't see them under the seats.

He'd done his walkaround an hour before Wednesday night's show. His men were there, and his buckets, but the extinguishers were missing.

> *Q.* Whose job is it to see that those extinguishers are in place?
> *A.* The boss electrician.
> *Q.* The boss electrician's name, please?
> *A.* Versteeg.

He would be the next to see the commissioner.

All through the night

On the lot, the show's diesels drummed, feeding the lights of the midway and around the perimeter. The kids on Barbour Street thought the army was searching for bodies in the dark woods.

At midnight, city and state police relieved the MPs from Bradley. They would guard the grounds till daybreak. Chief Godfrey's car detail patrolled the empty streets, taking license plate numbers, making up yet another list.

In Municipal Hospital, the detective's daughter Marion Dineen—now found among the living—shared a third-floor room with Shirley Snelgrove of Plainville, who, now that it was past midnight, was officially thirteen. July 7th was her birthday. The trip to the circus was supposed to be her party. The Snelgroves had first come in on Wednesday, but the matinee had been cancelled, so they came back Thursday. When the fire started they climbed the north grandstand to escape but lost their nerve at the edge. Her parents made it over the northwest chute; Shirley didn't. She ran up the grandstand again and jumped and someone dragged her out from under the sidewall. She had burns on her arms, legs and back. Her parents were still missing.

Marion wore the pearls she'd had on at the circus above her hospital gown. She'd had her brother Billy by the hand. As they reached the northeast chute, she lost her grip on him. "I dropped his hand to go over the animal cage and caught my foot there, but I yanked my foot out of my shoe and went on over. Then I ran toward a door, and I haven't seen my brother [since]. He was under the building when the thing fell."

The halls had gone quiet. Downstairs, volunteers folded bandages. Across the city at St. Francis, nuns watched over the injured. At Hartford Hospital, internes slept in four-hour shifts.

The armory was still open. Maurice Goff's husband, Arnold, a private in the army, identified her by her wedding ring. Her father Robert Wells identified Muriel by an arch support she wore. They couldn't locate the Epps boys.

There was no line outside. An announcement came over the sound car: The morgue would be closing for the night at 1:00 A.M. Upstairs, Albert Cadoret identified #4588 as his brother-in-law Bill Curlee with the help of a friend. Curlee's sunglasses had been on the wrong cot, but between the two of them they'd figured it out.

At 1:00, as promised, the armory closed, the state police and MPs clearing the building. Some people had been searching for hours, going through the rows again and again fruitlessly. Of the 135 bodies, only 60 had been identified. Guards locked the grate and closed the tall lobby doors. The morgue would reopen at 8:00 A.M., a voice over the sound car announced to the crowd outside. Long after they'd dispersed up Broad and Capitol, headed home, soldiers remained on guard under the spotlights.

Jennie Heiser got home exhausted. She poured herself a good strong brandy and knocked it back, fell into bed and slept like a log.

Thomas Barber dragged himself home to Edgewood and Garden Streets. He unbuckled his holster and put his service revolver away where the kids couldn't get at it. Barber was used to being awake this time of night. Sometimes when his shift was done he invited his buddies over and made a big pot of spaghetti and clam sauce and they played poker till dawn, dropping coins on the rug for the children to find. Now he found himself thinking of Harry, and the little girl in the front row, all those kids. The heat and the smell. The relatives. Tomorrow he'd be back, Ed Lowe, too. Eight o'clock wasn't far.

Downtown at fire headquarters, the switchboard received a call. It was fireman Joseph Viering's sister. He wouldn't be reporting for duty tomorrow. There'd been a death in the family.

And on till morning

Whitey Versteeg testified that he and his crew used their extinguishers on the light plant. He volunteered the information unbidden. It was all the opening Hickey needed.

Q. You have charge of the fire extinguishers, haven't you?
A. I have charge of the ones in my department.

Q. Only one?

A. The ones in my department.

Q. Are you charged with the duty of looking out for all the extinguishers that are on the lot?

A. The ones in my department.

As a former county detective, Hickey had interrogated thousands of suspects; he knew stonewalling when he heard it.

Q. What I want to find out is, how many fire extinguishers have you control of?

A. Well, I would say about eighteen altogether. Eighteen to twenty.

Q. How many has the circus?

A. Well, that I couldn't say exactly.

Q. They're all— You are the man that has charge of all the fire extinguishers, aren't you?

A. Not outside my department, like the trucks and things like that.

They went round and round like this. Versteeg said his men were supposed to set the extinguishers out (he didn't say where), but only if they had orders to put them out, orders from the front office, from George W. Smith or his assistant. If no orders, they'd set them out around their wagons. Hickey tired of this line and veered off. He came back minutes later. He believed Aylesworth, not this guy.

Q. Since you arrived in Hartford, and that would be yesterday, did you unpack or unload any of these fire extinguishers for distribution about the tents?

A. We unloaded them but they weren't distributed around.

Q. You unloaded them but they weren't distributed around?

A. They were taken out of the containers, of course.

Q. None of them were distributed about the main tent?

A. No, they weren't put around the main tent.

Q. And you don't do that unless you get orders?

A. When we get orders, we put them around.

Q. You got no orders from anybody?

A. No.

Q. And the ones that are to give you orders would be Smith or Kelly?

A. Yes.

Q. And since you started out on the road, and the first show was in Philadelphia, have you received any orders to put them up?

A. We had them out, I think, once since we left Philadelphia. I don't remember offhand which town it was.

Q. But that wasn't in Hartford?

A. No, it wasn't here; no.

Q. Neither yesterday or today?

A. No.

Hickey then tried to nail Versteeg down on precisely where the extinguishers were supposed to go. Again, Versteeg weaseled. Hickey was losing patience.

Q. You also know from your experience being around this circus, Ringling Brothers circus, and other circuses, that it has been the practice up to this year to have fire extinguishers distributed and available for service underneath seats for the seatmen to use, don't you?

A. Well, I had no orders to that effect.

Q. Please don't misunderstand me. I am not charging you with it being a requirement on your part, or a part of your duties. I am asking you if you know, from your experience as a circus man and an electrician that it has been the practice, prior to this year, to distribute these extinguishers in order that they would be available for fire purposes or fire prevention underneath the seats, especially in the main tent? Do you know that from your own experience?

A. Well, my common sense would tell me that they should be.

It was as close to an admission as Versteeg would make. The line of questioning couldn't have been a surprise. At McGovern's, being the first one to testify, he had the chance to frame things his way, laying blame on Smith and Blanchfield and Aylesworth. Here though, he must have suspected that Smith or Aylesworth had returned the favor. Still, to the end

Versteeg wouldn't admit the obvious: His extinguishers were supposed to have been beneath the seats, and they hadn't been.

In his opening answers, superintendent of trucks Deacon Blanchfield revealed that he had no fixed address at present, but that he was a native of Hartford. He and Hickey were the same age; as boys the two had known some of the same folks. The discovery of such common ground lifted the tone of the proceedings. Where Versteeg had been tight-lipped, Blanchfield was almost jaunty, though not completely forthright in his answers.

Blanchfield located the four water trucks for Hickey, putting one at the light plant (true), one at the back door (debatable), and two outside of the northeast chute exit (untrue—these were the two tucked back into the woods). His account of their actions once the fire started was accurate, and as Hickey went over their capabilities, Blanchfield revealed—contrary to George W. Smith's testimony—that the hose couplings on the four trucks were not the standard two and a half inches but only two inches. That is, they would *not* fit Hartford's fire hydrants. The circus only owned one fifty-foot length of standard hose that would.

Blanchfield also contradicted Smith's assertion that Barbour Street was a "tight lot," saying they had roads around it and that it was close to streets. A tight lot, he said, was where you had to crisscross things in and you didn't have roads. The lot was small, yes, but as long as they could move about, they considered it plenty of room.

Blanchfield had been in Cleveland and had vivid memories of the menagerie fire. He also recalled the Huntsville fire that killed so many horses, though he'd been with Barnum at the time. "If anyone has never seen a big tent burn, they don't know how fast it goes. . . . It's impossible to save a circus tent. There's no way to do it unless you was right there and put it out with your foot." He'd also seen smaller tops burn, and every time it was fast, because of the waterproofing.

> *Q.* So the minute you saw this fire today you knew that—?
>
> *A.* There was no chance of saving the top. The only thing you could save was what's around it, and get the people out.
>
> *Q.* You knew that?
>
> *A.* Yes.

Pressed, Blanchfield admitted that his water trucks weren't adequate to put out a fire of this size. But, by the same token, he said, "If you gave a general alarm, the Hartford Fire Department couldn't have saved that top today."

The problem was the waterproofing. Blanchfield had heard of fireproofing but he'd never seen it done. It was common knowledge among circus people that once a big top got going there was no stopping it.

> *A.* As I say, anyone that's saw one burn, gentlemen, anyone that's never saw a big top burn, cannot realize how quick it burns—that is, the canvas part of it. The chairs and seats and ropes make a big fire afterwards.

That was all Hickey needed from Blanchfield. Of the accused, he was by far the most personable—even entertaining, it could be said. When the commissioner asked him to wait, he called him David.

Circus chief of police John Brice had been in Cleveland, but Hickey didn't ask him about that. He was more concerned with police coverage, and whether the circus had its own fire department. Brice was pals with Hallissey, and there had been more than adequate coverage. And no, the circus had no fire department of its own.

Another senior person with the show had witnessed a big top burn before—John "Blinky" Meck, Aylesworth's assistant boss of the canvas crew. (The nickname came from a weak eye.) In 1912, he'd been in training with the Ringling show at Sterling, Illinois. He wasn't at the hearing tonight, but Coroner Healy would get him for his inquest.

At 2:00 A.M., during a break, Prosecutor Leikind announced to the press that charges had been dropped against John Brice. No other information. They still had some witnesses to go through.

William Caley related his movements just before the fire began, explaining how the chutes were supposed to be broken down and muscled out by the propmen.

Another seatman told of a fire on the sidewall in Providence—a large pinhole. Two or three times a week he saw that kind of fire. He reported them to the sailmaker so he could patch the untreated canvas.

And the stand before Providence, in Portland, somehow a piece of

Spanish web (cloth-covered rope for the aerial ballet) had caught fire twenty-five feet above the floor during a matinee.

City fire marshal Henry Thomas commented on the flammability of the waterproofing treatment: "I think as far as the gasoline is concerned, that hazard is nil, because the gasoline that would be used in the cutting of the wax has disappeared. That wax that remained would naturally add to the inflammability of that canvas. . . . It is also the cheapest way. . . . The ropes that hold that canvas were jute and sisal, both quite combustible."

Circus legal adjuster Herbert DuVal allowed that he didn't see any no smoking signs posted. In some cities this season they'd displayed the signs, but not in Hartford.

The hearing limped into the wee hours and beyond, the police present at the fire—like Detective Beckwith—the last to testify. Mayor Mortensen showed up to provide moral support. Circus radio publicist F. Beverly Kelley waited outside headquarters all night, wanting to be the first to talk with the accused when they were released.

The five Ringling employees originally accused of involuntary manslaughter. From left to right, standing: George W. Smith, James Haley, Whitey Versteeg, Leonard Aylesworth, Deacon Blanchfield. Seated: Court reporter, circus attorney Dan Gordon Judge. Seatman William Caley would later be arrested. PHOTO COURTESY OF ART KIELY

The hearing finally recessed around 5:00 A.M. Leikind finalized the warrants and instructed Beckwith and other city policemen to arrest Haley, Smith, Aylesworth, Versteeg, and Blanchfield on charges of manslaughter. The others were free to leave but asked to remain in town for the coroner's inquest. Beckwith escorted the prisoners to Hartford Police Headquarters to be booked and to arrange bail.

A storm of reporters waited for them. As Haley gave his fingerprints, he said, "I don't know what caused the fire. They have grilled me here since yesterday afternoon and I tried to help. All of us were overwhelmed by the catastrophe, and I know I can't seem to think that anything, any of the court arraignment this morning or the business about being released on $15,000 bond, is real. The only real thing is death and the grief the circus feels for the families of those who died. This fingerprinting doesn't bother me. It's the people there in the armory and in the hospitals. Our job is pleasing people and making them laugh. I never thought this could happen."

He said he'd helped carry the dead from the tent. "And now I'm charged with manslaughter and held in jail all night. I wish this were a dream. We all know the circus is hazardous, but none of us thought this tragedy possible. Does it do any good that I would have given my life to prevent the fire?"

Circus attorney Dan Gordon Judge represented the five men before a police court, which continued their cases until July 19th. All five stood silent at the rail while scores of photographers popped off flashbulbs. Unshaven, still in yesterday's clothes, they appeared haggard and downcast.

They were by no means the only people who'd stayed awake all night. Parents reported children waking up screaming, in shock. Janet Moore Sapolis had nightmares, and would for months. One young nurse's aide worked till 4:00 in the morning. New to the profession, she'd never seen death strike right before her eyes. When she got home, she went through the house, turning on every light she could find.

During the night, at Municipal Hospital, eighteen patients died. Among them was Mary Kay Smith's playmate, Agnes Norris.

A nineteenth survived till morning. At 6:21 A.M., Edward Cook died in his aunt Emily's arms. His mother was sleeping, her body trying to repair the damage. The doctors could not wake her.

July 7, 1944

Friday morning everyone wanted a *Courant*. A Torrington news dealer explained to his regular customers that he had none left. Before he opened up, factory workers on their way in to early shift had cut the wire around the bundle and cleaned out his entire supply. On his doorstep they left a pile of pennies, nickels and dimes.

The *New York Times* quoted a circus worker, "It was like you had opened Hell's doors, and you had all you could do to get your hands over your face and run the other way." The reporter said at least two-thirds of the dead and injured were children.

Circus radio flack F. Beverly Kelley took exception with a neighboring city's paper. It had printed a shot of the accused in the courtroom with the caption: They Saved Their Animals.

Everyone speculated on the cause of the blaze. On its front page the *Courant* said it originated from a cigarette thrown against the sidewall of the big top by someone using the men's toilet. People who were there had other theories: "Personally, I believe the fire was caused from spontaneous combustion from the heat of the tent and spotlights." Some suspected the fire was an act of vengeance by a disgruntled former employee—as the Cleveland fire at first seemed to be. (Coincidentally, three or four of Blanchfield's drivers who'd signed on in Portland had quit at noon Thursday—the same basic scenario as in Cleveland.) A circus hand claimed the fire had been started by a prankster sitting in the top row of the bleachers who lighted a newspaper and waved it against the roof of the tent while friends told him to quit kidding around. When asked for a comment on these rumors, Commissioner Hickey said, "In a disaster of this type it would be too smart-alecky for any police official to discount any theory."

The AP reported that a few hard-hearted residents around the grounds charged a dollar a phone call, one tenant clearing $200. Though many of the women had lost their pocketbooks, the chiselers were adamant—no cash, no call.

Flags across the city flew at half-mast. Survivors waking up at home were so bruised they had trouble walking. One woman couldn't lift her arms to button her dress; her son had to help her.

In West Simsbury, neighbors feared one family had been killed in the fire. They hadn't come home overnight; their dog was tied up outside and barking.

As morning papers hit stands and stoops across the country, inquiries concerning relatives from servicemen stationed as far away as New Mexico poured into the Red Cross. It was also the duty of the Greater Hartford Chapter to inform ten men overseas that relatives had died or been injured in the fire. That number would grow.

At Municipal, day shift was still cleaning up from last night. A new roster of injured and dead listed both an Agnes Morris (dead) and an Agnes Norris (injured). At Hartford Hospital, the most seriously burned patients woke up in the bright first-floor ward of the new South Building, its windows overlooking the hospital grounds and Retreat Avenue. Some had their faces bandaged, some their extremities, a few their whole bodies. None would be ambulatory for weeks; many couldn't use their hands. The majority were either children or grandparents. The staff assumed—not quite rightly—that the more able-bodied had died helping them out. Visiting hours for non–circus fire patients were summarily canceled.

It was going to be another scorcher. The temperature was creeping toward seventy as the crowd gathered outside the armory. The line was smaller and less edgy, the panic and confusion of last night cooled to a stolid resignation. The found children of the Brown School were all gone, the injured at the hospitals positively identified. Were there any other possibilities?

Some of the searchers from last night had returned. They knew the routine, and knew what was waiting for them upstairs. Others were fresh, late to discover what had happened or filling in for those who'd tried last night. Dorothy Bocek's mother and brother-in-law were there for Stella Marcovicz and Francis. At 8:00 sharp, the grates opened.

The morticians had sprayed again, but the smell was just as bad, and now on top of it the stink of decay: butyric acid and methane gas naturally given off by the bodies. Jennie Heiser and her girls were back to do the typing; Thomas Barber and Ed Lowe stood sentrylike by the checkout desk.

It went faster than last night. With the smaller crowd, the odds were better. There were more dentists along, and they'd had time to prepare. Ralph and Olive Snelgrove were the first, identified by Dr. Frank Boardman—orphaning their daughter Shirley on her thirteenth birthday.

Stella Marcovicz' husband Frank passed out but recovered. He helped her mother identify her by his mother's signet ring. As for Francis, his aunt Dorothy Bocek said the family claimed the body of what they assumed was a four-year-old boy. "Whether it was him or not we don't know, but they buried him with her."

In Keney Park, a passerby noticed the Epps boys lying together in the brush and went to fetch the authorities. They were fine, just hungry, achy from sleeping on the hard ground. The police took them home, where their aunt Theresa Wells had been out of her mind with worry. William and Richie learned that their mother was in the hospital and that their aunt Maurice and cousin Muriel were dead.

At 386 Barbour, Mrs. Dewey Howrigan looked out her back window to find all three cars from last night still sitting in her yard. She took down the license plates. The Howrigans didn't have a phone, so she couldn't call

The elephants vacation in Sponzo's meadow. PHOTO COURTESY OF THE CIRCUS WORLD MUSEUM

Wagons 36–39 suffered some fire damage. Behind them sits wagon 25, which carried seat planks. The elephant to the left is in harness. PHOTO COURTESY OF THE HARTFORD COLLECTION, THE HARTFORD PUBLIC LIBRARY

the police. She had errands to run. If the cars were still there when she got back, she'd have to call them somehow.

The lot smelled of ashes. Cageboys had slept on the ground under the menagerie wagons but were up at dawn to water and feed the animals. The elephant men tossed hay to their charges, staked in two lines in Sponzo's meadow. Police ringed the site, keeping the public out yet letting the press in.

Inside the black oval of ash, a United Press reporter turned up pieces of stories: "The woman's blue straw hat with the large flower ornament hardly touched and surrounded by ruins. The child's shoe over in one of the worst burned sections of seats, crushed but not burned. The burned remains of a woman's pocketbook. Police said the owner was on a cot in the Armory, dead."

Bored, one worker tipped over a charred shoe with his toe. Others sat in the shade of the wagons—more than 35 wagons were singed, their Ringling red paint bubbled and blistered. "I found a ten-dollar bill," one man said. "Burnt in half."

Clown Felix Adler scuffed around the site, staring at the blackened planks and chairs and poles as if to convince himself it had really happened.

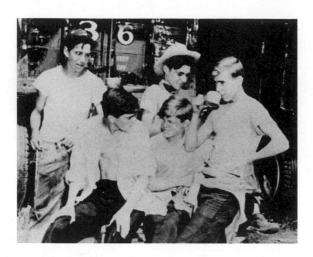

Teenaged circus hands with little to do after the fire. Some have speculated that Robert Segee is the dark-haired boy seated at left, but there's no proof one way or the other.
PHOTO COURTESY OF THE *HARTFORD COURANT*

Scattered about the ground were hard, dirty puddles that had been Coke bottles. Adler made out a perfect circle in the dirt, a coin. He bent over and pinched it up and thumbed the soot off—a Buffalo nickel, turned purple by the heat.

Gawkers filled the front yard, peering past the police lines with morbid curiosity. One woman described the scene as quiet, as if a giant had come along and pressed everything flat.

Hands had circled the animal wagons so none of them faced the wreckage. Inside, the animals were lethargic from the heat, panting as they lay on their sides like dogs. The United Press enlisted them in getting the story across: "The big cats whined like lost kittens." "Gargantua's screams turned into wailing that echoed across the Ringling Bros. Barnum & Bailey Circus grounds where death scarred the ground." "One lion refused to eat. A tiger crouched on the floor of his cage and mewed mournfully." "A roustabout explained the strange quiet of the menagerie which was broken only by the crying sounds. 'The animals just know when death is near,' he said."

Performers took the early bus up from the train yard. They were all worried about their trunks, some of which were burned on the outside, their costumes safe within. Exactly when they were getting back on the road was the hot topic.

Not long, they thought. In Sarasota, retired hands were reopening the closed-up barns and buildings of the winter quarters, sweeping out the per-

Aerial view of the Barbour Street grounds looking south, with the victory gardens in the middle, Kensington Street above them and Barbour Street running through the upper right corner. The billboard at the corner of Barbour and Charlotte marks the lot where the elephants were taken. McGovern's yard full of tombstones is clearly visible to the middle right. Mrs. Howrigan's yard with the cars is in the bottom right corner.

PHOTO BY ABE FOX, COURTESY OF ART KIELY

Aerial view of the grounds looking east, with Barbour Street in the foreground.
353 Barbour stands directly across from the sideshow tent. Kensington and Earle Streets
run up the right side of the picture. At the top of Kensington, note the barracks of the
antiaircraft unit on the right side of the street. PHOTO BY ABE FOX, COURTESY OF AP/WIDE
WORLD PHOTOS.

manent animal cages in anticipation of the show's return. The old-timers remembered other fires and blowdowns and train wrecks, even waging pitched battles with townsfolk, but none of those tragedies approached this one.

At the *Times,* the man who usually wrote the obituaries was in his eighties. Today the sheer volume overwhelmed him, and a cub drew the assignment. Aside from the spelling, which had to be perfect and often wasn't, the funerals were simple. The city was segregated into tribes by mortuaries. All the Irish were at O'Brien's, Farley's or Molloy's, all the Jews at Weinstein's, all the Italians at Laraia-Sagarino's, all the Poles at Talarski's. The phone rang and rang. The difficult thing was the number of children. One undertaker called and said, "I have a beautiful little girl for you."

In Bristol, a sixteen-year-old war worker read the morning paper and found out that she was dead. Her brother had somehow identified her at the morgue, checking the body out to a local undertaker. The girl called the Bristol Police and explained she'd attended the Wednesday night show. Yesterday she'd put in a regular shift at the ordnance plant. Everything checked, so the funeral home had to rush the body back to the armory and set it on a cot again.

In the women's section, Ludger LeVasseur, Jerry's father, identified his wife Marion. He managed a First National grocery store; she'd been a nurse. He needed to tell her parents. After he gave his information at the checkout desk, he headed for Providence by car. How he would tell Jerry he didn't know. He was still on the critical list; when he was strong enough the doctors wanted to cut the loose skin from his arms.

Joseph Budrick was the projectionist at the Eastwood Theater, Frank Locke his assistant. The two East Hartford men had married sisters and lived right down Hill Street from each other. Now they came to the armory together to claim them, as well as their children. Joseph Budrick had already lost his daughter Edith; she'd died overnight at Municipal. He was looking for his wife Edith and seven-year-old Joseph. Frank Locke's son Lawrence was the sole member of the party to escape. His wife Viola and six-year-old Elaine were still missing. In quick succession, with the aid of a dentist, the two men found all but Mrs. Budrick.

She should have been easy to identify; her platinum wedding ring bore their initials and the date of their marriage. Mr. Budrick checked all the cots in the women's section—once, twice, three times—until he was satisfied she wasn't there. Then where was she?

A detective compiling the official list of the dead for the city police wrote on his original: "Albert Toth previously reported dead on page 11 at Municipal Hospital is alive." The list is creased (still, after fifty-five years), as if he had it folded in half in one hand as he moved through the rows. Another handwritten note from Friday the 7th reads: "11:50 A.M. 18 children, 4 male adults, 1 baby, 21 female adults" (this just crossed off from 22). On the back of the next page, he scratched: "Elwyn Wakeman suspects wife here—Virginia Wakeman—not able to identify until after 6 P.M."

Blocks away, Commissioner Hickey interrupted his interrogation of six ushers to send a trooper down to Davis Field in Waterford. The World of Mirth carnival was playing there under tents treated with the same paraffin and gas waterproofing. Hickey wanted them shut down.

As undertakers drove one boy's body back to Lakeville, his mother was giving birth at Canaan Hospital to what would have been his second brother. The other brother had also been born on July 7th. The mother wondered how they would ever celebrate the day again. Her father was failing fast at Municipal Hospital; her mother was still missing.

In the middle of the afternoon an older woman died at Municipal. A maiden aunt, she was the third and last of her party to die. A native of Thomaston, for years she'd worked at Seth Thomas Clocks and been a communicant of St. Thomas's Church. She would be buried in St. Thomas's Cemetery a day after the feast of St. Thomas More.

Friday was hotter than Thursday. At 3:30 the temperature peaked at ninety-two degrees. Two grass fires broke out in Bristol. At Municipal, fans blew hats off nurses turning corners, lifting them on their bobby pins like sails. At Hartford the stench of the burned was so overpowering the Airwick Company donated hundreds of bottles of their liquid industrial deodorizers to be set out all over the wards and ORs.

South Building 1 was the new home of a brother and sister transferred last night from Municipal. The children were already familiar with a number of hospitals. In April, while riding the school bus, the boy opened the rear door and fell out, landing on his head; he spent most of May in the hospital with a fractured skull. In June the children were riding in a car with their father when they were involved in an accident. The father suffered a concussion, the girl a leg injury and severe lacerations, and the boy just some bad bruises. The family had been hoping July would be an easier month.

In a way, it was. Both children were alive, and neither was burned half as badly as Donald Gale or Barbara Smith at Municipal. There, nurse's aides changed the ice in Elliott Smith's oxygen tent, their hands beet red, freezing. Bluebirds cruised the rooms with trays of juice and Jell-O for their patients.

Word of the fire intrigued the nation, so newsreel crews showed up at the lot or outside the armory or on the lawns of the hospitals, shooting footage. Metro News of the Day and Paramount scooped the competition, buying fifty feet of 8mm film of the fire taken by a man from Bristol.

At city police headquarters, survivors came by to claim their wallets and glasses and compacts. One mother had shoved a bag of circus peanuts in her handbag as she ran from the fire; now her son cracked the shells and gobbled up the nuts. Some came looking for lost objects that would never be found: money, a dental bridge, a thermos of milk brought along for a toddler.

On Barbour Street, Mrs. Howrigan returned from her errands to find the Buick gone. The owner would certainly miss the blanket and umbrella she'd taken for safekeeping. She decided to call the police and let them know about the Chevys. It had been more than twenty-four hours.

Police succeeded in tracking down the missing West Simsbury family. Relatives thought they might have gone to New York to visit friends. A call located the family, all of them safe. For the sake of the neighbors, the relatives brought the dog in.

The *Times* editorial that afternoon weighed in with their take on the fire's origin: "A moment of carelessness, a cigarette butt tossed aside, and someone has on his soul and conscience today the death of at least 139 persons, largely innocent children." The paper announced the formation of a Circus Fire Victims Fund to help the families of the injured and the dead. They chipped in $500 to start. Mayor Mortensen, acting as honorary chair, gave $100, the circus employees $445.

From Evanston, Robert Ringling publicly insisted the circus had no priority for fireproofing. Locally, show folks tried to put the fire in a better light, saying it would have been worse if the spec had been on at the time, with all the horses circling the track and Emmett Kelly's float drawn by eight elephants. Equally lucky was the decision not to raise the menagerie top. The *National Fire Protection Association Quarterly* would later bring up another, worse scenario: What if it had taken place at night, the crowd forced to flee through the maze of stakes and ropes with just the reflected light of the fire to guide them?

Journalists shredded Robert Ringling's excuse of not having priority even before it hit print. The *New York Daily News* reported that the Big Top Circus failed a burn test there the past June and then spent $6,000 to flameproof its main tent. They also cited, along with every other paper, the post–Cocoanut Grove laws prohibiting inflammable curtains, drapes, costumes or decorations in any public theater, and how thousands of nightclubs had complied by using fireproofing.

That argument settled, writers and circus publicists turned to the origin, as yet undetermined. Along with cigarettes, spotlights were obvious suspects. An editor at the *Windham County Transcript* wrote: "Shortly after the performance started, there seemed to be a flash from one of a dozen spotlights which illuminated the performers and at that moment I happened to glance up at the flash and noticed a flame had started about as round as a half dollar which in no time had ignited the whole canvas." This account matched that of a circus hand given yesterday at the scene to a policeman: "I saw the fire start. It was right over the cleanest part of the ring there [pointing to a spot at the west end] and there was a flash among the spotlights at the top of the pole." Several larger papers also mentioned that authorities were first suspicious of the lights "which sat high in the corners of the main tent."

In the *Times,* circus flack Hal Olver flatly denied that the fire started near the men's room. "The fire definitely started at the roof of the tent." One prosecutor said his investigation had established the same point. Asked how it could have started on the roof, Olver said, "We have a theory, but we're not making it public now. We expect to make an announcement later." As for speculation that it had been a cigarette: "I defy anybody to set the canvas afire with a cigarette."

A private eye in Washington, D.C., sent a cryptic telegram to Commissioner Hickey saying he had information "worth your while."

The National Fire Protection Association (NFPA) noted that these kinds of terrible fires brought about safeguards: the Iroquois Theater fire in Chicago spawning theater regulations; the Triangle Shirtwaist Company fire doing the same for factories; the Cocoanut Grove for nightclubs; the Lakewood School fire in Ohio for schools. Perhaps, they said, the circus fire would do the same and in that way serve some purpose.

The thought that the city would be remembered for providing a bad example was no consolation to Hartford. The fire would have been a civic embarrassment anywhere, but to have it fall on Hartford, whose fire prevention techniques the NFPA and other organizations had lauded as exemplary, awarding them national prizes for fire safety, was especially cruel. To the insurance industry as a whole it was a humiliating blow.

In the minds of the city fathers, the question of who would pay the damages had already been decided. Mayor Mortensen said he'd been informed that the circus carried $500,000 worth of public liability insurance. With no apparent irony, city officials announced that they were investigating the question of the city's liability. One city councilman asserted that he was convinced the city had no liability whatsoever because the Barbour Street grounds "had been leased to Ringling Brothers in their entirety and without reservations." No one in the city government argued with him.

The first claim granted in probate court was an application appointing Salvatore DiMartino as administrator of the estate of his wife Anna DiMartino. Immediately following the appointment a writ was given the deputy sheriff for service on the Ringling Bros. and Barnum & Bailey Circus Inc., with instructions to attach the rolling stock of the show at the Windsor Street yards, preventing any removal of equipment until adequate security could be provided. The deputy was directed to appoint the yard superintendent of the railroad as keeper. The flood of writs on top of DiMartino's kept the deputy busy writing up attachment papers the rest of the night.

Around 7:30, Commissioner Hickey assigned a state trooper to assist Emily Gill in trying to find her niece Eleanor Cook. She'd heard from a nurse's aide and a social worker at Municipal Hospital of a girl fitting Eleanor's description who had died there last night. Along with another man, she'd tried to find the girl in the armory, but had only seen 1565 again. Now the three of them and a Hartford police officer set out to check all the funeral homes in the area that had taken away bodies of girls

Eleanor's age (eight). They looked at all the children at Dillon's, Pratt's, Farley's, Talarski's, Newkirk's and Hartford Memorial, but couldn't find anyone who fit Eleanor's description.

The trooper called Municipal Hospital to see if he could talk to the nurse's aide, but she was off duty. He got hold of the social worker at home; she described the child at Municipal as having severe burns from the waist down but only slight burns on the left side of her face.

The trooper asked Emily Gill for a picture of Eleanor. They stopped by 4 Marshall Street and got one, then retraced their steps. No luck. The case remained open.

Back at the armory, another body returned, #1522, previously identified as Joan-Lee Smith. Though it matched the five-year-old's general description, a tooth she'd lost the week before didn't fit the jaw. William Menser attached a new tag with a different number to the body and set it on a cot.

Mary Kurneta's brother-in-law identified her by shreds of clothing, leaving of their party only Raymond Erickson still unaccounted for. His father was on his way home from Gulfport, having been given compassionate leave.

The machinist from Waterbury who'd been notified at work learned from his wife that the initial report had been wrong; their daughter had *not* gotten out of the tent. He found his mother-in-law and his daughter under one blanket. They were the woman and child discovered together beneath the sidewall.

The armory would be closing at 9:00 P.M., the sound car announced. Besides the nurses and troopers and clerks, the floor was nearly empty, only ten or so searchers, twenty bodies. And still, to Barber and Lowe's surprise, 1565 lay there on her cot, her face seared on the left cheek but otherwise untouched. The rest of the bodies were charcoal.

At Emanuel Synagogue at the corner of Greenfield and Woodland Streets, two girls who escaped the fire attended a special service dedicated to the victims and their families. The rabbi intoned the names of congregation members who had passed away, and those in need of prayers for recovery. The temperature was in the eighties and the building was packed. The two girls had trouble staying in their seats, inching toward the aisle. They were afraid they wouldn't be able to get out if there was a fire.

At Municipal, nurses readied nine patients for transfer to Hartford Hospital. Mildred Cook was among them, in fair condition. With Edward gone, the doctors had no reason to keep her there. Hartford would be better for her. Aides placed the stretchers in the rear of the ambulances, then closed the doors. Riding downtown with Mildred Cook was the birthday girl, Shirley Snelgrove.

At the armory, the night ended with a flurry—which may have been desperation. There were no plans to open the morgue on Saturday, and both Dr. Weissenborn and Mayor Mortensen had made public statements about the necessity of burying the unclaimed dead. At this point, families may have taken whatever they could get.

The man who'd told the detective keeping the list that he couldn't make it to the armory until 6:00 finally came to identify his wife and their six-year-old son. During the fire, the man had their daughter on his shoulders as he made for the northwest chute, hoping to go out the front door. When he realized his wife and son had fallen behind, he threw the girl to a man on the far side of the bars and fought his way back into the mob. He never found them, fleeing as the top collapsed, burning his neck and back. He'd been treated as an outpatient at St. Francis, then tracked down his daughter at Municipal. Now he found the rest of his family.

A cousin identified one mother. After telling her son to jump, she'd done likewise, but the tent came down on top of her, pinning her to the ground. She never got up.

An East Hartford policeman escorted an older woman who was looking for her companion. The woman said her friend had a clubfoot. The policeman searched the women's section but couldn't find anyone with a clubfoot. Some had legs that were just stubs; maybe she was one of them. He went back to the woman and asked for another identifying feature, something she wore, perhaps. She had an odd watch, the woman said, an old one. He inspected the wrists of the bodies and this time he found her. Her feet had been burned off.

The cop told the woman that it was her, but he didn't want her to look at the body because it was so badly burned. As he said this, the woman moaned, "Ooohh," as if to faint. He went to support her, a hand on her back. When he touched her, she screamed.

Her back was raw. She hadn't realized she could suffer burns through her clothing, and for more than a day had tried to ignore the pain, thinking it was temporary. The policeman flagged down a Salvation Army officer, who took her to Hartford Hospital.

The last body identified at the armory was that of a little girl whose mother couldn't hang on to her in the crush. She was four years old and their dentist confirmed that these were her teeth.

Minutes later, at the strike of nine, a guard locked the grates and closed the doors. Of the 135 bodies brought to the armory, all but fifteen had been identified—two men, six women and seven children. Of these, many had no hands and feet. One woman was almost entirely missing her head. Among them, oddly, was 1565, in excellent condition yet unclaimed. The Cocoanut Grove contingent conferred briefly with Dr. Weissenborn. At this point they could offer him no more help; they would be flying back to Boston tonight. Weissenborn agreed with their assessment. Publicly he doubted whether any of the fifteen would be identified.

It was too hot to keep them here another night. Hartford Hospital offered their refrigerated morgue, and Weissenborn accepted. A mortician embalmed the unidentified as best he could, registering as evidence any effects left on the bodies. The Red Cross enlisted several Sage-Allen delivery trucks to move them. Detectives Barber and Lowe helped load the bodies, then followed them down Broad and onto Capitol, the procession passing beneath the streetlights.

The state guard and the Red Cross and the War Council finalized their lists and packed their typewriters away, folded their tables and their cots, unplugged their silent phones. They cleared the drill floor, leaving the shed empty, its windows open to the night air.

By the circus grounds, police tow trucks were pulling the Chevys out of Mrs. Howrigan's backyard, bumping over the grass. Down the street, a wrecker's winch lifted the front tires of a fancy black sedan—Michael Norris's '41 Olds. Besides Agnes, dead at Municipal, so far the car was the only trace left of the family.

July 8, 1944

At 3:00 A.M. Saturday morning the deputy sheriff attached the seventy-nine flatcars and coaches owned by the circus at the Windsor Street yards, leaving copies of the writs with officials of the New Haven, New York and Hartford Railroad.

Salvatore DiMartino's was the first suit listed. As administrator for his wife's estate, he was asking for $15,000, the maximum penalty for a death by accident in Connecticut. The complaint said that while Mrs. DiMartino "was sitting in said main show of said circus, a fire broke out which engulfed the tent and surroundings like a wild fire, causing a terrible conflagration, and catching said Anna DiMartino in its force and violence, and burning her to death." In addition to the circus, defendants in the action included Messrs. Haley, Smith, Aylesworth, Blanchfield and Versteeg.

It was the first of hundreds of suits against the circus, the accused, and the city of Hartford. Alert attorneys instructed their clients to hold on to their ticket stubs.

The cause had still not been determined. Commissioner Hickey asked city police to assign the same officer the task of locating the man who'd told him "that dirty son of a bitch just threw a cigarette butt." The policeman succeeded in broadcasting the man's description over WDRC and getting the *Courant* and *Times* to print it, but no one came forward.

Saturday morning, a Connecticut company bus driver showed up at city police headquarters with a strange story. He'd been standing at the end of the sideshow banners near the menagerie connection, watching a diesel generator. An Indian with long hair and no shirt walked around the back of the diesel with a bucket in one hand and a gas can in the other. He hollered to a fellow worker that the motor had stopped and he needed some gas. He gave the can to the other man, who disappeared through a flap in the menagerie sidewall.

In itself, the driver's statement established little, but the police took it seriously. Both Hickey and Coroner Healy would call on him in their investigations.

Early that morning the *Courant* and the radio stations made a special appeal for donors of Type O blood. In hours, volunteers stocked the Hartford Blood Bank to overflowing.

Like many soldiers overseas, one sergeant on the march in France first read about the fire in the *Stars and Stripes.* He immediately sent home both a V-mail and an air-mail letter but couldn't wait to hear back from his wife. He collared a Red Cross worker and explained his anxiety. Meanwhile in Hartford, his wife had called the Red Cross. They sent a cable to the sergeant: "Family all well. Not at circus."

In England, an army corporal wouldn't receive word of his mother's death for several days. His father had identified her at the morgue last night by her wedding ring.

At St. Michael's on Clark Street, Father Looney presided over a funeral mass for Anna DiMartino. The neighborhood had taken up a collection for the DiMartinos, chaired by the barber whose shop was right beside Molly Garofolo's beauty parlor and Jaivin's Drugstore. Later that afternoon, Father Looney would perform another mass for a neighborhood boy. St. Michael's was busy the next few days. An altar boy from Nelson Street remembered how the fire shocked the parish. The DiMartinos lived right around the corner from him, and he'd been in the same class as Marion Dineen at St. Michael's. The rumor among the boys was that Billy Dineen hadn't been burned, he'd been trampled or suffocated (a rumor partly true: his death certificate lists "trauma to head and torso/fourth-degree burns" as the cause). Father Looney said mass for all of them. His parishioners knew he suffered from ulcers, and worried for his health.

The sheer number of dead put a strain on area funeral homes. One ran out of coffins and had to send to Worcester and New York for more. Tiny white caskets for children were at a premium.

A family friend had to make arrangements for the triple burial of one mother and her two sons. Their father was too distraught.

To aid families of the dead and injured, the Hartford War Price and Rationing Board informed the mayor that survivors could request increased gasoline rations. Local boards made extra five- and ten-gallon coupons available.

Two co-workers of Michael Norris from the Russell Company and a dentist drove up from Middletown to examine the fifteen unidentified bodies at the Hartford Hospital morgue, but had no luck.

The officer who had assisted Emily Gill in her search for Eleanor Cook yesterday gave her a call. He'd showed the picture of Eleanor she'd lent him to two policemen who'd been at the armory, also to Dr. Weissenborn and the nurse's aide he hadn't been able to find yesterday. They said the photo resembled the little girl they'd all seen—1565. Would Emily come down to Hartford Hospital and look at the body again?

Barber and Lowe were there, and William Menser. She looked at the girl, saying this was the same one she'd looked at in the armory. The only thing that made her say this wasn't Eleanor was that she thought Eleanor had eight upper permanent teeth, whereas this body had four upper and four lower adult teeth. If it hadn't been for that, she would say that the child could be her niece. The doctor advised her to get a chart, which turned out to be impossible; the dentist was in Canada on vacation.

As Emily Gill had looked at all the other bodies, there was nothing the officer could do for her. Later he learned that Dr. Weissenborn had declared her incompetent to identify the body of Eleanor Cook—though precisely why is unclear. At a dead end, the officer marked the case closed and wrote his report to the commissioner.

John Cleary and his father-in-law found a body at the morgue that seemed to fit Grace Fifield's description, down to the pink Spencer corset she wore. #2109 was short and stocky, in her late forties. Cleary asked Dr. Butler to check her teeth so they could match her dentist's chart in Vermont. The dentist up in Newport compared the two. They were not close; it wasn't her. Mr. Fifield unexpectedly accepted this as good news. Now he was even more convinced his wife had suffered some kind of nervous shock and wandered away. Cleary realized that some other family must have claimed the wrong body as they themselves had almost just done. For years he would regret asking the dentist to make sure—her body would never be found, and the family would never know what happened.

One father had found his daughter at the armory last night. Now he phoned from New Hartford to ask police for a watch and a ring she wore; he wanted to bury her with her jewelry. The coroner's office gave the pieces to a policewoman since she was headed out to Canaan anyway.

The heat wave lay heavy on the city, even worse than yesterday. At noon it was eighty-eight degrees and climbing. The health department inspected the train cars at the Windsor Street yards and found a nuisance being created by careless handling of the slop pails. The inspectors took the matter up with the porters and "the scavengers who remove the material to the sewer opening on Kensington Street between Hampton and Barbour Streets." They also did a walkaround of the circus grounds, discovering garbage from the cookhouse, "a considerable amount of animal manure (elephants and horses)," and a general lack of sanitation. They appealed to the courts and managed to get two circus trucks released to clean up the area.

On the lot there was nothing to do. Legally, show folks weren't allowed to touch anything inside the police line. One sixteen-year-old clown working with his father remembered that circus people stayed close to the trains, fearing the North End residents were angry with them.

The temperature peaked at ninety-two and the power went out at Municipal Hospital, the fans slowly going still. The diesels of the emergency reserve system kicked in, providing energy for only those areas deemed necessary. The cafeteria was dark; in the halls, every other bulb glowed. It was a blown transformer, the Hartford Electric Light Company said. It would take them till late afternoon to restore service.

Typically, Hartford Hospital had no such problem. Down in the chilly morgue, under the eyes of Detectives Barber and Lowe, a Plainville man discovered fragments of one of his sons' belts among the effects. Away on a business trip, he'd returned to find the house locked and his family gone. They were here, his wife, his two sons, his daughter. Of the man, Dr. Weissenborn said, "I saw one father identify his whole family. He was superb."

Lowe's of East Hartford handled the bodies. There were eleven left.

On the lot, a team of state police secured the following evidence: a section of canvas from the dressing-room tent not involved in the fire but treated with the same solution as the big top; three jacks and small boards from the southwest bleacher section, the purported origin of the fire; one length of the animal chute; and the steps and remains of the steps that originally bridged the chutes. The troopers fit everything into the trunks of their cars and delivered it all to the office of State's Attorney Meade Alcorn, where he and Commissioner Hickey held a long conference.

The *New York Times* said that unofficial speculation pointed more and more toward the possibility of a short circuit.

Mayor Mortensen convened his own board of inquiry behind closed doors—first posing for a photo. The board would look at what the city government had or had not done in an official capacity, and draft corrective legislation, if necessary. To represent his police force, Mortensen included both Chief Hallissey and Deputy Chief Godfrey. The city fire marshal testified that no one from his department inspected either the circus tents or their firefighting equipment, and that that had been the custom for years. While not condoning the practice, the mayor said it wasn't clear from existing statutes just whose responsibility such an inspection would be, the city's or the state fire marshal's.

Mortensen rightly worried that the press might bring charges of negligence against his administration. Publicly fire chief John King had dismissed the notion that a city fire truck on the lot might have prevented the blaze from growing out of control—an unpopular and ill-advised comment. King claimed the department had never had any apparatus on the lot in the past. City ordinances required either policemen or firemen to be present at circuses. Since the police were there, King declared, there was no need for firemen.

At this point the mayor was trying to find one city office that had done something other than accept the show's money and free passes. The only instance he could cite was building inspector Joseph Hayes being on the lot Wednesday. He gave Hayes credit for determining that—at the time, at least—the circus provided nine unobstructed, clearly marked exits. That Hayes had left the grounds before the big top was fully set up, the mayor did not divulge.

At Municipal Hospital, a chicken farmer from New Hartford died. It was his Chevy Suburban that had sat by Mrs. Howrigan's garden all night.

At St. Francis Hospital, a six-year-old boy visited his mother for the first time since the fire. The mother had crawled on top of her son as the flames rolled over them. It worked; the boy was only slightly burned. The mother was in serious condition, but she would live.

At Municipal, the staff tried a similar reunion between a mother and son. The woman had bad burns on her face and feared it might be too early.

When they wheeled the two together, a nurse asked the son, "Do you remember who this is? It's your mother."

"No, it's not!" the boy screamed. "No, it's not!"

At home, survivors were surprised to find new bruises blooming where people had stepped on them.

In Jeffersonville, Indiana, the military quieted people's fears. At the army's quartermaster depot there, an officer showed reporters how flameproofed canvas could withstand a blowtorch without burning. As planned, the material merely charred, the fire didn't spread, and the reporters all got some copy for the Sunday papers.

Back in Hartford, Chief King announced that the department was saddened by the deaths of the wives of several firemen.

At the morgue, Barber and Lowe watched the last successful attempts of the day. Friends of the Norrises sent a dentist from Mrs. Norris' old hometown to establish her identity. He claimed as Eva Irene Norris #4540, the body formerly thought to be the woman from Glastonbury.

The identification left eight bodies unclaimed: three women, two girls, two men, and one boy. Among the missing were Mrs. Edith Budrick, Grace Fifield, Eleanor Cook, Judy Norris, Michael Norris, Raymond Erickson and eighteen-year-old war worker Ermo Flanders. Mayor Mortensen announced that all bodies still unidentified at 11:00 A.M. Monday would be buried "with dignity and reverence" in individual graves at Northwood Cemetery and urged any persons with knowledge of missing relatives, friends or neighbors to report it to the State War Council at the armory.

Later, Commissioner Hickey took to the airwaves and made a public appeal, asking the man who had told the policeman that that dirty so-and-so threw a cigarette to please come forward. The commissioner read his description, as if the man were a criminal, or missing: white, about thirty-seven, five eight or nine inches tall, wearing dark trousers and a white sport shirt.

Minutes after Hickey addressed the city, a fire started in a ten-story building on Main Street downtown. The fire began in two hampers at the rear of the first floor. It never had a chance to become fully involved; only the hampers were destroyed. The cause would be listed as undetermined. The building's owner: the Aetna Fire Insurance Company.

All night, Trooper Francis Whelan had been nursing his drinks in the bar of the Bond Hotel, undercover, hoping to pick up information on the fire from the show people staying there. Another detective "was going to be in this barroom at the same time but we were not to recognize each other."

Whelan struck up a conversation with George W. Smith, who was steamed by a *Times* article about the city fireman who tried to direct water on the tent only to be pushed away by Blanchfield's men. Smith groused that Hartford was one of the few cities this size that didn't station a piece of firefighting equipment right on the lot. He had a date to keep and left Whelan at the rail.

The clown Felix Adler sat down beside him, and Whelan bought him a bottle of beer. Adler told him he'd helped people out, then run back to his dressing tent to rescue his pig and his duck. He gave Whelan the burned nickel he'd found as a souvenir. His theory was that some drunk must have tossed a cigarette in a wastebasket. The fire definitely started in the men's room. Whelan bought him another beer.

His daughter was a spinner, Adler said, with the aerial ballet. She had guts. After the fire both of them went over to the armory, and she insisted on going in and seeing the bodies. She asked a trooper how she could get in; the officer told her she needed to be looking for a particular person. Adler himself refused to, but she gave a name and saw the bodies in the company of a Red Cross nurse and another trooper.

*Felix Adler with his pet pig
(one in a long series).*
PHOTO COURTESY OF THE CIRCUS
WORLD MUSEUM

Adler said the troupe would be drinking at the Hofbrau House on Trumbull Street later. Adler was going to catch a quick nap; if Whelan was still in the bar at 11:00, Adler would bring him along and introduce him to the Wallendas and other stars. Whelan said he'd probably be here since it didn't look like his date was going to show.

Across the room, the other detective had spoken with Leonard Aylesworth. In the lobby of the Bond, his partner slipped a note to Whelan. It read: "I am Supt. of that Department, an engineer and a graduate of Yale. I know textile. I was in Springfield, Mass. when this fire took place. In the year 1799 Geo. Washington attended a circus and from that day to this day the tents have been always treated the same. Now who is lax the circus or your city officials. I was before some of the 'Big-Shots' until six o'clock this morning then thrown in jail. 'What for?' 'That's my business?' 'I will never tell you.' 'I did the best I could but they are not kidding me.' 'Of course there may have been some laxity but at these times, what can you expect.'"

At 11:00, Adler returned with a man named Bill Hudson from New York City. He wasn't part of the circus, just someone—like Whelan—he'd met at the bar. Hal Olver, the press flack, came along and told stories about how he'd broken people's cameras during the fire. Adler said he'd busted one too. Olver was sore about a fellow named Roden or Rodent who apparently was "a weak sister, who he told to shut his mouth." He was surprised the cops hadn't picked him up yet. Adler wondered why they hadn't questioned Blinky Meck.

Olver left and Adler suggested he and Whelan and Hudson go out to a bar called the Spinning Wheel on Albany Avenue. Whelan said that was fine but he couldn't stay out too late. He excused himself to go to the bathroom, then ran outside and across the street to his car and removed its fishing pole antenna and hid it in the high grass of a vacant lot.

At the Spinning Wheel, Adler introduced the two men to Frankie Saluto, the famous midget clown. Adler and Saluto reminisced about the good old days in New York and signed autographs for people at the bar. Show folks there were wondering where "Cookie the Blow" disappeared to after the fire.

After last call, Adler said he'd buy them beers back at the railroad cars; porters sold them by the bottle. When they got there, Hudson paid. Two midgets drank with them. When Hudson went outside to pee, Whelan learned that Adler didn't know the man at all. Adler mentioned it was the first beer Hudson had bought in a long time, and when he returned, the show people seemed suspicious of him. Hudson told a circus story from years back, and another fellow tripped him up in his details. Whelan thought they might gang up on the man if he didn't get him out of there, so he said it was time he was heading back.

He dropped Adler off at the Bond. Once he was alone in the car with Hudson, he asked him a few offhand questions about New York. Hudson clammed up. Whelan asked him who he was and who he thought he was kidding. The remark sobered Hudson instantly. Whelan said he didn't think he was even from New York. He asked if he was a government agent.

"I could be," Hudson said.

Whelan told him who he was and showed him his credentials. He demanded to know what Hudson's business was. When Hudson refused to say, Whelan told him he was taking him in.

Just short of the barracks, Hudson broke down and confessed that he was just a fireman from Stamford. He showed him his badge. Whelan hauled him in anyway, asking the duty officer to make a record of Hudson in the logbook. Hudson was terrified, afraid he'd lose his job. He'd been suspended for being drunk on duty a few weeks before. He begged Whelan to take his name off the log.

Whelan was sick of him and his stories. He dropped him at his hotel, swung back to the Hotel Bond and retrieved his antenna, then drove home. The nickel he stuck in an envelope and attached to his report to the commissioner, along with a cocktail napkin autographed by Felix Adler, King of the Clowns.

*J*uly 9, 1944

Sunday no one celebrated the one hundredth anniversary of Tom Thumb's first visit to Hartford. They were too busy with funerals.

Mt. St. Benedict Cemetery on Blue Hills Avenue had all of their employees working overtime. They would bury twenty people today, with fifteen more scheduled for tomorrow.

The papers were full of announcements. In New Hartford: "The local Girl Scouts will attend the funeral of Lorraine Wabrek Sunday afternoon in a body. They will meet one-half hour before the funeral in the parsonage, in uniform."

In Hartford, the triple funeral of one mother and her two young sons drew a crowd to Talarski's. Her husband didn't attend; he'd collapsed upon hearing the news and was in seclusion. Thick tributes of flowers blanketed the white caskets, the boys on either side of their mother, two small crosses of white roses at their feet. As the organist played "Nearer My God to Thee," the woman's mother cried, "Alice, my Alice, why did you go, why did you go?" The reverend chose an appropriate verse: "Jesus said suffer the little children to come unto me, for such is the kingdom of heaven." Emotion overcame both grandmothers; they had to be helped out of the chapel. A cortege of fifty cars wound its way to Fairview Cemetery. Again, the women nearly fainted. It was already hot, haze hovering above the trees. Relatives plucked rosebuds from the wreaths and cast them into the open graves. The crowd dispersed, gently shutting their doors. The sexton lowered the boxes, the workmen uncovered the dirt.

There were so many dead that the funeral notices' normally acceptable platitudes—true or not—now rang false and hollow. "Mrs. Goff was well known and had a wide circle of friends." "Mrs. de la Vergne was widely known and had a large circle of friends."

The heat was unbearable, in the nineties before noon and staying there past supper time. At the baseball stadium, John Stewart and the St. Michael's Boys Brigade roamed the stands, collecting money for the *Times'* Circus Victims Fund.

Strangely, at the air-conditioned Roxy Theater off Broad Street, along with a short of Bing Crosby and Frank Sinatra (*Swooner vs. Crooner*), they were showing *Under the Big Top,* a collection of clips from Ringling's Madison Square Garden dates. For the Roxy, though, this was not in questionable taste but absolutely fitting; their features Sunday were *Delinquent Parents* (See . . . Youth on the loose!) and *Rebellious Daughters* (What do they do at night?).

In Sarasota, the *Herald Tribune* ran an editorial about the fire on their front page.

> In time, it will probably be decided no individual or group was really to blame. Canvas has been weatherproofed the same way for years. We shall probably decide the catastrophe may be attributed to any one of a number of causes, from a cigarette to a match carelessly flipped.
>
> Human beings, subject to human limitations, learn primarily by experience. There was, in this case, no criterion worthy of the name. Now that the criterion exists, you won't have to worry further about another Ringling circus fire.
>
> Detention in Hartford of five key men on a technical charge of manslaughter is merely a normal step in [an] official investigation. Not one of the five but would have given his right arm, his very life, to have prevented the holocaust. Authorities realize this. So will the public, once hysteria dies.
>
> Whatever the cost in lives and immeasurable anguish, whatever the official aftermath, there will be no more inflammable canvas stretched above circus audiences. Not because of what the law will do, but because those operating the Ringling circus HAVE NOW LEARNED FROM EXPERIENCE. Doubtless Ringling's new "big top" will not only be unburnable but so constructed that multiple exits will safeguard against panic of any type. Ringling executives will see to this regardless of investigations or popular sentiment.

Commissioner Hickey didn't read the editorial. He spent the day going over all the testimony he'd collected since Thursday night, trying to figure out who he should talk to next.

Mabel Epps came home from St. Francis to her boys—safe, thank God. Why her sister Maurice and her niece Muriel were taken, she couldn't understand. Everyone wanted her to rest. She tried, but how did you rest your mind? How did you not think?

At the morgue, a dentist from Middletown identified Michael Norris by his teeth. He checked the two girls who were left, but neither of them was remotely close to Judy.

Seaman Raymond Erickson Sr. came all the way from Gulfport to find his son. He didn't know what to make of Stanley Kurneta's story about the priest. He went to the morgue, hoping to find a child his son's size with no dental work whatsoever and the knotted shoelace his wife had tied. And Raymond had just recovered from a broken arm; an X-ray could verify that.

The one boy left was far too large to be Raymond. There were no others.

The police escorted Mr. Erickson to Municipal Hospital, but no one there offered any clues, and all the patients had names. He returned to Middletown. What else could he do? It didn't matter that it wasn't his fault he'd been away. He'd come too late and his son was gone.

As the day waned, the morgue fell quiet. Everyone on the missing list had been checked into except Ermo Flanders, and none of the six bodies fit his age.

Dr. Weissenborn was just as puzzled as Thomas Barber and Ed Lowe by 1565. He suggested the possibility that the one person who could identify the girl might be among the critically injured, or perhaps she was the only child of one of the three nameless adults laid out on the tables. Maybe someone had claimed the wrong body. The detectives wouldn't rule anything out.

Tomorrow the city would bury those left. The mayor's office had a ceremony planned.

Weissenborn set to work cataloguing the bodies, carefully taking their data—height, weight, head circumference, estimated age. He helped Dr. Butler to shoot dental X-rays of all six, then Butler pulled out his clipboard and patiently started charting. A detective gathered the information together in one place. Maybe someday people would need it.

*J*uly 10, 1944

As the courts and law offices opened, scores of suits against the circus clogged the docket, dozens of them naming the city as co-defendant. Always the populist, Mayor Mortensen spoke with the president of the local bar on behalf of citizens who couldn't afford legal counsel.

The mayor also appealed to storekeepers and owners of vacant buildings to take circus posters out of their windows. He personally paid to have a large billboard with the Ringling banner stripped.

The forecast for Monday was cloudy with showers, a warm rain breaking the heat wave. It ruined Coroner Frank Healy's last day of vacation. He'd missed all the commotion, down on the shore in Milford. Now he had to shut up the beach house and head north. His inquest started tomorrow.

The morgue opened at 8:30. No one was foolish enough to be hopeful at this point, though they showed up just the same: Barber and Lowe and Butler and Weissenborn. William Menser called in sick. They waited in the chilly room, blowing into their hands; when it was apparent nobody was coming, Weissenborn called in a state police photographer to take some pictures for the files.

From the official notes, the six unidentified were:

1503—9 year old female, white (probably), 3'11", 55 lbs., slender build, light brown hair with red glow. Upper and lower permanent incisors and first molars present. All baby molars present, the four baby second molars all have fillings, these are the only fillings in the mouth.

1510—11 year old male, white (probably)—badly burned. 4'4" (estimated), 70 lbs., muscularly developed. Wore white ribbed shorts, undershirt with shoulder straps. Only three baby teeth present (upper cuspids and lower left second molar); five fillings in four teeth.

1565—6 year old female, white, blue eyes, 3'10", 40 lbs., moderately well developed, head circumference 20½", blond or light hair, shoulder length. Curly hair. All baby teeth present except lower central incisors, the incisal edges of which are even with the occlusal plane of the lower lateral baby incisors. Brown shoes (pair); flowered dress.

2109—30 plus female, white, 5'1", 148 lbs. (approximately), small boned, stocky, head circumference 22", light brown or blonde hair, appendix operation about 8 years ago. Wore Spencer corset, pink pants, and tan rayon stockings. Gold crowns in upper left laterals; other dental work indicates intermittent care.

2200—55 to 60 year old male, white (probably), 5'3", 170 lbs. (approximately), short moderate build, head circumference 20". Well kept, regular dental care; good deal of gold work and bridges.

4512—30 to 35 year old female, Black (probably), 5'2", 160 lbs. (approximately), short stocky build, wide hips, head circumference 21", married and probably a mother. Wears ornamental ring on right ring finger, wedding ring on left ring finger. Very good teeth; all teeth present except lower left first molar.

While the photographer popped away, Dr. Weissenborn filled out the death certificates. Where the form calls for "Name of Hospital," he filled in "Barbour St. Circus Grounds" for all six, though at least 1565 had died at Municipal. He gave all six the same cause of death: "Burns by fire, 3rd and 4th degree."

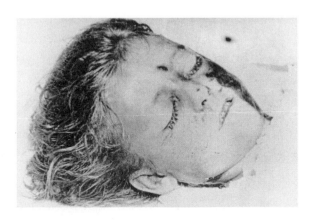

Little Miss 1565, the famous shot taken at the Taylor & Modeen funeral parlor. PHOTO BY ROBERT GLYNN, COURTESY OF ART KIELY

Six different funeral homes had offered their services free of charge. At 10:30, as planned, Weissenborn turned the bodies over to them.

At noon, on orders from Commissioner Hickey, Adolph Pastore gassed up the Cadillac and set off for Rochester with Hartford police officer George Sanford. Hickey trusted only Eastman Kodak themselves to develop Sanford's 8mm film.

The police photographer followed 1565 to the Taylor & Modeen Funeral Home, unwilling to give up so easily. The undertakers there touched up her face and combed her hair back, and he took two more shots for future identifications, one head on, one a profile.

Apparently Robert Ringling was worried about the possibility, as president of the corporation, of being arrested like James Haley. Circus attorney Dan Gordon Judge checked with associates at his New York firm, one of whom wrote back: "Dreyfuss has found authorities (both New York State and Federal), indicating clearly that Mr. X is not subject to extradition." Rumors placed Ringling in New York City, holed up in the Plaza Hotel under an assumed name, but of course these were only rumors.

The burial of the six unidentified victims at Northwood Cemetery, Monday July 10th, 1944. Rabbi Morris Silverman officiates while Father Thomas Looney and Reverend Warren Archibald pray with him. PHOTO COURTESY OF THE *HARTFORD COURANT*

The cortege left Hartford Hospital shortly before 3:00, six hearses escorted by city police and firemen behind Chiefs Hallissey and King. The procession turned from Jefferson onto Main Street, private cars falling in behind, rolling slowly through the canyon of office buildings and department stores. Around them, traffic stopped; men on the sidewalk doffed their hats. At city hall Mayor and Mrs. Mortensen joined the mourners. The cortege proceeded up Main and through the North End, passing within blocks of the circus grounds before turning into the iron arch of Northwood Cemetery.

The cemetery was the city's Soldiers Field, its veterans from the Spanish-American War and Pershing's Mexican Expedition and the Great War laid out in neat rows, the identical gravestones even as teeth. A small private corner backed up to Keney Park. Here the city had selected a plot large enough for all six. The graves were open, framed by boards crossed to hold the coffins. 1565's was conspicuous, the only white one; even the two other children had adult boxes.

It hadn't rained, but the air was thick. A reverend read the 23rd Psalm. The rabbi from Emanuel Synagogue read the Kaddish and the Mole Rahmin. Finally Father Looney read in Latin the committal service and sprinkled the graves with holy water. The crowd joined in prayer.

As the last cars filed out, gravediggers lugged the coffins aside and jumped down into the holes. They hadn't finished digging. On the grass lay six stakes, each bearing a number.

By the cemetery entrance stood the nameless dead's opposites—rows of graves with no bodies. Headstones commemorated local men killed in faraway places or buried elsewhere: Manila and Tunisia, Belgium and Honolulu. Killed in Action, one said, the location insignificant. Lost at Sea. Missing in Flight.

In Center Cemetery in Southampton, Massachusetts, a cenotaph would remember Eleanor Cook, her brother Edward's stone right beside it. The children held their own memorial service. Rev. James Yee led a procession from the town center, gathering neighbors and friends from Eleanor's grade and Edward's Sunday school class as they moved down East Street toward the Parsons' house. The boys wore church clothes—slacks and a shirt and tie—the girls their best dresses. Edward's casket was in the Parsons' three-season porch, a long room with a hardwood floor and windows on three sides. On the lid stood a picture of the Cook children, a flower arrangement blocking Donald. Rev. Yee conducted a full service for the town's children; later at the Congregational Church he would perform another for their parents.

Thomas Barber missed the services for the dead he'd watched over for the past four days. He had to give his daughter Gloria away. Because Orville Vieth was going overseas, they couldn't postpone the wedding. Father Looney married them in St. Michael's before a small crowd of family and friends. They needed to cut the pictures short and head off to the reception; the church had a hectic schedule with all the funerals. Immediately following the ceremony, the hearse from Farley's rolled up with Billy Dineen's coffin.

The Barbers and Dineens were good friends. Last Friday, knowing they wouldn't be able to make the boy's funeral, Barber and Gloria had visited with them to pay their respects. The Dineens apologized for having to miss the wedding.

Cities as far away as Houston held services for the dead. Hartford's namesake in England, Hertford, sent its official sympathy. Telegrams rained in from across the country. Hartford and St. Francis Hospitals had to ask well-wishers not to send any more flowers, citing the extra heavy load on maintenance workers.

In Chicago, where the circus had an office, the *Tribune* noted that "a report by Ringling Bros. and Barnum & Bailey investigators, prepared independently of the official inquiry, said that sisal hemp, a product of the Yucatan and as combustible as dry kindling, was employed for the lacing which held the six-sectioned big top together. Flames raced along the shoestring fashion lacework of these seams to reach the center pole bail rings supporting the canvas, the report said."

The vault at police headquarters reeked of the fire. Among the items still unclaimed: a child's shiny black patent leather sandal, a Glastonbury Fire Department badge, draft cards, blankets (taken from car trunks to cover the dead), checkbooks, snapshots, and several yards of "summer cotton dress goods." Police were especially impressed with the honesty of people turning in ration coupons for food, shoes and gasoline.

Not everything could be replaced so easily. One daughter wrote to the coroner looking for a sizable diamond ring and large emerald her mother wore. Circus performers The Four Macks beseeched the police; they needed a new table built for their roller-skating act but weren't allowed back on the lot to measure the old one.

The lot itself was becoming cluttered—specifically the backyard. The mayor met with health department officials, hoping to find a solution. A homeowner at 95 Cleveland Avenue made a complaint about the latrine behind the cookhouse. Its six toilets, servicing several hundred workers, stood just thirty yards from his back door. The circus cleaned it twice daily, but inspectors said their sanitation was only fair. The health department discussed it with the chief steward.

Worse than the toilets for some neighbors were the smells and sounds of the animals. The elephants and big cats were loud, sometimes in the middle of the night, and with the heat, Sponzo's meadow was decidedly aromatic. And who knew how long they would be there?

On their end, the circus was running out of supplies. They were supposed to be long gone by now, finished with Springfield, doing tonight's show in Albany, then heading for Schenectady. Instead, they were stuck on Barbour Street, paying inflated prices for ice and meat and hay, and no end to it in sight.

The crackdown on tent shows didn't let up. At the city's insistence, the Colored Elks Club on Bellevue Street removed a tent from their lot, and the building and fire departments refused a permit for a revival show hoping to set up in the North End. Yet somehow Dick's Paramont Carnival met Commissioner Hickey's strict criteria. They opened that night in Berlin, under the lights, playing through the 15th with a fat lady as well as snake, posing and ape shows.

At Hartford and St. Francis, the night was quiet, but early that morning the halls at Municipal were suddenly busy. The boy who'd shared a bed with Jerry LeVasseur right after the fire weakened after midnight. He hung on through the early morning, the doctors working elbow to elbow over him until he was gone. Down the hall, his mother slept, her face and arms scarred. She had another son, but this was her baby. The doctors wouldn't tell her for months.

*J*uly 11-July 15,
1944

Tuesday at 10:00 A.M. Coroner Healy opened his formal inquest, calling six ushers and seatmen first, hoping to discover the fire's origin.

One seatman offered his opinion: "Probably somebody was sitting on the back row of seats that struck a match on the tent, or maybe it started at the men's toilet. . . . That is about the only two ways I could say."

Head usher John Carson testified: "I think probably somebody lit a cigarette and threw the match out the other end and it caught that way. They never do burn with a cigarette."

Witnesses mentioned the Spanish web fire in Portland and the pinhole in Providence, yet none brought up a more serious blaze. In Philadelphia, their first stand under canvas, flames had broken out on the sidewall of the dressing tent. Oddly, this incident never came to light in any of the Hartford investigations.

Commissioner Hickey continued to gather evidence, corralling as many photos of the fire and its aftermath as he could find.

He resumed his hearing by recalling James Haley and asking him again about the show's fire and liability coverage. Haley had the facts now. Five different companies carried their fire insurance for a total of $578,000, Lloyd's of London their liability at $500,000. The answers satisfied Hickey; he dismissed Haley after five minutes.

City detectives visited witnesses at their homes to take their testimony. William Dineen spoke to families in the North End. Ed Lowe handled mail about missing children. Thomas Barber interviewed people who'd been in the southwest bleachers, including one man who sat seven rows up and said he "smelled something like paper burning" minutes before the fire started. Another man in section B had heard a combustion engine running just outside the tent, right where the fire started.

That afternoon the *Times* ran photos and the story of the burial ceremonies at Northwood on page 2. Directly across from them an article headlined GIRL STILL MISSING SINCE CIRCUS FIRE described Eleanor Cook. She was "tall for her age, was dressed in a blue and red plaid playsuit, red socks and white summer shoes. Her hair is light brown and bobbed and her eyes are blue. She was first reported in the hospital with her mother and brother but this proved to be untrue. . . . A member of the family said the little girl who was buried yesterday among the unknown victims was not Eleanor."

Children who'd survived the fire unharmed—and there were thousands—became neighborhood celebrities, telling their tales of escape over and over. For some, it was an adventure, the first big event they'd been a part of. It was exciting to see their own names in the paper. "In our innocence," one said later, "we didn't have a clue." For the same reason, many never had bad dreams.

The aftermath could even be comic. One girl's father had been burned on his bald spot, a blister rising like a tiny cap. One evening while he was reading the paper, the blister broke, the water trickling down over his brow.

Others like Betsy Kurneta couldn't sleep for weeks. When they did, they dreamed of the fire, waking bolt upright in the dark, screaming.

. . .

Wednesday the *Courant* brought up the issue of Unidentified #1: "Parts had been cremated immediately after the fire because of the absolute impossibility of identification." The author didn't commit to whether #1 represented a seventh unidentified person, but later that day the *Manchester Evening Herald* built on his lead, saying, "The remains of one body, entirely indistinguishable, had been cremated earlier."

This description may be a gloss of Weissenborn's write-up on #1's death certificate. After the fire, "dismembered parts of a body were found. Left hand, left foot, part of skull and brain and right hand. These rapidly deteriorated and were destroyed. It was impossible to determine what sex from these. It is my impression that this body was crushed by a falling pole and the rest of the body burned and trampled beyond recognition. Was disposed of by incineration at the Hartford Hospital on July 7, 1944."

Weissenborn called #1 a single body for convenience. The pieces came to him in different containers, and not all (if any) came from the same person. The state police list of the parts—given to them by Weissenborn himself—included three left feet, one of which came from a child. So many bodies lost hands and feet that these could have easily been from them, and the piece of skull fit with the description of the unidentified woman in the morgue on Saturday whose head was almost entirely missing. #1 had no torso and no limbs, just the very extremities.

How #1 evolved over the years into the incinerated baby is unclear. Reporters knew it as a seventh unidentified body, and perhaps the fact that it was small enough to be both indistinguishable and incinerated may have tempted one to make the leap. The label stuck.

The lists balanced perfectly now, seven missing and seven unidentified, until Wednesday when detectives located war worker Ermo Flanders at his East Hartford rooming house. Flanders had attended the circus; he'd been out when investigators checked earlier. Understandably, he was not happy about his name being in the paper all week.

The missing list was now six: Mrs. Budrick, Mrs. Fifield, a Mrs. Woodward from Storrs, Eleanor Cook, Judy Norris, and Raymond Erickson.

On page 2 the *Times* ran a small article titled ELEANOR COOK, 8, ON MISSING LIST, topping it with a grainy shot of her. On page 9 the words "Who knows this child?" capped a picture of 1565.

The burial Monday of the unidentified piqued the nation's interest, unleashing a flood of mail from parents of runaways and couples locked in ugly custody battles. "Mr. F—— keeps Lila more or less in hiding because he does not want his wife to have the child."

A New Jersey woman wondered if 2200 might be her brother, missing for over a year. Ed Lowe wrote back, asking for a dental chart, but the woman didn't have one. She thanked him anyway. "I wish I could find my brother," she said. "We are the only 2 left out of a family of seven. I am the oldest and I allways tried to keep in touch with him."

The Philadelphia Police were searching for two boys, thirteen and seventeen, rumored to have run away with the circus.

A Worcester woman was looking for her son, working with the show. The timekeeper said he'd received his pay on July 8th, then left town. A year later, his mother was still sending letters.

A mother from Stockholm, Maine, wrote: "Will you be kind anofe to look and fine my girl."

One writer suggested to Commissioner Hickey that all civilians wear steel ID tags on fine metal chains—not cotton string, as some servicemen had lost their dog tags at the Cocoanut Grove that way.

Mail concerning the cause of the fire was even heavier. From Philadelphia, a man wrote to Hickey, saying he'd spoken with a suspicious character in a lunch car when the circus played there. The man was a circus employee who confided that the elephants weren't poisoned back in 1941 but had in fact been asphyxiated by fumes in their railroad cars. He mentioned that in case of fire, a "master rope" freed the horses, and that his wife, a tightrope walker, had been killed some time ago in an accident. The writer said the man didn't make sense, but figured Hickey might be able to use some of the information.

Also from Philly, a woman reported that a spotlight blew up and caught a wire on fire the last night of the stand. A Hartford man remembered getting an electrical shock from a cable lying on the ground where the southwest bleachers met the track.

Some letters were obviously the work of cranks, others the ramblings of disturbed people drawn to the news. "Falling due on my blisters for Roosevelt—a former president's son. I told you before, you have to name all the living sons of the former presidents. I almost died of strep like Calvin Coolidge Jr. Now, if you haven't saved his life, you'll be having some uproar on account of him, and it might be the circus burned up on account of it."

But many of the leads seemed plausible. A Hartford woman testified that she and her son saw a man with a bloody shirt hurriedly wrapping his wrist with a roll of bandages or rags in a circus wagon about thirty feet west of the main entrance. He couldn't have been injured in the fire because she was one of the first ones out. She "thought that if there had been such a fight it might be connected with the origin of the fire. He was a white man, heavyset, had dark hair. He was apparently alone in the wagon."

The most promising letter came from the warden of Deer Lodge Prison in Montana. He had an inmate who'd worked for the circus last year. In November, in Nashville, the show let go a man he worked with named Cox. Cox swore that he would burn the show out, that it wouldn't get far in '44. He also told the inmate he'd served five years for burning down a hotel. The warden felt his prisoner's story would hold up. Hickey sent back a telegram, asking him to interview the man at length and get a full description of Cox and any other friends then working for the circus. He also got in touch with the chief of police in Nashville, hoping his people might be able to locate Cox.

Meanwhile, the legal front was heating up. Seeing that survivors' claims would easily outstrip the show's holdings—leaving clients who filed later with nothing—attorneys Edward Rogin, Julius Schatz and Arthur Weinstein applied with the superior court to place the circus in temporary receivership, nominating Rogin to be the receiver. The court agreed.

The circus didn't. Legally, the appointment of a receiver required a federal court order, not merely a state court's. But the alternative to a receivership was some form of bankruptcy, meaning the current officers would lose control of the corporation and the victims would receive little or nothing. This way, the circus could operate as usual, feeding their profits to the receiver over time to pay the damages. After discussing the situation with Rogin, Schatz and Weinstein, and then among themselves, Dan Gordon Judge, Aubrey Ringling Haley and Mrs. Edith Ringling agreed to the receivership. Rogin would process all claims and disburse all payments.

First though, he needed to help the circus get out of town. In the last twenty-four hours, complaints from neighbors on Cleveland had swamped the health department. Again, inspectors went out and toured the lot; this time they recommended the animals and cookhouse be relocated, possibly to the North Meadows, down by the river. The situation at the trains was no better.

As receiver, Rogin would take possession of the train cars, the wagons, the animals—all of the show's property and assets within the state of Connecticut. The court charged him to preserve and protect those assets, yet the only way he could restore the corporation to a moneymaking basis was to get the three sections back to Sarasota as fast as possible. To release them, he needed the circus to put up a sizable chunk of money. The insurance policies were a start. The rest he'd have to finesse.

In Rochester, Adolph Pastore and George Sanford walked out of Eastman Kodak headquarters with an original and a duplicate print of the film, got back in the Caddy and drove.

That night Mayor Mortensen went on WTHT, making a long speech. He lamented the lack of fire laws concerning carnivals and circuses—not merely here but around the country. The nation would be watching Hartford. "We cannot renew to life a single one of those who have died so pitifully, but we can make certain that never again need so ghastly a toll of this kind be taken of a civilized community. If we were to fail to learn the sobering lesson of the disaster, this tragedy would only remain what it is today, completely senseless and cruel."

At Municipal and Hartford, three more patients died, bringing the total to 161. One was the Lithuanian immigrant, Charles Tomalonis. Fellow tobacco workers said he had no family here, and with the war, finding anyone in his home country was impossible. The search for his next of kin would last twenty-five years.

. . .

Thursday, a week after the fire, the *Courant* issued a special edition reprinting just their fire coverage from the 7th and 8th at the regular price of 4 cents a copy. It had no paid ads and, like their original run of 90,000 the previous Friday, sold out instantly.

Troopers delivered to the state's attorney's office a section of khaki canvas that had been part of the south wall of the men's room, also a portion of the menagerie sidewall. Commissioner Hickey adjourned his hearing till July 18th. So far eighty witnesses had testified, their names withheld from the public.

Detectives Thomas Barber and Edward Lowe, who'd helped at the circus grounds and then the armory and finally the Hartford Hospital morgue, began their own investigation in their spare time. They sent pictures of 1565 to every primary school in Connecticut and her dental charts to hundreds of area dentists, hoping for any lead. They questioned teachers and priests and mailmen, sure that somebody somewhere would remember her face.

"Within a couple of weeks," Lowe said, "we were discouraged. The missing children all turned out to be on vacation, at camp, or visiting relatives. In fact, so many children were reported missing that it made our search practically impossible. We decided to wait until school reopened to check reports of missing children."

Instead, they tried a more direct but much harder road. They spoke to parents who'd claimed bodies at the armory that fit 1565's description.

"These interviews were extremely painful," Lowe admitted. "People who had lost relatives in the fire wanted to forget the whole affair. Most didn't want to talk about it and we couldn't blame them. We got nowhere."

At Municipal, each nurse's aide tended one patient. One aide's was a woman whose condition was critical. Every time the aide changed her bandages, more skin would come off. The woman's six-year-old son had died in the fire, but they didn't dare tell her that. They told her he was in the pediatric ward, doing all right.

"They didn't tell her for a long time. She would ask me to go down and read to him. We had strict instructions not to tell her her son was dead. I would say, 'I'd be happy to.' I would go out and be lost for twenty-five to thirty minutes. Then I would come back and tell her all the stories I read to him. And for that twenty-five to thirty minutes, I would be out in the hall, crying like a baby."

Finally doctors told the woman the truth. Later the aide came in to face her.

"How could you do that?" the mother asked.

"I'm sorry. I was told to."

"Oh, my dear, I'm not yelling at you," the woman said. "I just don't know how you did it."

Hartford Hospital restored regular visiting hours. In those days, children weren't allowed in the wards. Martha Ann Moore's bed was close to a window. Outside, across the street, her granddaughter Janet Moore Sapolis waved up at her.

Elliott Smith's father came to Municipal every day. He worked downtown at the Factory Insurance Association, and took the bus up at lunch and then again in the evening. Elliott had developed pneumonia and lay in his coffinlike oxygen tent, talking up at him through the plastic windows. Ironically, his worst burns were where his rescuer had touched him—the hand the man with the mustache had clasped and where he'd lifted Elliott, across the back and thighs; the friction had ripped the cooked skin off. Mr. Smith shuttled between the fifth and third floor, where his wife Grace was recuperating. He stayed till 8:00, the end of visiting hours, then said goodbye and took the bus down Main to the Isle of Safety and caught another one to Vernon. All summer he ate late.

Joan Smith had gone to live with her aunt and uncle in Wilson. The first week, her cousin Janet was still away at a lake. She had a large collection of Bobbsey Twins books; Joan read one a day till she returned. The girls went to summer school, making games and pictures for Elliott. Joan made up stories to tell him when she visited.

Their mother had suffered burns on her scalp and shoulders and on her ankles where the firemen had carried her out. The first time Joan went to visit her, she began crying before she even reached the room. The nurse was cross with her and said she couldn't go in like that. She gave Joan some ginger ale to calm her down. It worked, but when she went in it was obvious from her eyes that she'd been crying for some time. She couldn't hide that from her mother.

. . .

On the lot, Edward Rogin checked the circus' inventory of equipment, assisted by George W. Smith. With the stroke of a pen, Rogin officially took possession of everything on the lot. Then he went to the Windsor Street yards.

In Sarasota, the Ringling front office vigorously denied the show was in receivership.

About supper time, the radio stations broadcast a general call for information about the fire. Police were asking anyone who'd been in the southwest bleachers to please register at headquarters on Market Street. They repeated the request at 8:00 A.M. the next morning, receiving dozens of calls and letters.

The question of what to do with the circus was still up in the air. Acting under the mayor's direction, Dr. Burgdorf of the Board of Health ordered the circus off the lot by midnight Friday; precisely where they were supposed to go wasn't clear. Rogin wanted them gone from the city altogether. Hickey said they were not to leave Barbour Street until he completed his investigation.

That morning, Rogin, Schatz and Weinstein met in Schatz's office to find a way to break the deadlock. They needed to reassure the state before they could pull out. The key was getting the circus to put up enough money to cover the value of their rolling stock and equipment as a good faith gesture. The three men conferred with the show's attorneys and came up with a plan. The circus would surrender $380,000 in cash, assign two fire insurance policies worth $125,000 each to the receiver, and devote their Lloyd's policy solely to paying claims. All afternoon, Weinstein and Ringling lawyers ironed out the final draft of the agreement. The court approved of the solution. By 7:30, razorbacks were lining up the wagons for the short haul to the runs. Mayor Mortensen's hand-picked liaison Deputy Chief Godfrey watched over them.

A little past 8:00, the sun dropping in the west, a heavy black sedan with Florida plates rolled over the dirt-covered sidewalk and onto the lot. Leonard Aylesworth stepped out and set to gathering his crew. Not long after, Commissioner Hickey's Cadillac pulled in, Adolph Pastore at the wheel. The circus attorneys were there too, and Dr. Burgdorf, all of them originally at cross purposes now working to ensure their concerns weren't lost in the rush to bug out. Hickey needed a guarantee that thirty-three employees both he and Coroner Healy had asked to testify would remain in the city. Burgdorf wanted the lot cleaned up. The circus was amenable to everything, their lawyers said.

Around midnight, trucks towed the first string of wagons over the sidewalk and up Barbour Street, headed for the Pleasant Street siding. By 3:00 that morning, the workers finished cleaning up, leaving nothing but the fallen poles and charred stands.

The first section left for Sarasota at 7:00 A.M. Saturday, seen off by Rogin himself, the trains accompanied by a deputy sheriff whom Rogin had appointed custodian in his stead. Knowing it was a once-in-a-lifetime assignment, the deputy brought his teenaged son along. They chatted with the performers as they rocked westward through the green hills. Just after lunch, the train crossed the Newburgh Bridge high above the wide Hudson and pulled into the junction town of Maybrook, New York. The deputy and his son got off. The circus went on.

July 15-July 31,
1944

A ten-year-old boy from Magnolia Street in the North End had escaped the fire. His best friend from the Vine Street School had died. The boy's father was a rabbi, and instructed his son to say the Birkat ha'Gomel, a prayer upon deliverance from peril, on the following Sabbath. So on Saturday, as the circus trains pulled for winter quarters, the boy went to Agudas Achim Synagogue on Greenfield Street and prayed: "Blessed art thou, O Lord our God, King of the Universe, who vouchsafest benefits unto the undeserving, who has also vouchsafed all good unto me."

That morning, Commissioner Hickey sent a memo to all local fire marshals and police chiefs. Since the fire, his office had handled hundreds of inquiries concerning the licensing of traveling shows. It was the season, especially in the distant towns and down along the shore; every meadow seemed to sprout a carnival. In his memo, Hickey asked local inspectors to examine the seating arrangements. If patrons stood, officials could allow one per every five square feet; if sitting in fixed chairs, one per eight square feet; if in loose chairs, one per ten square feet. Shows should provide ample aisles and exits, shorten their rows, and limit capacity. Lastly, he suggested strict enforcement of all No Smoking laws, citing specific sections and fines.

In the early afternoon, WTIC presented a speech by Governor Baldwin. The day before, he'd suddenly announced that he'd reconsidered his position and would indeed run for a third term. Now he briefly recapped the fire and gave the most current death toll before outlining the state's response and the ongoing hearings. "In lives lost and in personal injury," he said, "this was the worst disaster in the history of Connecticut. A thorough investigation is being made to determine how and why this tragedy occurred. If any criminal negligence or neglect is involved, everything in the power of the state will be done to bring to justice those who may be responsible."

Like the mayor, he praised Hickey and the War Council, the Red Cross and the hospitals. "These volunteer forces were organized for protection against enemy attack . . . a bombing raid which has never come. But a bomb attack could not have struck more swiftly, with less warning, or with more cruel force than this circus fire. The injuries, indeed, were much the same as could have been expected in any enemy raid with incendiary bombs—many severe burns and a smaller number of fracture cases. We regret the tragic event that called the emergency organization into action. We shall always be grateful that it was ready for the job."

Closing, he spoke of how a thousand volunteers had responded, putting in long hours of hard, sometimes impossible work. "The circus disaster has saddened the state. We shall not soon recover from this blow. But we can be intensely proud of the spirit with which the people of Connecticut met the emergency. There are heroes, nameless and innumerable, in this tragedy."

. . .

Unpublicized was the death of Mabel Epps's baby. She was eight months when she went into premature labor. The baby was stillborn, the result of a separation of the placenta, probably caused by her fall from the top of the bleachers. It would have been her first girl. Ten days after the fire, she was still crying hysterically and suffering from mysterious headaches. The doctor took X-rays but couldn't find an answer. He let her go home, red-eyed and sniffling into a tissue.

At St. Francis, a twenty-two-year-old West Hartford woman died. She'd received only first- and second-degree burns, and as early as July 7th had been listed by hospital staff as "not serious."

That night in Denver, a fire destroyed the Old Mill ride at Elitch Gardens, killing six, including two attendants who ran into the tunnel of love to rescue patrons. Officials suspected either a short circuit or a lighted cigarette tossed into one of the niches of the winding tunnel. The owners insisted they'd sprayed all their scenery with liquid fireproofing and that electricians had just checked the wiring that spring.

Later that night in Port Chicago, California, a tragedy of much greater magnitude struck. Two docked munitions ships exploded, leveling the town and killing over three hundred fifty people, many of them instantly vaporized. The blasts came two seconds apart, rocking the state like an earthquake. With the town's power out, the Spartan Bros. Circus cranked up their diesels and lighted the site. By midnight, searchers had recovered only four bodies. The navy declared martial law and shut Port Chicago down. Authorities said no death list would be made available and that an investigation was pending.

The next morning, Governor Baldwin wrote a note to Hickey about the Old Mill fire, saying Hickey should prompt local officials to inspect "all places of amusement." He also forwarded the commissioner a letter from the head of a chemical company whose firm had fireproofed canvas for both military and civilian use. The man asked that Baldwin use his influence to push through laws requiring all tents to be similarly treated.

That afternoon, both Hickey and Healy listened to witnesses. It was convenient for reporters; the two hearings were right across Washington Street from each other. As Chief Hallissey testified before the coroner, the circus train barreled down the Atlantic Coast line south of Richmond.

The first section pulled into Sarasota shortly after noon on Tuesday, the second and third not far behind. Several reporters and photographers who'd waited much of the night had left, called away to more pressing assignments. Only a small gathering of friends and relatives welcomed the circus, staring at the fire-blackened wagons as the flats and stocks and Pullmans rolled in. Razorbacks bandaged from rescue efforts grimly unloaded them.

"We are all dazed," Karl Wallenda said. "It was a nightmare. Those bodies piled high and that roar that I can never forget. . . . I still cannot understand why so many had to die . . . but the show must and will go on. We want to go out again and we will."

Free on bond, their manslaughter trial continued till August, George W. Smith and James Haley would only say they'd held an executive conference on the train which included Robert Ringling.

In Hartford, Raymond Erickson's mother Sophie toured Municipal Hospital, looking for any trace of her son. A social worker there let her dig through a box containing effects taken from the victims. Mrs. Erickson found Raymond's brown sneakers, the knot she'd tied for him that morning still tucked inside the eyelet so it wouldn't show. Someone had removed his blue socks and carefully pushed them into the toes of his shoes so he wouldn't lose them.

. . .

Wednesday the fire department submitted a list of grass fires that had occurred on the Barbour Street grounds to Commissioner Hickey. Over the last five years the lot had seen more than fifteen, most of them in the spring, but just the year before there'd been one the afternoon of July 3rd.

Hickey's driver Adolph Pastore was in Portland, Maine, tracking down runaway Roy Tuttle. Allegedly Tuttle had passed remarks that he knew how the fire started. The night before, he'd been admitted to Maine General Hospital, where he was recovering from third-degree burns to his arms and legs.

According to the local police, Tuttle was the village idiot, a homeless, illiterate victim of apoplectic fits. He did odd jobs around town for pocket money.

At the hospital, Tuttle told Pastore that he'd signed on with the circus in Portland on June 30th, helping to erect the bleachers. On July 6th, he ate lunch at the cookhouse and took a walk down Barbour Street. While he was in front of a store, he heard women screaming that the big top was on fire. He ran back to the grounds and rushed into the tent just as the poles were falling. He was near the animal chute when he had one of his spells and fell down.

When he woke up, he found himself in an open lot. He slept the night there and the next day started hitchhiking back to Portland. It took him nine days. To relieve the pain of his burns, he sat in water wherever he could find some; now they were infected.

That was it. Pastore got nothing out of Tuttle about how the fire started, just this vague, implausible story. Perhaps he felt Tuttle was harmless, or that it was pointless to dig further into his recollections. In any case, he took his statement and left, hearing from the Portland police once more about the fire on the Spanish web.

The next day Hickey himself went to the lot and took as evidence a small piece of melted iron and a four-foot length of wood sheathed in steel. City police still guarded the interior of the tent, and would for months, but the rest of the grounds reverted to the neighborhood kids. The boys had tired of picking through the grass for coins and scraps of clothing; they went back to playing ball, aware of what had happened but drawn by force of habit. One explained: "You go up there, you always think of that, but you still go up there."

In their winter quarters the circus retooled, scraping the blistered paint from the damaged wagons, redesigning lost props. The animals had been inactive so long that their trainers had to put them through a crash re-training program. The fliers needed all new trapeze rigging. Everyone pitched in, from bally girls to sideshow performers; sunburns and busted knuckles were the fashion, and beach parties at night.

Thursday, F. Beverly Kelley announced to the press that the circus would leave Sarasota without a big top and play in open air arenas and ball-parks. It was probable they would use all-steel seats in the future, but that plan could not be realized this year. "We will never go out under a main tent of canvas until a suitable fireproofing process has been discovered and the cost is within the circus's reach," he pledged. The show already had a carload of flameproofing compound on its way. "It is planned to fireproof the sideshow tent which will be the only tent to which the public will be admitted, and all sidewalls to be used by the circus when the show resumes its tour." They would also treat the sidewalls of the dressing and horse tents, but not the tops themselves. "This fireproofing compound had not been available to the circus until this time," Kelley said, and "it has passed the board of underwriters' specifications and [is] recommended by the bureau of standards in Washington."

The show would include the same acts as before the fire, but there would be more headroom for the aerial acts. "The world-famed Torrence and Victoria team will present their act on a 135-foot pole, which has never been done in the circus's history."

Karl Wallenda was used to even greater heights; in Germany he'd made his name walking between church spires. "We're no longer limited by the big top. I can't tell just how much higher we'll go, but it will be a more thrilling act than ever. There is more danger under the new plan because of the wind. We'll get in as much practice as possible." He promised the act would "go higher than ever has been presented before circus audiences."

"What does your wife and the rest of the Wallenda family think of the plan?" a reporter asked.

"They don't ask questions," said Karl. "I tell them to do it and they do it."

Back in Hartford, a state policewoman took the Ericksons to see Stanley Kurneta in the hospital. Again, Stanley told his story of leaving the badly burned Raymond at Municipal—the elevator, the mattress, the ruddy priest with the straw hat. The shoes were proof he'd been there.

The policewoman escorted the Ericksons to Municipal one more time, where they talked with the superintendent. No one had been allowed out of the hospital unidentified unless they were dead, in which case any clothing had been tied to the body before it was taken to the armory. There was a possibility a disoriented patient may have wandered out in the confusion, but they'd preserved all the effects of the dead. The only priest fitting the description Stanley Kurneta had given was Father Thomas McMahon, but he remembered nothing of any boy.

They checked Hartford and St. Francis—no luck—then went back to Middletown again.

The less badly burned were home now. Their family doctors took care of them, changing bandages and applying clean salve. It grew into a routine, mothers walking their children to the offices, followed by ice cream.

One family heard that salt water was good for burns and arranged for their girls to spend the rest of the summer down at the shore. People noticing their livid scars understood immediately.

The country's sympathies were with the victims, and this included the circus itself. The Ringling front office received bushels of condolences, one from a twelve-year-old Richmond, Virginia, boy with a quarter in it. The boy suggested they use it to start a fund donated by all the boys and girls in America who enjoyed the circus as much as he did. "A chance to see the circus is something every boy should have. It is part of the America which our Army, Navy and Marines are fighting for. I am buying all the war stamps I can but don't think Uncle Sam would mind if all children would give to a fund to help bring back the circus so I am sending you 25 cents to start the fund and I hope you will come this way again some time."

James Haley wrote back, thanking him and assuring him they'd be on the road again in no time. He returned the boy's money, saying that if they ran into financial trouble, he'd be the first person they called.

The PR struggle was desperate, but they were winning. Few could hold a grudge against the circus. It was like hating ice cream.

In Hartford, late on Saturday the 22nd, Roland Butler announced to the Associated Press that the circus would reopen in the University of Cincinnati football stadium on August 2nd for a two-day stand. Sarasota rescinded this statement within hours. Sunday the front office said the new show would debut August 4th in Akron's Rubber Bowl, playing a three-day run, two performances a day, as usual. Monday the show would begin rehearsals in winter quarters.

The carload of Hooper Fire Chief fireproofing arrived from Baltimore. F. Beverly Kelley had prepared a release for the *Sarasota Herald Tribune*. "The assistant manager spent several days in Washington, D.C., convincing governmental agencies of the need of this compound, hitherto denied the circus because of certain wartime priorities," he added. Fire Chief had the consistency of liquid chalk or thick milk. Applied with a paintbrush, it changed the color of the canvas from khaki to a grayish-white. Hooper advertised it as flameproof, water repellent and mildew resistant.

Monday the circus gave a public demonstration of its efficacy. A crowd of circus executives, newsmen, and photographers watched as "for nearly a minute a blowtorch was applied to a section of the chemically treated sideshow tent. As the first flames touched the canvas it began to glow a bright red. . . . When the flame was removed the glow died out, leaving a blackened charred-edge hole in the fabric."

Hooper's chief chemist performed the test. He'd invented Fire Chief in 1936. While all branches of the services had used it for years on truck and lifeboat covers, it had never been available to civilians. George W. Smith told reporters that efforts to obtain the compound had been made as far back as a year ago. Because of government priorities, he said, the circus was unable to get any until these 1,200 gallons were released.

Meanwhile, in Hartford, the policewoman continued to search for clues in the case of Raymond Erickson. She talked with Drs. Weissenborn and Onderdonk, making a list of all boys in that age range. At the coroner's office, she found four brass buttons that seemed to be from Raymond's shirt—though the shirt was nowhere to be seen. The coroner said the city police had taken the clothing from the victims, but the property officer on Market Street only had two scraps of fabric, one red [Eleanor Cook's playsuit?] and one figured. The policewoman checked the funeral homes with the same persistence Emily Gill had, with the same result.

She tried Municipal again. A priest from St. Joseph's also fit Stanley

Kurneta's description. He remembered a young boy, but not well enough to be certain. He'd have to ask a nurse who was with him.

Over the next three days, three more patients died at Municipal, all of them older women, bringing the total to 165.

In Boston, the police commissioner reinstated a police captain who had been the last city official cleared in the Cocoanut Grove case. Prosecutors had charged him with failing to enforce laws with respect to the presence of fire hazards. The club's owner was serving a twelve-to-fifteen-year sentence for manslaughter. While the courts granted another continuance for the five circus fire defendants' criminal cases, Hickey and Healy nursed their inquiries along.

For patients still recuperating in the hospitals, time moved differently. Mildred Cook was still fading in and out. She remembered holding Edward's hand, and then the doctor separating them, taking him away. Vaguely she recalled a doctor coming into the room to tell her something. She knew it would be about the children. "She didn't make it," he said, or was it, "They didn't make it." Maybe it didn't register correctly. She couldn't move. It was dark in the room and then it was bright. Sometimes the hall was loud.

Donald Gale woke up in an oxygen tent, fascinated by the canvas and sectioned plastic panels. Boy, this is neat, he thought; it looks like the inside of an airplane. Outside, inquisitive faces gathered around him. Like Elliott Smith, he'd contracted pneumonia; his parents were afraid he'd die. In the tent, he'd puffed up, grossly bloated with edema—"moon face," the doctors called it. A nurse's aide came in, took one look at him and ran out. He'd been unconscious for three weeks.

The luckier patients were under the care of a dietician, trying to replenish lost protein the body needed to build new tissue. There was no way to do it with regular food; they'd have to eat twenty steaks a day. Mead, Johnson and Company had developed a product called Amigen which did the job, except that it tasted nasty. It came in either a powder or a solution thick as a milkshake, tomato paste red, the taste unsubtly and unsuccessfully disguised with cherry juice concentrate and sometimes a dash of grenadine. Adults couldn't keep it down, and they were serving it to children. The staff couldn't get away fast enough; the kids threw up on their starched uniforms, their nice white shoes.

At Hartford Hospital, because of the rapidly changing techniques of treating burns, doctors asked patients if they would become part of a study. The patients signed forms permitting them to use their data and photograph their scars for publication in medical journals. After what they'd been through—despite what they'd been through—they were glad to do it.

The circus kept working on their image, Herbert DuVal opening a local office on Pearl Street to process claims and hear complaints. Patrons with tickets for Thursday night's show could exchange them here for cash or have their refund added directly to the *Times'* Fire Victims Fund. DuVal also presented the Hartford Chapter of the Red Cross with a check for $10,000, a "small token" of appreciation for all their work.

It was perfect timing. The next night in Sarasota, Friday the 28th, the show performed a full dress rehearsal under the lights. Acts played to just one side of the arena instead of the traditional in-the-round. Three-quarter poles supported the lighting and aerial rigging. The troupe was rusty and tired but good enough.

Having failed to find any more evidence of Raymond Erickson, the policewoman met with Mrs. Erickson one last time. The navy had recalled Raymond Sr. to Gulfport. The officer told Mrs. Erickson that Dr. Weissenborn believed some other family had claimed Raymond. Mrs. Erickson said she didn't want to disturb any of the other parents and that she would be satisfied if the policewoman checked with all the undertakers to see if they had Raymond's clothes. The officer did as she asked, though she knew any clothing would have been removed before the body reached the embalmer's. The net result of her investigation, she wrote, was that though great care was taken in the identification process, some errors had been made. She left the case open. It remains open to this day.

In Sarasota, the circus spent the day at the runs, loading everything to go out on the road again. Sunday morning at 9:00 A.M., the first section left for Akron via the Atlantic Coast line. The flats used to carry the big top, poles and seats stayed behind, cutting the train from seventy-nine to sixty-eight cars. The show traveled in three sections, the second riding light. Canvas and seat personnel shifted to other departments, easing the labor shortage.

They made two feed stops en route, the first early the morning of the 31st in Atlanta, letting the elephants and horses off to dip at the tubs and

tanks.

While the train waited, a reporter collared May Kovar and quizzed her about her heroics.

"If you'd ask me now what I'd do in case of fire," she said, "I'd duck, and quick. But I didn't. I don't know why."

A day later they stopped in Cincinnati, shooting to arrive in Akron August 3rd for a one-day rehearsal at the Rubber Bowl. The show would be the same basic program they last performed the night of July 5th in Hartford, with one notable exception—there would be no clown firehouse.

August–December,

1944

The Blue Heaven Circuit, as the newspapers called it, got off to a bad start in Akron. As they arrived at the runs Wednesday morning, George Smith realized the flats with the wagons were facing the wrong way for unloading. That section had to swing north fifteen miles to another yard at Hudson, Ohio, uncouple the flats and reattach them.

Since the fire, John Ringling North had been sniping from the sidelines, saying he'd told the current administration since the beginning of last year that shortages and war regulations made it foolish if not dangerous to take the show on the road. He questioned the intelligence of going back out now—a position that worried receiver Edward Rogin. The only way to pay the claimants was for the circus to tour and make money. If North took control of the show again, he might let it sit in winter quarters until the war was over. It seemed that Aubrey Haley and Mrs. Edith Ringling—the two halves of the Ladies' Agreement—would honor their debt to the survivors, but North played hardball, and it was clear he didn't consider the fire his business.

Robert Ringling accompanied the show to Akron, riding in his private car. From the empty stands he oversaw the set up with Smith, wearing a pink shirt and making small talk with performers. The Rubber Bowl sat tucked into a hillside by the airport, and workers stood gawking at the parade of planes. The famous Soap Box Derby course ran down the hill. They raised the newly fireproofed sideshow tent by the stadium's main entrance. The layout was strange, and it took them till midnight.

The next day they rehearsed the entire program twice without costumes, the women in bathing suits and shorts, the clowns doing their walkaround without makeup. In the afternoon, while May Kovar was running through her routine, a black panther swiped a paw at her and tore her baggy shorts. She rapped him with her wand and backed him onto his stand. Outside, hundreds of spectators pressed against a wrought iron fence to catch a free peek. The late rehearsal took place under the stars. Satisfied, Robert Ringling sent his troupe to bed around midnight.

In Akron, Robert Ringling sits in the stands for this posed publicity still, surrounded by bally girls in their Changing of the Guard costumes.
PHOTO COURTESY OF THE CIRCUS WORLD MUSEUM

The circus was so intent on doing well the next day, so isolated by their work, they never heard the news—as Hartford did—that Janet Moore Sapolis's grandmother died. Martha Ann Moore was sixty-five and strong enough to overcome her burns, but developed a strep infection in her leg that proved to be both penicillin- and sulfa-resistant. She was victim num-

The afternoon practice, Thursday August 3rd, 1944. In an undershirt, Joseph Walsh puts his mixed group through its paces.
PHOTO COURTESY OF THE CIRCUS WORLD MUSEUM

ber 166. Janet, who wasn't allowed to visit her in the hospital, saw her at her funeral.

That week the Hartford Police and Fire Departments played a benefit baseball game, donating the $3,000 in proceeds to the *Times'* Fund. The papers said little about the circus, content to let the issue rest.

Friday the show went on. Legend is, Emmett Kelly always painted a tear under his left eye after Hartford, or a dot to signify his grief. He would be doing that now, getting ready in the dressing rooms beneath the stands (plush compared to the dressing tent; no more bucket baths!), except that photos from the era show Weary Willie with neither a tear nor a dot. The legend, irresistible to newsmen, was untrue. Kelly was more pragmatic. "We must forget the fire. We must entertain. In wartime, it's more important than ever. It's going to be great in the open air."

It wasn't. Weather for the matinee was threatening, and like any heavy manufacturing center, Akron was busy. On top of that, the Rubber Bowl was seven miles from downtown, the bus line running by it was strictly for defense workers, and the city was in the midst of a polio epidemic. A pathetic crowd of two thousand showed up, seeming even tinier in the vast arena. The airport was distracting, and the band didn't carry well outside. The evening show drew sixty-five hundred, but a sudden downpour spoiled the opening. Later a full moon rose over the Bowl's rim, but the tone was set for the stand. Saturday rain stopped the show twice. They played in a steady drizzle and ended up cutting two numbers. Spectators huddled under sopping newspapers. In the papers the next day, Robert Ringling jokingly announced the show would follow baseball's policy. If they hadn't completed half of their twenty-two displays before the rains came, you got a rain check—not a reassuring proposition.

Next on the schedule was the University of Detroit stadium, a twelve-day run. Opening night was Bond Night, so they sold out. The remainder of the stand, afternoon temperatures hovered around one hundred, and the crowds stayed away. Thirty-five hundred attended one rainy weeknight. For the Saturday matinee only fifteen hundred people showed up. John Ringling North was licking his chops.

While the circus struggled in the Midwest, a hepatitis outbreak swept Municipal Hospital, infecting Elliott Smith just as he'd gotten over his pneumonia. The doctors isolated him again, putting him in a room with

Friday August 4th, 1944. The first show after the fire was an economic and public relations disaster. Only two thousand fans showed for the matinee and suffered through a rain-dampened performance (note the umbrellas in the crowd). The show has just started here; Walsh has both lions and bears in the east cage with him. PHOTO COURTESY OF THE CIRCUS WORLD MUSEUM

The show that evening had more magic to it, but more rain as well. See the three fans in the left foreground huddled under a scrap of cardboard. PHOTO COURTESY OF THE CIRCUS WORLD MUSEUM

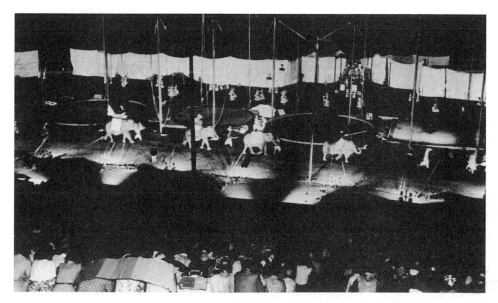

three women similarly afflicted. He received penicillin shots every three hours, the nurses waking him up to swab his skin cold and push the needle in until he'd beaten it. Then the doctors began the long process of skin grafting.

His hand and his back were the worst. The doctors would slice patches of undamaged skin from the fronts of his thighs, paint the burned area with a plasma preparation that would act as a kind of glue, then paste the new skin to it and wrap him again in Vaselined gauze. Elliott couldn't lie on his back, so the doctors rigged a sling to keep him on his hands and knees while it healed. His hand they tented so he wouldn't brush it against anything, the brass clips holding the grafts visible inside. Outside his window, Keney Park was a blaze of green.

Donald Gale was his new roommate. The doctors wanted to remove Donald's fingers and keep just the thumbs; his father said no and brought in a surgeon from Hartford Hospital to save his hands. The surgeon said it was touch and go but that he'd try.

First the surgeon cut away the dead skin from a finger, then amputated it from the first joint, wrapping a flap of skin over the nub, hoping a cover would grow. When it didn't, the doctor did a pedicle graft, slitting Donald's stomach, inserting the damaged hand and grafting the stomach skin to the finger. For eleven days, Donald lay in bed like a mummy. When the doctor cut his hand free, the graft had taken.

Barbara and Mary Kay Smith were split up, Barbara rooming with Marion Dineen. Marion was almost completely better. Her father would come every day, bringing the girls hot-fudge sundaes from the Lincoln Dairy, a pleasant change from the Amigen. When Marion went home, Barbara and Mary Kay were reunited, sharing the room next to Elliott and Donald's with Patty Murphy, whose parents and brother had died in the fire.

By now, only the worst cases remained, a total of seventy among the three hospitals. Across the hall, in a triple with Barbara and Mary Kay's mother, two women who'd lost children passed the days, commiserating. The two became close friends; when they got out they continued to see each other, getting together for lunch or coffee, staying in touch.

Fridays a specialist came down from Boston to change the patients' dressings, a routine the children feared. If the grafts hadn't taken, layers of flesh peeled off with the bandages. The kids screamed and fought so much that soon the doctors took them to surgery and put them under. The ether made Donald Gale nauseous; it felt like falling, spinning in a whirlpool, and afterwards he couldn't eat.

Elliott Smith remembered lying on a gurney like a piece of meat, his new skin open to the air, waiting for the specialist to dab the infected places with a Q-Tip impregnated with silver nitrate. Having withstood this torture, he was rewarded with newly Vaselined bandages. They went on cool and soothing.

A machine called a microtome sliced the skin from his thighs, each piece slightly wider than the burns on his back; they would shrink during the grafting. The scars on Elliott's thighs were almost as bad as the ones on his back. His father volunteered to donate his skin, but medically at the time there was no way to do it.

The idea of a father wanting to take his child's pain upon himself may have struck the doctors as common, but a letter they received shortly after the fire did not. It was from the state prison in Wethersfield, from an inmate. He'd been justly convicted eight years before of a crime he said involved "a person's life." Since then, he'd tried to think of a way to repay his debt to that person by saving another's life. He donated blood every time the Red Cross came, but it didn't seem enough. "Offhand I couldn't specify the exact type of skin I have," he wrote, "but so far as I know I am perfectly healthy, am twenty-six years of age, and am more than willing to offer my skin to any person needing it. I would then feel that I had done something to give new life and new hope. Won't you please consult your files and let me know if there is anyone burned at the circus fire who is in need of a skin graft? I'm sure there must be."

The warden approved the prisoner's letter and sent it on, but, as with Mr. Smith's offer, the doctors sadly had to decline.

Ludger LeVasseur could not save his son from another, even more debilitating pain. For weeks, visiting him, he carried the secret that Jerry's mother was dead. He waited until his son was recovering—safe, in a way— to tell him. They both cried. And then at 8:00, the PA announced the end of visiting hours, and he had to leave him again.

One girl in Hartford Hospital didn't know that both of her parents had died. Her younger sister had learned from their grandparents, "and the way they did it was awful." She wanted their parish priest and a nun from the girl's school to tell her sister.

The hospitals wisely matched patients with similar injuries and family situations as roommates, relying on them to keep each other's morale up. But some things were beyond the powers of empathy or medicine. At night nurses heard children crying and calling out for their parents. One boy asked an aide the same question over and over: How could he get out of the hospital if there was a fire?

Those at home suffered the same anxieties, some more deeply than people who'd been burned. One mother reported that her daughter had a serious mental condition as a result of seeing people trampled, the equivalent of a nervous breakdown. Another girl dreamed of a woman sitting in the bleachers alone, untouched; her clothing wasn't burned, her hair wasn't scorched, but when the dreamer reached out to touch her, she disintegrated into a pile of ashes.

Memories of the fire ate at one girl. She had recurring nightmares of burning babies. When she tried to hide under her bed, her parents dragged her out. Sirens sent her into hysterics. Her family distanced themselves from the fire, rarely mentioning it, a tactic she could never seem to master. She withdrew from the world, developing a stutter and crying in private.

Some parents became wildly overprotective, seeing disaster in the most harmless activities, never letting their children out of their sight. Some parents refused to talk about the fire. The topic was forbidden, especially with friends. Later, people who'd been children at the time of the fire would find themselves doing these exact same things with their kids; they constantly had to guard against it.

One boy had been lost at the circus, his mother knocked to the ground. Later he went to the movies on a humid night, insisting, as always, that he sit on the aisle. In the middle of the film a huge crack of thunder outside sent him running from the theater into the street.

A mother had the same kind of panic attack at the eye doctor. With no warning, in the middle of an examination she jumped up and ran out the door. Her daughter could smell smoke when others couldn't and refused to light their gas stove. Another woman dreamed there was a fire in her room and would wake up and search for it.

As if to prove their fears weren't imaginary, a series of fires swept amusement parks up and down the East Coast. At Whalom Park in Fitchburg, a fire leveled the midway, destroying the Dodgem, the penny arcade and the shooting gallery. Early the morning of August 12th, the boardwalk at Wildwood, New Jersey, went up. That afternoon a blaze practically wiped out Luna Park in Coney Island, the heat so intense the huge swimming pool reportedly boiled. The very next day, flames gutted most of Palisades Park, seven people dying on the Virginia Reel; the fire roared over the bathhouse and two hundred cars in the parking lot, leaving people with no clothes and no way home.

The August issue of *Fire Engineering* magazine speculated that overheated spotlights just under the canvas may have started the circus fire—an old theory by this time—but also listed two new blazes: in Baltimore the baseball stadium, Oriole Park, and in Detroit, the racetrack at the State Fairgrounds.

In Hartford, a West Hartford girl died at St. Francis, following her mother and younger sister. On July 25th, while hospitalized, she'd turned seventeen. She'd survived trampling and fourth-degree burns only to weaken from shock and sepsis after skin grafting, finally succumbing to congestive heart failure. She was the last to die from the circus fire, number 167.

The next day, responding to Mayor Mortensen's recommendation, Municipal Hospital announced it would waive all charges for fire victims, unless patients requested a bill, and then they would only be asked for a flat $6 a day. Hartford Hospital followed Municipal's lead, giving the Red Cross credit for providing nursing services at no cost.

That same day, a Hartford detective arrived at Deer Lodge Prison to interview the warden and the prisoner. The inmate was doing time for passing bad paper; he'd completed the seventh grade, was a model prisoner, and subject to epileptic fits. He'd joined the circus in September of 1943, working as a helper on a water truck for Deacon Blanchfield. Cox drove a water truck. In Detroit Blanchfield fired him for being drunk, then rehired him the next stand in Chicago; later they repeated the same act in Nashville and Indianapolis. It was after Nashville, after a couple of beers, that Cox supposedly told the inmate, "So help me God, they're going to pay for this. One of these days I'm going to burn the goddamn tent down. Wait and see. The goddamn show won't get very far next year."

The detective tried to mix the prisoner up, but he stuck to his story, and the warden believed he was telling the truth. The inmate didn't seem to want anything; he was being released in a few weeks.

The detective had two leads to pursue: Cox had worked for Rubin and Cherry Shows as a Ferris wheel operator and had a married sister in Nashville. Hickey sent the detective after the carnival first. He caught up with them in Billings, at the State Fair. The show had changed hands and personnel since Cox had been with them, and no one could remember him.

The circus was in Chicago, drawing disappointing crowds to Soldier Field. The detective talked with Haley, who told him their records were in Sarasota.

"I'm glad Mr. Hickey is finally getting around to see us," he said. "We could do a lot to help if he'd talk with us." The fires at Luna and then Palisades Park made Haley suspect a pyromaniac might be on the loose. Old-timers with the show felt the Hartford blaze was arson.

Blanchfield said he didn't remember any Cox but that he had two drivers on a water truck he regularly fired and rehired on account of drunkenness, always keeping one with the rig. One of these men had been in Waterbury this year [June 19th or 20th] bothering him for a job. He'd heard the man had also been on the lot in Providence. One of the men was named Walsh or Welsh; maybe the other was Cox.

Another man was also a possibility—Blanchfield's ex-assistant, who left the show in Philadelphia after an argument with Blanchfield. The man was a native of Hartford.

The detective conferred with Hickey over the phone that night. Hickey told him to deliver this message to Haley: "We are investigating this case from every angle, and it is immaterial to us who did it or who is involved. We will report it to the court. We are making a thorough investigation."

The next day Blanchfield had the name of the driver who accosted him in Waterbury. The other's name was Emmet Welch, driver of water truck #128, fired repeatedly for drunkenness, with a married sister in Nashville. Haley seemed pleased that they finally had a suspect; he asked the detective to let the FBI know and questioned him about the state police's methods. The detective assured him—like Hickey—that they would follow the case wherever it led them.

In Nashville, he found Welch's sister's husband. The sister was visiting friends in Williamsburg, Virginia, but the man referred him to another sister who said the family rarely heard from Welch, but that six months ago he'd been in Miami, his address care of General Delivery. The woman described her brother as a tramp who, as far as she knew, didn't work and was no good to anyone. The most recent picture she had of him was at least ten years old. A local bank told the detective that the man had gone bankrupt in 1929 and his credit was no good.

Amazingly, the detective turned up an old friend of Welch. He said Welch had made his home in Miami for about ten years now, and that he was okay when he was sober, but not too good when he was drunk. The detective tried Williamsburg next, but the sister couldn't come up with an address for Welch. When the detective returned to Connecticut, Hickey sent a telegram to the Miami Police.

In days they picked up Welch for skipping out on a hotel bill. He'd just come off a ten-day drunk. They kept him in jail till the detective could get down there and question him. Welch admitted that he'd been with the circus and that he'd known the inmate, but denied ever having been arrested for arson. In 1943, before he joined the circus, he'd been living in a boarding house and dropped a cigarette in his room, starting a fire that caused some damage, but the police had never questioned him about it. He was driving a city bus for Miami Transit now, and had been since June.

It was true. The company had time sheets to prove Welch had been at the wheel July 6th. After all of their legwork, the state's best suspect turned out to be a dead end.

Labor Day, more than forty patients still lingered on the wards, none of them critical. Dr. Burgdorf at the Board of Health released his final figures: 487 people had been injured, but only 140 required hospitalization. (In the future, the number of injured would commonly be quoted as 655— the incorrect total of the dead included—and sometimes as high as 1,000.) Burgdorf broke down the dead statistically. Of the 167, just 10 were men between the ages of fifteen and sixty. The small number was not due to their ability to escape more easily, but to the fact that, as the show was a matinee, most of them were at work.

As school started, teachers made up their seating charts, the gaps from last year apparent. In Wethersfield, one had to explain to her puzzled first-graders: "Judy's not coming back to school again." Thomas Barber and Ed Lowe were relying on some teacher out there noticing an empty seat and letting them know. But none did.

For one girl, school became a stage to tell her story of the fire and show off her scar. Don Cook took the opposite tack, withdrawing from his playmates, not talking about what happened.

In the North End, students traditionally went from Brackett to Northeast and then to Weaver High. Everyone knew someone who'd been in the fire. In gym, burns were a common sight, unremarked upon, understood.

One girl's family saw a father-and-daughter team of dentists. The father took care of the parents, his daughter the children. She kept an album with pictures of all of her patients. The children would go downtown to J. J. Newberry and use the photo stall, smiling hard; the daughter picked the best one of the strip. After the fire, these dentists helped identify the dead by their charts. In the album, the daughter drew a border around their pictures and a tasteful notation giving their age. "It was sad to see those smiling faces," the girl recalled, "and also to realize it could have been me too."

A tutor schooled the children left in Municipal Hospital, but the age difference between the youngest and oldest was so broad that the job was impossible. The kids gave her a hard time. No one did their homework; they were too busy getting better.

Once the doctors got Donald Gale's hands started, they grafted skin from his legs onto his arms. When the new skin took, it welted and raised up, turned fibrous and tough, shrinking so it tugged at the untouched skin. The doctors bombarded the patches with X-rays, smoothed lanolin on the grafts to soften them, and still the skin cracked and bled, pulled drum-tight.

Both Mrs. Smiths went home in September. Between grafts, Barbara Smith read a lot—the whole series featuring nurse Cherry Ames. Her classmates from St. John's sent cards and letters; her pastor sent a big doll; people she didn't even know sent fudge.

Elliott Smith had established a bond with his nurse, Becky Beckshaw. "She was my guardian angel, she could get me to do things that the others couldn't. She just had that knack of cajoling a child to eat, to take the shots and drink the potions."

His father played a game with him. Elliott closed his eyes and Mr. Smith rolled his wheelchair through the winding hallways, into and off elevators, to some far corner of the hospital. Then Elliott had to guide them back to his room.

The doctors splinted Donald Gale's hands to flat paddles, wiring his fingers to evenly spaced brads so they'd remain separate. Donald learned to use his feet. His father dropped coins on the floor; Donald could keep everything he picked up. Soon he could manipulate a wheelchair; Municipal still had the old-fashioned kind with the big wheels in the front. He and Elliott Smith staged races in the hallways, both of them pushing the spokes with their feet. Occasionally a door unexpectedly swung open in their path and they crashed, sending a nurse's tray clattering, both of them tearing out of there.

The staff let them roam around the other departments. Donald Gale's favorite place to hide was the lab downstairs, watching the old men play cards. The elevator operator let him work the switch. He went up to the polio ward and visited.

Elliott, Donald, Barbara, Mary Kay and Patty Murphy formed a core. Together they made it through the painful Friday sessions and choked down the Amigen and hid from mean Mrs. Amari. They played a game in which they lowered the shade and turned the lights out in the room; one person sat on the bed while the others tried to creep up on them in the dark. The person on the bed threw things—pillows, wadded paper towels. Donald once whipped a blackboard eraser and hit Mary Kay square on a graft and tore the skin. The doctors threatened to suspend the game entirely, and didn't only after the children promised to use softer objects.

The mayor visited, and people from the National Red Cross. They had assemblies in the cafeteria—a clown act, a three-piece band. The nurses took them out on the roof overlooking Keney Park and let them color.

Mostly it was boring. Elliott and Donald couldn't use their hands, so cards and board games were out. They even needed help reading. Donald's father came every day and read Edgar Rice Burroughs to him, slogging through the entire Tarzan series. Like William Dineen, he brought a daily treat—milkshakes. When Donald got sick of them, he switched to sundaes, until Donald got sick of them too. It was no fun being in the hospital, but then, as his hands slowly healed and he progressed through his exercises—

squeezing rubber balls, touching his thumb to his pinkie, his index finger, his middle finger—he began to worry about what it would be like on the outside.

Like Jerry LeVasseur at Hartford, they'd been bedridden so long they had to learn how to walk again, and they hadn't been around other children for months. Their parents and the staff couldn't help but pamper them. The world, they feared, would not be as kind.

The circus had discovered much the same thing. Chicago had been a disaster, with rainouts and skimpy crowds. One night show under threatening skies drew only fourteen hundred to massive Soldier Field. During a matinee, a veteran clown had finished the walkaround with his fox terrier—the dog jumped through a door in the front of the clown's barrel-like costume, then leapt out the rear—and was walking to the backyard when he dropped dead of a heart attack. The doctor tried to revive him, but there was nothing he could do. High on their 135-foot platform, fliers Victoria and Torrence watched the scene below, then answered their cue.

Haley felt it was hopeless. The heat didn't quit; in Toledo it was over a hundred. They were losing money on a daily basis. They'd gone out without enough lead time for their publicity, so there were no advance sales, no guarantees. It was his opinion they should fold up and go home.

The rest of the Midwest was better, as temperatures cooled, as was Texas. Karl Wallenda was upbeat: "The awful fire has called up in all of us the spirit of the circus trouper." Originally they'd planned on staying out until November, but the front office, heeding Haley, decided not to do the deep South. Citing the heavy college football schedule, they canceled their last three weeks, finishing in the rain and mud at New Orleans's Pelican Stadium on October 8th. For the whole open air tour, the show managed to turn a profit of just $100,000.

On the legal front, Rogin, Schatz and Weinstein cobbled together a draft of an arbitration agreement for claimants to sign. A panel of hand-picked arbitrators would set the amount of the awards, the receiver then paying the claimants. Survivors would have until July 6, 1945, to file. If the lawyers could produce one hundred signatures from claimants involved in death cases, the court would enforce the agreement. Rogin himself vowed not to accept a penny until all claimants were paid in full—a position he would come to rue.

Mayor Mortensen's board of inquiry reported their findings in November. There was practically no communication between different city departments, it said. While critical of the manner in which its government operated, the report—mostly by omission—implicitly absolved the city itself of any true wrongdoing. The board recommended setting up a coordinating authority between all departments and adopting a standard safety and health code then under preparation in Washington. For the short term, it urged that the building, police and fire departments adopt stopgap measures concerning temporary public structures.

For Thanksgiving, Elliott Smith's doctors let him go home. Just overnight; the next day he'd have to come back. After being in a huge institution for so long, he found his house tiny and confining, the rooms airless, the ceilings lowering over him. He went out in the backyard and walked around by himself, kicking through the leaves. At supper the family said a prayer.

The next week, police supervised workmen as they removed the ruins from the circus lot. All that fall, cops had stood on guard night after frosty night, protecting the grounds from ghoulish souvenir hunters. Days ago Chief Hallissey had pulled those officers back to first shift. Now they watched for any stray effects or human remains. "Nothing of any note was found."

At the end of the day, the workmen piled all the loose wood in a bonfire. A flame rose up and gave color to the gray light. They stood around it with their gloves off, warming their hands, watching the sparks corkscrew into the winter sky.

Christmas Eve, all the Municipal children had gone home except Donald Gale and Patty Murphy. Around the city, parents who'd lost sons and daughters prepared to celebrate the day.

At Northwood Cemetery, Thomas Barber and Ed Lowe laid a bouquet of flowers at the grave of 1565, both of them squatting on their haunches by the numbered stake. If it had been their daughter, they would have wanted someone to remember her. They were surprised they were the only ones there.

1945

Once the press got ahold of Barber and Lowe's visit to Northwood, the story shot across the wires. Interest in the case revived. Papers across the country published not only the morgue picture but artists' sketches of an idealized, living 1565. Leads poured into Hartford, and Barber and Lowe chased them down. Not one panned out.

People wrote to them with baroque theories. Her mother was killed in the fire—at precisely the same time her father died fighting in Europe. She was the illegitimate daughter of some prominent family. She was actually a midget. It was all right; her face was out there now. Surely someone would come forward.

In mid-January, the city passed all the stopgap legislation recommended by the mayor's panel. Days later, Commissioner Hickey finalized his official report. Like Mortensen's board, he found the coordination between departments deplorable, but as state fire marshal he also concentrated on the origin of the fire and the charges pending against the six show folks.

He set the stage, noting the grass fires and lack of inspection, then repeated in full the officer's tale of the man informing him that "that dirty son of a bitch just threw a cigarette butt." Beyond the obvious problems of the inflammable canvas and the animal chutes, Hickey blamed the accused individually for contributing to the circumstances that led to the catastrophe. Blanchfield's drivers were untrained and unprepared. Versteeg never distributed the extinguishers. Aylesworth noticed them missing but did nothing, then the next day took off for Springfield, leaving no one in charge. Smith knew and approved of Aylesworth leaving. Caley and Cook abandoned their posts.

As for the origin, Hickey quoted one usher as if he were a forensic expert: "I couldn't see what caused it; the only logical thing would have been a cigarette or throwing the match down without putting it out. A cigarette would have smoked for a while, but this came all of a sudden and it evi-

dently was a match." He cited the Portland and Providence fires, saying
there had been a dozen pinhole fires so far that season. He could find no
evidence of arson and no plausible suspects after the bus driver Welch. "All
information reported from various sources relevant to this inquiry, concerning discharged and/or disgruntled circus employees, was fully investigated with the assistance of local and state police officers within and
beyond the borders of Connecticut."

Therefore, Hickey concluded: "I find this fire originated on the
ground in the southwest end of the main tent back of the blue bleachers
about fifty feet south of the main entrance and was so caused by the carelessness of an unidentified smoker and patron who threw a lighted cigarette
to the ground from the blue bleachers stand." He backed this up with pho-
tographic evidence—shots of the jacks behind the men's room. "It indicates
this ground fire at the point described above burned the immediate grass
area, the wooden supports for the blue bleachers structure, the sidewall canvas upward, then the tent top."

Hickey felt satisfied that the fire did not start in the men's room,
though he never explained his position. Likewise, he quoted but then ig-
nored testimony like the usher's (and a New York fire chief's) that favored
a lit match over a smoldering cigarette.

The results of Healy's inquest were nearly identical, except the coroner named a different seatman and not John Cook derelict in his duties. He
also found that Blanchfield allowed his wagons to block the exits.

Neither report charged James Haley with any specific act of criminal
negligence. Tacitly, as the ranking member of the circus on the lot that day,
he was held liable for the actions of his employees and the policies of the
corporation.

For Mayor Mortensen, the case boiled down not to law but moral
obligation. That it was not his administration's fault never crossed his
mind. Like George W. Smith, he could have made changes, assigned re-
sponsibilities. He hadn't. He recalled: "One woman who lost her daughter
called me up every night for almost a year afterwards and she would review
the thing so often, but I never dared to tell her that I couldn't take any more
of her calls."

Meanwhile, Edward Rogin had been busy keeping up his end: 451
survivors had signed the arbitration agreement, 105 representing death

cases, putting it into effect. In early February, the board heard their first case, the estate of William Curlee.

The maximum accidental death benefit in Connecticut was $15,000. In the eyes of the board, few of the dead were worth it. They came up with a formula to determine the correct figure of each individual settlement. The *Courant* explained: "The life expectancy of the victim was figured according to regular mortality tables. Next, his financial condition and earning power were examined. And in the case of women, matters of education and social responsibility, such as her assistance to her husband in business, for example, were given an economic value. In the case of children, a more arbitrary basis was employed, with a minimum, for children 3 to 7 years old, set at $6,500."

Not only was this formula patently absurd and insulting, it was calculated almost as if to minimize the circus' liability. There were few men of working age who died in the fire; the victims were overwhelmingly women and children. Bill Curlee's widow would receive the full $15,000, since he was young, healthy, educated and well employed, while the estate of Lithuanian tobacco worker Charles Tomalonis would collect only $6,650. Children almost always brought $6,500, some—like Billy Dineen—slightly more for hospital or funeral expenses. Likewise, the elderly went cheap; being both aged and female, sixty-nine-year-old Margaret Garrison's life was worth only $5,000, seventy-five-year-old Mary Bergin's $4,000.

The awards included the missing and presumed dead. John Cleary accepted $9,000 for Grace Fifield's estate, Judy Norris' estate the standard $6,500, Raymond Erickson's the same. Mildred Cook got $7,000 for Eleanor and $6,500 for Edward, compared to $30,000 for her own burns.

The board reserved the larger awards for the severely injured. Former dancer Katherine Martin of West Hartford received the largest, $100,000, with Patty Murphy right behind her at $90,000, Jerry LeVasseur at $80,000, and Donald Gale at $75,000. All four were still in the hospital.

The hearing process ate up months, the last death claims to be arbitrated Maurice and Muriel Goff's—the only African Americans confirmed to have died in the fire. The settlements themselves took the circus years to pay off.

As the arbitration hearings dragged on, the criminal trial began. Each of the six defendants faced ten counts of involuntary manslaughter. The lawyers for the circus threw their clients on the mercy of the court, pleading nolo contendere. Show people of the time spoke of a gentlemen's agreement, balancing the freedom of the accused against the willingness of the circus to bear complete liability for the fire. It may have seemed a fair trade. The city, co-defendant in so many of the civil suits resolved under the arbitration agreement, would not pay a single penny.

State's Attorney Alcorn, who prosecuted the case, had obviously not heard of the deal. Neither had the judge. The defense said they'd entered a no-contest plea not because they expected dismissal but because a long trial would keep these key men from preparing the circus for the start of the season. Whatever the reasoning behind the tactic, it backfired. After hearing the evidence, the judge found all six guilty and fined the show $10,000 for the hazard of the tent. He sentenced Blanchfield to six months in jail, Caley and Versteeg to one year, then gave Haley one to five years and Smith and Aylesworth two to seven in the state prison. The court granted a stay of execution until April 6th so the accused could get the show on the road. Only Caley declined the stay, choosing to begin his time right away.

The sentences stunned the men, and a good part of Hartford. The issue of criminal negligence had never been clear to the public; many still believed Robert Ringling's original claim that the circus had wanted to fireproof the big top but couldn't without military priority. The fire was an accident, letters to the editor cried; it was unfair to punish the circus for it. Two men who had lost their wives and children in the fire wrote to the *Times*, asking why the city, being equally guilty, wasn't held equally accountable.

In all the commotion, as if admitting the city's culpability, Mayor Mortensen announced that he'd accepted Chief Hallissey's resignation. Privately, the mayor offered him a sweet deal to move on, and Hallissey was smart enough to take it. In a move that surprised no one, Mortensen named Deputy Chief Michael Godfrey as his replacement.

"The show will go on," Robert Ringling declared, but, groping for any leverage he could get, said the prison terms could endanger their moneymaking ability. As the Florida state house debated a formal letter expressing their concern, two ex-governors made a public plea for the judge to overturn the convictions. Circus attorneys filed a motion to withdraw the nolo contendere plea, saying it had been a hasty and ill-considered measure only meant to save that year's show—for the benefit of the claimants, they implied. The motion also disputed the Portland and Providence fires, and the dozen fires on the sidewall; first, there was no official record of them, and second, the pinholes were not technically fires at all. It was here that the attorneys for the first time brought up three other fires—one each in Portland, Providence and Philadelphia, and all in either straw or grass, none of which threatened any tents.

The judge agreed to listen to arguments before executing sentence—not on the fire itself (since the new information seemed off the point and unverifiable) but on the nolo plea and whether the convicted men were truly irreplaceable. His decision brought Robert Ringling and John Ringling North to the stand, the two enemies once again facing off with the future of the circus at stake. To make the drama even sweeter, that week the show was opening in Madison Square Garden. With their men looking at jail time, Sarasota chose a route that skipped not just Hartford but Connecticut altogether, breaking a fifty-year-old tradition.

There would have been no place to play anyway. The same week, with little fanfare, the city turned the Barbour Street lot over to the War Garden Committee. A Parks Department tractor plowed the grounds, adding another one hundred plots to the forty-five behind the snow fence. A spokesman for the garden committee described the soil as excellent for raising vegetables.

As the trial reconvened, Robert Ringling testified that imprisonment of the five would affect the show's ongoing management. It "would not be impossible but would be desperately jeopardized." Circus historians believe that Robert didn't come on strong enough here, and paid for it later. Rather than fight for Haley, he merely said of his vice president, "He was a great help to me." The only passion he showed came the morning of his cousin's testimony. In the hall outside the courtroom a deputy sheriff attempted to serve him with papers naming him a co-defendant in several suits stemming from the fire. Robert dashed the papers to the marble floor and stalked away.

John Ringling North could not be lukewarm. He swore he'd warned the show not to go out last year, and that he was contemplating a suit against the present executives for mismanagement. None of the accused were irreplaceable, he claimed, and went on to name able seconds for each of them—Arthur Concello for George Smith, William Curtis for Leonard Aylesworth. Not only that, but Robert Ringling himself had assured North that the circus would tour regardless of what happened in Hartford. The defense attacked North, hoping to paint him as unfriendly to Robert's administration. North deftly took their argument away by flatly admitting that he was, and that it was hardly a secret. When asked if he had wanted to "wash out" the claims of the survivors by putting the circus into bankruptcy, North denied it, conceding only that, as one of the vested directors of the show, he'd voted against the arbitration agreement, finding it unsatisfactory on several counts.

After hearing the accused themselves, the judge reduced the sentences of Haley, Smith and Aylesworth to a year and a day minimum, five years maximum. Under this arrangement, they'd be eligible for parole in eight to ten months. Blanchfield, who testified that he was not indispensable to the circus, impressed the judge so much that he revoked his sentence altogether. Once again, he suspended the sentences of Smith and Aylesworth, this time till June 7th, so they could return to Sarasota and prepare the canvas setup before the show opened under the new Hooper Fire Chiefed big top in Washington, D.C. Haley and Versteeg started their sentences the next day, reporting to Wethersfield State Prison.

Two days later, Monday noon, the circus delighted New York with an old-fashioned mile-long street parade through Times Square, complete with elephants and plumed Percherons drawing the classic Five Graces wagon, menagerie cages and fantastic floats from the season's new spec, *Alice in Circus Wonderland*. Ostensibly in support of the Seventh War

Mugshot of inmate James A. Haley.
PHOTO COURTESY OF THE CONNECTICUT DEPARTMENT OF CORRECTIONS AND THE CONNECTICUT STATE LIBRARY

Loan, the parade effectively erased the general public's memory of the fire, showing the troupers' can-do spirit and celebrating the allies' imminent victory in Europe. It was just the first of many publicity stunts that season designed to engender goodwill; the next involved a special morning show at the Garden for fifteen thousand blind and disabled children—"a must performance," Karl Wallenda piously informed reporters.

In Mansfield Center, near the University of Connecticut, one survivor honored his wife by planting a tree in her memory on Arbor Day. Another couple had a different kind of reminder—a daughter, born exactly nine months after the fire. "I guess my mother was happy my dad was alive."

Of the children in Municipal Hospital, only Patty Murphy remained. One doctor remembered her vividly. "She was a cute little redhead with curls. She reminded me of Shirley Temple, she was a little doll. She had nobody but her grandparents and an aunt and uncle. She was in the hospital for many months. There was a custody battle to see who would get the child. I used to take her out occasionally to see a movie. Her hands were all scarred. She had burns on her face and chest. I don't know whatever happened to her."

On April 22nd, more than nine months after the fire, Patty Murphy left the hospital to live with her aunt and uncle in Plainville. A boy remembered her walking down Henry Street for exercise, the scars on her legs pink.

In New York, the circus was having an excellent opening run until the evening show of May 9th. Above the center ring, Victoria and Torrence were finishing their spinning act, descending from the peak of the rigging. Frank Torrence hung from a rope above him by one hand while Victoria lay horizontally across his spread feet—her head pillowed on one, her ankles clasping the other. In front of a crowd of ten thousand, Victoria slipped and fell seventy-five feet to the sawdust, spinning half over and landing on her face. Merle Evans cued the band, bringing on the next act. An ambulance rushed Victoria to a nearby hospital, but her head and chest were crushed. She never regained consciousness. The accident served as a reminder of last year's tragedy, exactly what the circus didn't need. The circus chaplain came down from Boston to do the service. No one talked about Hartford—it was taboo—but everyone thought it.

Decoration Day, Northwood was busy, the Parks Department plant-

Hartford Police Detectives Thomas Barber (left) and Ed Lowe (right)
visit the grave of Little Miss 1565, Decoration Day, 1945. PHOTO COURTESY
OF JUDITH LOWE

ing flags on all the graves. Thomas Barber and Ed Lowe came out to make
sure the six unidentified weren't forgotten, bringing flowers again for Little
Miss 1565.

A few days later the circus opened under canvas in Washington, D.C.,
the local fire marshal performing a burn test on the canvas first with a candle and then a match. Inside the menagerie tent, he climbed atop a cage
wagon to check the roof. It passed too.

A more stringent test was that of public opinion. The circus aced it
with the help of General George Marshall, recently victorious chief of staff
in the European theater. Like Eisenhower, Marshall had the reputation of
being a cautious, hardworking leader. The circus invited him to be their
guest, and he accepted, showing up in full uniform with his grandson. A
picture of Emmett Kelly shaking the boy's hand as he sat on his grandfather's lap made papers across the country.

Mugshots of inmates George W. Smith (left) and Leonard Aylesworth (below).
PHOTOS COURTESY OF THE
CONNECTICUT DEPARTMENT OF
CORRECTIONS AND THE
CONNECTICUT STATE LIBRARY

Quietly, two days later, George Smith and Leonard Aylesworth entered Wethersfield State Prison.

In Hartford, no one had forgotten. As the school year ended and temperatures rose, residents naturally cast back to last July. The anniversary was also the deadline for any claims against the circus. In the last weeks, Edward Rogin processed dozens. The injuries weren't always physical. Julius Schatz's clients included a child with a "morbid fear of fire and noises caused by oil burner at home"; and women with "psychoneuroses due to psychic trauma, insomnia, nightmares, spells of melancholy, fear of crowds and closed places, spells of panic, much pain, suffering and mental anguish and a severe traumatic shock to her nervous system all of which are permanent in nature"; "fainting spells"; "headaches, dizziness"; and one woman whom the fire rendered "hysterical, panicky, tearful and insomnic so that her confinement was necessary to Norwich State Hospital."

Another, more positive legacy of the fire was the Aetna Ambulance Service. When the co-owners of the Aetna Florists came back from the navy they both had first-aid certificates. They purchased a used ambulance from a Manchester undertaker and started their own company. Fifty-five years later it was still serving Wethersfield, Rocky Hill and Newington.

July 6, 1945, Thomas Barber and Ed Lowe visited 1565 a third time, laying a bouquet of flowers on her grave. A *Courant* photographer accompanied them. The photo of the two detectives ran on the front page, along with a joint statement. "Somebody, somewhere, must have cared enough for that little girl to take her to see the circus. In her own neighborhood, there must have been playmates, milkmen, grocery clerks, mailmen and adults who noticed that some little girl was missing from their everyday lives. It just doesn't seem possible that a child like that little one could disappear from her own small world without somebody noticing that she had gone and never come back." They'd checked with the families of the six unidentifieds, but had come up with nothing. For the sake of completeness, they named the missing and gave the descriptions of the unidentified, in case some reader had information.

The response was immediate. The wire services ran with the story, eliciting letters from across the country, some including money for more flowers. One memorial company in New Jersey offered to carve 1565 a proper headstone. When Ed Lowe went out to the grave a few days later and found the flowers and flags they'd left had been stolen, he and Barber and Godfrey put together a committee to decide how best to permanently commemorate all six. Eventually three Hartford companies as well as the New Jersey firm donated uniform markers.

Each wanted their stone to be Little Miss 1565's, so the committee came up with a fair way of choosing which it would be—in the process devising a ceremony to promote their cause. They would line up the six on the ground and a girl the same age who'd survived the fire would circle them three times, holding a white rose, then select 1565's by placing the rose on the stone.

Patty Murphy was the obvious choice to do it—the right age and the last to go home, and also a darling of the public like 1565. Apparently her aunt and uncle had no qualms with the ceremony, because in mid-August she charmed everyone with her curls, her white dress and her corsage of sweet peas, curtseying to lay the flower on a marker. The photographers blasted away at her.

In prison, James Haley received a parade of visitors. Edward Rogin re-

August 1945. Patty Murphy selects the stone that will mark Little Miss 1565's grave. PHOTO BY THE *HARTFORD COURANT,* COURTESY OF JUDITH LOWE

lied on the vice president to keep him informed—to teach him, really, the money side of the circus. Mayor Mortensen went out of courtesy. Haley pulled work detail on the Enfield Prison Farm, bending his back as he hadn't in years, his fingernails packed with dirt. If he expected Robert Ringling to stop in and thank him for taking the rap, he was disappointed. His brother-in-law never even wrote him a letter.

Ever scheming, John Ringling North attempted to visit him. Haley refused at first, then relented, meeting North in the warden's office. The two discovered they had much in common, and much to offer the other, regardless of their differences.

William Caley, having begun his sentence immediately, earned parole first, in September. He hadn't planned on rejoining the show, but the front office thought it was important—so important that they dispatched him by train and then tracked his progress by telegram all the way from Hartford to Chicago to Dallas, where they were playing.

Days after he signed on, a twister hit the big top during a matinee. In the stampede for the exits, patrons knocked Fred Bradna to the ground, badly fracturing his hip. At seventy-four, the equestrian director wasn't coming back. He'd ruled the show for so long with his whistle and perfect posture that the rest of the season seemed strange, missing a key ingredient. They closed November 3rd in Charlotte, the same day workmen installed a large slab at Northwood for the six nameless victims. Beneath a carved wreath, the inscription read:

THIS PLOT OF GROUND
CONSECRATED BY THE
CITY OF HARTFORD AS
A RESTING PLACE
FOR THREE ADULTS AND
THREE CHILDREN WHO
LOST THEIR LIVES IN
THE CIRCUS FIRE
JULY 6 1944

THEIR IDENTITY
KNOWN BUT TO GOD

Just before Thanksgiving, newly reelected Governor Baldwin remembered the fire in a different manner. In a ceremony at the State Capitol he awarded Donald Anderson the Connecticut Medal for Distinguished Civilian War Service. Without his quick thinking, the citation read, the death toll would have been much worse.

But as a reminder of the fire, no day in 1945 approached Christmas Eve. That morning, James Haley left prison after serving eight months; that afternoon, Thomas Barber and Ed Lowe kept their vigil at Northwood Cemetery; and late that night, as a final, inescapable echo of last year's disaster, a fire tore through the Niles Street Convalescent Home, killing nineteen senior citizens. If the rest of the country had forgotten, Hartford still remembered.

1946–1950

All five men who served time for the fire went right back to work for the circus—out of loyalty or perhaps a lack of options. A grand homecoming banquet greeted James Haley on his return to Sarasota, but at that point nothing could have placated him. He'd lost weight in prison, and lost patience with his position in the show. No one had looked out for his interests, or those of his wife, and he let Robert and Edith Ringling and the circus attorneys know it in no uncertain terms. Among themselves, they decided that his months in Wethersfield had affected him, and that in time he would return to the reasonable man they knew.

In April, Haley arrived at the annual stockholders' meeting without Aubrey, who was supposedly sick. Though Edith voted her shares for Robert as president, Haley broke the Ladies' Agreement and voted his wife's shares for himself, and for John Ringling North as vice president. Victorious, Haley and North didn't wait around to discuss the legality of the matter; they got up and walked out of the room.

As the show opened in Madison Square Garden, both factions made an appearance. Edith and Robert had challenged the election in the Delaware courts, but the wheels of justice turned slowly; it would be another full year before the judge ruled. Till then, they had to stand on the sidelines and watch Haley and North operate.

Again, the route purposely skipped Connecticut. The state had passed such stringent fire laws governing tent shows that other circuses also stayed away. The only show that regularly played the city of Hartford in those years was the Shrine circus. While well attended, and for a worthy cause, their appearances made some people queasy, for good reason. They played in the State Armory.

The Barbour Street grounds underwent another change. Now that the war was over, returning soldiers needed a place to live. The mayor's Emergency Housing Commission approved a plan to move empty barracks from Bradley Field to the lot and subdivide them into ninety-six single-

John Ringling North (left) and James Haley became unlikely allies after the fire. Here they confer in 1947, a slippery year for the big show's ownership. PHOTO COURTESY OF AP/WIDE WORLD PHOTOS

family apartments. By the second anniversary of the fire, the city had laid out two intersecting streets ending at a cul-de-sac back by Sponzo's property. Carpenters banged away inside the wooden shells. For protection, the city installed three fire hydrants, one where the front door of the big top had been, another near the bandstand.

North End residents considered the Barbour Street Veterans' Housing Project sacrilegious, in bad taste. When the workmen were driving the foundation piles, a neighborhood woman served them sausage-and-pepper grinders for lunch and listened to them talk about the things they found. "Every time I went by," Thomas Barber's daughter Gloria Vieth said, "I'd think, how can they live there? They said the odor was there for a long time—the odor of smoke." Stories went around that the place was haunted, that the city couldn't keep their tenants because of the unearthly screaming; eventually, people said, so many of them left that the project was a ghost town, and they tore it down. This may be a legend in itself. The project was always meant to be temporary, there only until builders could meet demand, which they soon did.

The second anniversary also brought the first major lead in the case

of Little Miss 1565. The *Courant* ran the morgue photo, along with a cap-
sule of facts. After reading a wire story on Barber and Lowe, a Michigan
woman thought the description of the girl matched her granddaughter. The
woman's daughter had divorced the girl's father. She was a wanderer, and
the two had last been heard of four years ago in South Bend. The girl would
have been six at the time of the fire.

Though Lowe doubted "very seriously" that this was her, he provided
the grandmother with the photo. A comparison with an early picture of the
girl convinced the woman. Her two sisters agreed; they were all positive she
was Little Miss 1565.

The identification meant that either 2109 or 4512, both adult
women, was probably the woman's daughter. Her mother would have to locate her latest dental charts; the last dentist to work on her in Michigan had
moved to another state and for some unknown reason had discarded her
records.

The *Detroit Times* story that broke the news said, "The Hartford detectives are certain that is the answer to the mystery," an assertion Barber
vehemently denied. He also seriously doubted the woman's story. Chief
Godfrey backed him up, saying 1565 was in all probability from the
Central Connecticut area, her family mistakenly claiming the wrong body
and leaving her at the armory.

In Portland, Oregon, the girl's mother read the story about herself in
the newspaper and immediately wrote her mother a letter. She and the girl
were fine.

The woman from Michigan chalked it up to an honest mistake, and
it was true, the two pictures were an uncanny match. Lacking forensic evidence, the identification probably would not have gone through, but she
still would have been satisfied. This was even better. "If the story had never
run in the papers," she said, "I might never have heard from my daughter
and granddaughter." The case remained open.

The circus had burned down over two years ago. WTIC's Fire
Prevention campaign kept the issue in the public eye. A reporter who'd
been on the grounds that day chaired the effort. The station sponsored a
poster contest for area schoolchildren, with savings bonds as prizes. Bill-
boards along the shore reminded beachgoers that FIRE TAKES NO HOLIDAY
and asked, HAS YOUR CIGARETTE CAUSED A FIRE LATELY?

But much of the circus fire's true legacy was private. Well after they'd left Municipal, Barbara and Mary Kay Smith regularly returned to Hartford Hospital for X-ray treatment to stop keloid tissue growth. Barbara's grafts grew so rigid she couldn't bend her arms. She had to travel to Mass General, where doctors broke the tissue at her wrists, grafting more skin from her stomach, legs and rear to form pliable joints. It worked, yet she still walked with her arms oddly bent.

Their mother took the deaths of the Norrises hard. She passed the empty hours sewing the girls long-sleeved dresses, though no one stared at them. As time passed, they wouldn't wear the dresses anymore. The kids at St. John's treated them just the same.

Donald Gale wasn't so lucky. The doctors took the bandages off his hands, but he couldn't do much. Now he had to wear shoes, so his feet, with which he'd learned to manipulate objects, were useless too. His parents had to dress him. He returned to the hospital often for therapy, and did his exercises at home, but at school he was an instant freak, an outsider. He couldn't do anything to risk hurting his hands, and turned into an easy mark, the other kids beating him up. At Mayberry Village, his mother came outside to find other boys sitting on top of Donald. She chased them home, scolding their mothers as well. Eventually, Donald's parents took some of the settlement money and moved him from public school to Suffield Academy, where he discovered a godsend—soccer. The school was all boys, which was easier. He was self-conscious, and it would be a long time before girls would even associate with him.

Jerry LeVasseur wore a hat to cover the burns on his head. The other kids made fun of him, and Jerry ended up getting into fights and into trouble. He spent several summers at Presbyterian Medical Center in New York where the doctors fixed his left hand so he could grip objects. The settlement money covered the bills. While he was recuperating, a nurse there took him under her wing, easing him through therapy. By the end, they were playing tennis. Back at school, Jerry rediscovered baseball, wearing his glove on his right hand and taking it off to throw.

Elliott Smith's mother wore a full wig to hide her bald spot. Monthly Elliott went back for X-ray treatments like Barbara and Mary Kay's. He was frail, and the kids in the neighborhood treated him more gently than before. His family spoiled him rotten. One thing that bothered him was being put on display. Relatives asked to see his scars, and he had to bear their curiosity in the fern-shaped grafts on his back. The other kids didn't care much; once when Elliott was wearing a bathing suit, another boy said his back looked like a checkerboard—but not cruelly, just a good-natured observation, and taken that way. He didn't have any nightmares.

Many did. Eleven-year-old Sarah Goodwin Austin had been at the fire and seen horrible things. "I learned so much that day. I learned that people die. That they stink when they die. That they can be burned up. That they can kill each other to survive." She'd seen people clawing each other, and the sight never left her. In '46 her father, A. Everett "Chick" Austin, then director of the Wadsworth Atheneum, became the curator of the John and Mable Ringling Museum of Art in Sarasota. The owners of the circus regularly entertained the family. "He loved the circus," Sarah Austin said of her father. "Neither of my parents was able to understand what I had been through. I always felt set apart from them."

And then there were the parents of the dead, the wives and husbands and brothers. Mildred Cook went home to Southampton to recuperate, staying with Emily Gill and her daughter Carolyn Moon. She had only limited motion of her arms, and Carolyn had to help her get dressed in the morning. As she recovered, work became her salvation. She would work as hard as she could all day so she could sleep at night. Eleanor was still officially missing. Whenever Mildred and Emily left the house empty, they set a note on the kitchen counter telling Eleanor where they were. Just in case.

On the legal side, the change in circus leadership only increased the resentment between the corporation and its receiver. A circus attorney wrote to James Haley of Schatz and Rogin so far not discussing payment for their services, "I think they are beginning to lick their chops in anticipation of fat fees and expenses."

For his part, Rogin was tied up with literally hundreds of cases and their residual duties. The money attracted all kinds of people not related to the case, and Rogin found himself taking care of his claimants' personal finances. One man's creditors applied directly to the receiver for permission to garnishee his settlement to pay his bills. The arbitrators had awarded the man over $40,000 for the deaths of his wife and three children. Rogin told the creditors to get the money themselves.

A rougher battle engulfed the estate of Patty Murphy and her younger brother. The uncle they were living with died, and the court awarded custody of the children to another aunt and uncle. Even before their guardian died, their grandparents the Coughlans had challenged the original placement, taking the case to superior court. Now they instituted a new suit. The Murphys were Catholic and the Coughlans Protestant. Between them, Patty and her brother had received over $120,000 for her injuries and the deaths of their parents and their other brother. The case and its associated appeals would go back and forth for more than two years.

Meanwhile the circus made their first payment to the claimants, nearly a million dollars, exactly 25 percent of the total judgments. The second came in January of 1947, almost $1.5 million, or 37.5 percent. The show had done well under Haley and North, playing more dates and making more money than ever before.

The city government had been busy as well. They approved the city-manager concept, making communication between departments a priority, and established a formal civil service system. Cities around the country adopted Hartford's thorough new fire codes.

One survivor took his family to New York during the show's opening stand at Madison Square Garden. He hadn't planned on going; it was just a coincidence they were in town. He didn't have tickets, but since the fire he'd kept their stubs from July 6th in his wallet. The clerk at the box office said the show was sold out. The man produced his stubs. "Think these will get us in?" The clerk got on the phone. Minutes later, John Ringling North was escorting the family to his private box.

That same week, Katherine Martin, who'd received the largest settlement for her burns, gave birth to a daughter. Mrs. Martin was a tiny woman. She'd barely made it over the northeast chute and had been burned over most of her body. Her back still carried the thumbprints of the man who carried her to the circus bus and rode to Municipal with her, holding her up so her raw skin didn't touch anything. At first she couldn't move her arms, couldn't stand up, couldn't walk. It took her months until she could comb her hair and feed herself. She'd been facing another painful grafting operation when she told her surgeon she was going to have a baby. "That's the kind of miracle we need," he said. Pregnancy naturally stretched the tissues; she wouldn't need the operation. They did a caesarean. The baby was healthy and perfect, and the mother healed easily. The Miracle Lady, the papers called her.

As the circus opened under canvas, the Delaware courts supported Edith Ringling's claim that Haley had illegally broken the Ladies' Agreement. The presidency reverted once again to Robert Ringling. Two weeks later, Haley and North staged another power play and took control again, with Haley as president.

Never robust, Robert Ringling's health failed that summer. He suffered a bad stroke, and couldn't pursue his mother's interests as he had for the last five years. It appeared Haley and North had won.

But the new president and his vice president did not get along. They quarreled on basic management issues, and, though technically subordinate, North would not give in to the less-experienced Haley. After prison, Haley trusted no one but himself. He was the president, and his wife controlled more of the show than North. They would do things his way.

While Haley ran the show, North worked the other members of the board. He'd just won an old dereliction of duty suit against Robert for five million dollars. He parlayed this into a compromise with his former enemy, offering to drop his litigation. By October he replaced Haley as president, giving Robert the mostly honorary roles of executive vice president and chairman of the board. The Haleys, understanding they'd been skunked, sold off their shares and quit the business. North now controlled 51 percent of the corporation. After six long years, the circus was his again.

North was a showman in the style of Barnum, bold, abrasive and shameless when it came to the bottom line. From now until the final payment of the arbitration settlement, the relationship between receiver Edward Rogin and the circus would be difficult at best.

A week after taking control, North announced that he intended to bring the big show back to Hartford in '48. It made great press. Chief Godfrey welcomed the idea, saying the new laws were in place for just such a reason. The citizens of Hartford were nowhere near as understanding. Despite new and ingenious seat wagons with fixed steel chairs, too many people remembered the fire.

One widower wrote to the *Times* that families who'd also lost loved ones in the fire had asked him to protest. "We absolutely do not want the circus here. We want no billboard signs or advertisements of our tragedies."

A mother who'd lost a daughter seconded his opinion: "It would be unnecessarily painful for myself and others like myself who lost two or more [to] see the day that the circus returns here."

Editorials were mixed. Eventually, they reasoned, the circus would have to come back. When would the proper time be?

As if to soften up the opposition, the show delivered its third payment against claims, 10 percent, in late April. At that point, North said he was still hoping to find a lot in Hartford for the big top—maybe Colt's Meadows, where they'd set up in the early thirties. The circus was ready to comply with all the new laws. They were already scheduled for Bridgeport, Waterbury, and New London. They'd have to deal with Commissioner Hickey anyway.

In the end, they didn't come back to Hartford. They'd tested the waters though, and when a circus fan from Plainville said he had a lot they could use anytime, they accepted his offer. June 17th the show rolled into the smallest town the big top ever played. Patty Murphy begged her aunt and uncle to take her to the matinee, which they did reluctantly. The show was sold out, and she had a fine time.

In the fall, James Haley ran for and won a seat in the Florida house of representatives. Earlier, the same house had passed a special bill restoring his civil rights, even though his felony conviction came from another state.

All this time, Thomas Barber and Ed Lowe had been going to Northwood. Three times a year they made the trek, carrying magnolias and carnations and sprays of pine branches at Christmas, the stories in the paper growing smaller and smaller until they disappeared altogether. The wire services no longer picked them up. They were stale—old news.

In '49 the circus returned to Plainville, playing just the one day. It was becoming a tradition. Maybe they'd try Hartford next year, people speculated. John Ringling North said nothing; like any good showman, he left them guessing.

That year the show paid two installments of 5 percent each through Edward Rogin. He also helped them negotiate the dramatic rights for Cecil B. De Mille's *The Greatest Show on Earth,* which began shooting that winter in Sarasota. While the circus was occupied with Hollywood, in Miami, Gargantua the gorilla died of pneumonia complicated by a kidney disorder and rotted wisdom teeth. Show folks called him a trouper to the end; he'd gutted it out until the season was over. Even in death Gargantua remained an attraction. Henry Ringling North donated his bones to the Peabody Museum at his alma mater, Yale, and the picture of his reassembled skeleton ran worldwide.

Right after Christmas, May Kovar—now May Kovar Schafer—was rehearsing at a wild animal farm in California. She'd left Ringling and gone out on her own, but things hadn't panned out. She was developing a lion act, hoping it would solve her money troubles. Her three children were there, tagging after her on a slow day.

She stepped into the cage with her wand. Outside, her grown son slid a steel door open to let the first lion in. Sultan, his name was. It had been raining for three days, and he'd been locked up in his cage, missing his regular exercise.

He rushed May Kovar. He charged and knocked her to the ground with his paws, then closed his teeth around her throat and dragged her to a corner of the cage.

May's son ran in with his sister and beat at the lion with sticks, but couldn't get him away from his prey. Another trainer rushed over from the elephant barn with a pitchfork and an iron pipe. He speared the lion, and as it turned on him, bashed it between the eyes with the pipe. Sultan tipped back on his hind legs, stunned long enough for them to drag May Kovar out of the cage. It was too late. Her neck was broken, probably from the first blow. She died right there.

"I'd like to get out of this business," her son said, "but what can we do? This is all we know."

The day after New Year's, Robert Ringling collapsed of a massive stroke and died. He was fifty-two. Julius Schatz praised him for his help in securing the arbitration agreement. His obituary listed him as both the head of the show and an opera singer, but one line told the whole story: "His close associates said he never cared much for circus life." He was survived by his mother.

1950

In April, Officer George Sanford approached Julius Schatz and said his 8mm film was available. He wondered if the circus would be interested in purchasing it. Schatz wrote to John Ringling North and received a reply from his brother Henry. "We would be interested in getting these pictures of the fire, providing we were getting the original negative and not the prints."

Whether the deal went through, no one knows, but the film has never been seen again.

That month, near Columbus, Ohio, the state arson bureau picked up a young man named William Graham in connection with a fire at a local grain elevator. Graham admitted setting it. During questioning, police learned that a friend of his, Robert Dale Segee, had told Graham he once set a fire in Maine. Two weeks later, they arrested a cousin of Graham for another fire; after getting a confession from him, investigators decided to find out more about Segee. They talked to Segee's parents in Columbus, who told them he'd been with the circus at the time of the Hartford fire. Police spoke to Graham again, at the Circleville jail; this time Graham implicated Segee in several alley fires there.

Armed with extradition papers, the Ohio State Police arrested Segee in East St. Louis, Illinois, and brought him back to Columbus. On May 18th, Segee confessed to setting fires in Circleville and Columbus, and in Portland and Old Town, Maine.

"He stated that he was with the Ringling Brothers Circus June [sic] 6, 1944, when they had a large fire at Hartford, Conn. He stated that his starting of numerous fires was caused by his seeing a burning man which he called the 'Red Man' and the Red Man would tell him to start fires and that if he did not start fires he would himself be burned and that the first appearance of the Red Man was immediately prior to the Hartford, Conn., fire while he was with the Ringling Brothers Circus. He stated that the first recollection at the Hartford fire was that he was awakened and came to himself and he was then at a tent near the place where the horses were kept but that the only thing he remembered prior thereto was seeing the Red Man and seeing a man strike a match and set the wall tent on fire at a point where the tent had been soaked in oil to make it waterproof; that the flames shot on up to the large tent to the top of the big top. He stated that it could be that actually what he saw was himself starting the fire or it could have been a dream and the first appearance of the Red Man. He stated that after he had been awakened he recalled helping to get people out of the big tent."

Segee next confessed to a fire at a Columbus hotel which he started in a clothes hamper and a wastebasket in a broom closet—much like the unremarked-upon fire at the Aetna building in Hartford while the circus was barred from leaving town.

The following day, investigators drove Segee around Circleville so he could identify the buildings he claimed to have set on fire. He pointed out three barns and garages; the police verified the specific fires and provided dates. They charged Segee with arson, attempted arson and malicious de-

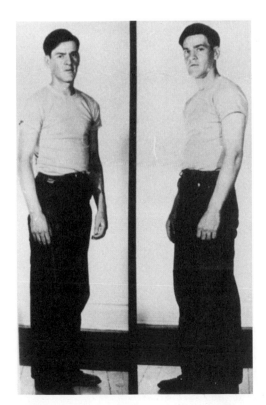

Robert Dale Segee upon his arrest in Ohio, 1950. PHOTO COURTESY OF THE *HARTFORD COURANT*

struction of property. He pleaded guilty to all three. They held him for psychiatric evaluation.

Segee was only twenty, meaning he'd been fourteen at the time of the fire. There was some question whether he could have actually worked with the circus at that age.

As the story broke in Ohio, a reporter for the United Press called Commissioner Hickey to let him know. So far Segee hadn't actually admitted setting the Hartford fire, but Ohio fire marshal Harry Callan had told the reporter he thought they would "have a good story by the first of the week."

Hickey got on the phone to Ohio, trying to find out whether he should send a man. One of Callan's deputies said the probe wasn't far enough along to justify that, and that they had no hard evidence that Segee was with the show. If anything developed, the deputy assured Hickey, Callan himself would call him.

The next day Segee's face was in the papers, and the story had added details. The Red Man turned out to be the logo of the National Board of Fire Underwriters—a flaming Indian astride a fiery horse. The board called him "The Fifth Horseman." Segee's mind would go blank; when he came to, he'd find the fire already blazing. Though Haley's defense attorney said this was vindication and that show folks had always held that the fire was set, articles quoted Hickey as not "getting excited" about the case. "They haven't enough on the suspect at present with regard to the circus fire here." He cited Segee's age at the time of the fire and said he had no plans to send any investigators to Ohio.

Later that morning, Ohio authorities said they were convinced that Segee had been with the circus. He'd been called "Little Bob." Segee said he'd been asleep just before the fire, and when the Red Man woke him up from his blackout, the tent was in flames. He slashed the canvas to let a man escape, then tried to rescue another. "As I drug, his arms came out of his socket. I guess it turned my stomach." Like the runaway Roy Tuttle, Robert passed out. He suffered burns on his hands.

Hickey sent two investigators the next day, secretly. While they were en route, Segee kept talking and the arson bureau kept feeding releases to the press. Now Segee believed he *had* set the circus fire, but couldn't be sure. He had blank spots. "We've gone as far as we can with him," one interrogator said. "Psychiatrists will have to work out on him now and I think we'll get the Hartford case cleared up."

A Ringling spokesman traveling with the show doubted Segee worked for them when he was fourteen and said they didn't have employee records going back that far. But a subsequent check with circus attorneys in New York determined Segee had been telling the truth. He'd signed on June 30th in Portland with Whitey Versteeg's light crew and been dismissed July 13th in Hartford.

In Columbus, Ohio officials brushed off Hickey's men. They weren't allowed to speak to Segee, his relatives or William Graham. One of Hickey's men pumped local investigators for information, finding out that the night before the fire Segee had allegedly dropped a cluster of spotlights, breaking them, and Versteeg slapped his face and cut his pay. Segee and Graham, they said, were "for quite some time sexual perverts, in effect, 'sweethearts.'"

A psychologist at University Hospital began his examination of the suspect, asking that no one else question him. The process would take at least three days, possibly as many as ten.

Hickey's men again tried to get interviews with the principals in the case. Failing, they spoke to the members of the arson bureau who'd talked with Segee's relatives. His sister mentioned that as an infant Robert had had a severe case of undulant fever, followed by rheumatic fever as a child, and sunstroke. He'd been confined to bed for a year. At present, she believed her brother was mentally unbalanced.

One of the investigators said that when he was driving Segee from the psychologist's office back to jail, Segee asked what Connecticut authorities would do if he admitted to setting the circus fire. Members of the arson bureau were unanimous in their opinion of the suspect, the men reported to Hickey; based on their investigation, they thought "that Segee was definitely a pervert, a 'psycho,' and a pyromaniac."

With Segee under the direction of the psychologist, Hickey's men could have no contact with him. They asked Callan's office to send them a copy of the examination when it was done, then packed their bags and snuck out of town.

The psychologist tried to gain Segee's trust, saying that by discovering why he set fires, they might prevent other boys from making the same mistakes. The doctor also assured him that since most of his crimes had been committed while he was a juvenile, there was little chance of adult punishment. Without concrete proof, any confession he made—"even if true"— would not be grounds for conviction. "As a result," the doctor wrote, "Robert was completely co-operative, at least to the 18 yr. or about age. From that time on we can only give him credit for using his intelligence, although he did plead guilty to the Circleville fires."

Robert Segee confessed not only to more than twenty fires, including the circus fire, but also to four murders, the first occurring when he was only nine years old. On a riverbank in Portsmouth, New Hampshire, he'd beaten a neighbor girl to death with a rock. In Portland, he strangled a night watchman when the man caught him setting fire to a warehouse on the docks. At Cape Cottage, Maine, he'd strangled a boy on the beach. And in Japan, less than a year ago, while in the army, he strangled a Japanese boy who called him "chop-chop-chimble," or damn cocksucker.

Ohio sent an investigator to Portland to check up on his story. He found a rash of fires around the Segees' many different homes, and placed Robert's family in Portsmouth at the time of the girl's murder. In 1943, a warehouse two blocks from the Portland waterfront burned; in the basement firemen found the body of the janitor. But police in Cape Cottage had no record of any unsolved murder. And while Segee said the army had court-martialed him for killing the Japanese boy, and that was why he'd been discharged early, no one ultimately verified this.

Meanwhile, the psychologist was fitting together a neat Freudian puzzle of Segee's early life. Robert's father, according to Segee, had punished him for masturbating by beating him and burning his fingers with a match. His hostility toward his father forced him to identify with his mother, and Robert took on a more feminine role. "It has been noted that feminine boys are more addicted to sex stimulation than are normal boys," the psychologist wrote (he would make a point later of stating that he was not a psychiatrist). "It is as if both male and female glandular tissue were demanding satisfaction." Segee's later fires, the doctor discovered, all followed unsatisfying hetero sex. The suspect said he wanted to burn away any bad memories.

The doctor also wanted to tie Robert's firesetting to malnutrition, a pet theory of his. He said he never rated Robert's intelligence, since it had no bearing on his behavior, though on two I.Q. tests in 1943 Segee scored a 78 and a borderline 60.

As if Segee's father supposedly burning his fingers for masturbation wasn't striking enough, the doctor posited an "undiscovered traumatic event" that lurked in Robert, waiting for a "trigger event" to release his repressed fury—probably the neighborhood girl calling him names. Everyone called Robert names—"Dopey" and "Dummy"; he hated it.

The psychologist believed Robert Segee. He considered him capable of the crimes to which he'd confessed, consistent with the circumstantial evidence of proximity and opportunity unearthed by investigators. He recommended the suspect be held at Lima State Hospital for further observation, and treatment, if possible.

In Portland, one of Hickey's men followed the trail left by the Ohio inspector. He found Segee's old neighborhood and interviewed people who said the whole family was "queer" and "funny-acting" and "crazy." After the circus fire, Robert had come home with a burned hand and gone around telling stories about how he'd slept with the daughter of one of the show's owners. He also said he'd beat up a man who was stealing money from the dead.

The Segees' neighbors in Dover, New Hampshire, were of a similar opinion, considering the entire family to be mental defectives—as the police chief put it, "half wits right down through." A doctor who knew them professionally said they were morons of the lowest type and didn't consider their word worth much.

The two investigations went on separately, with little consideration or cooperation between the two states. Occasionally Maine—out of some New England kinship, perhaps—leaked documents or accounts of the Ohio investigation to Connecticut, but more often Hickey found out his information from the morning papers. In early June he sent a telegram to Callan officially requesting any statements by Segee concerning the circus fire. It had been ten days since his men had been denied permission to interview the prisoner. Once the psychologist finished his exam, Hickey would appreciate a copy of the results.

Callan called Hickey two days later and assured him that Segee was still incommunicado, with the psychologist. Then where were the papers getting their information, Hickey wanted to know. Callan blamed the

Circleville authorities. Hickey again pressed Callan to provide any and all information on Segee with regard to the circus fire; Callan promised that he would.

Two weeks later, Hickey got his first look at Segee's initial statement—now almost a month old—not from Callan, but slipped to him by Maine.

Meanwhile, Ohio was taking formal statements from Segee's family. His sister knew of Robert setting two fires when he was five or six years old, but none after that. He kept to himself. He and their father didn't get along. She did remember that when they were living in Portsmouth, Robert had witnessed a little girl who'd been raped being pulled from the river. She also thought that the army had given him an honorable medical discharge.

Segee's mother cried through her interview. His father was always very mean to Robert, and the boy was sensitive. He spent most of his time in his room, staring into space, biting his fingernails. She knew there was something wrong with him, but, a mother, she didn't want to admit it. His dreams were so bad he hated going to sleep; he'd wake up sobbing and tell her he didn't want to die. As for the army discharge, Mrs. Segee said Robert felt bad about that; he didn't know what they'd let him out for. She seemed bewildered by it all. "I never knew that Robert had anything to do with any fires and never realized that Robert was responsible for as many fires as he has been responsible for. I feel that possibly his father's treatment in his early life and all through his life has had a lot to do with his condition; also the general treatment by the schoolteachers and other children, including his brothers and sisters."

Segee himself was making pencil and crayon drawings for the psychologist—the red horse and a fiery demon with fangs and flames coming from his head. This was the Red Man Robert dreamed about. "I want to burn again," ordered the demon. A series of pictures showed Robert killing the girl and strangling the other three victims—the two boys kneeling before him. One drawing of a woman's face remarkably like his own on a wall of flames represented "a dream," "like a voice at the circus fire"—the victim telling Segee, "You are the cause of that." Another series showed Robert as an Indian in a sunlit, mountainous land, menaced by a flying eagle.

Of the horse and the Red Man, Robert explained: "The fire would burst up in front of me and it would change into this flaming horse and a man would appear either afterwards or slightly before I saw the red horse. They would come after I would light a match. It would please me for a split second and then they would frighten me and I would run away. The horse and the man would run after me. I never knew how far they chased me. I would generally end up at home but by the time I got there the fiery horse would be gone. He was running but his hoofs wouldn't be touching the ground. The man would be running like any other man but his feet wouldn't be touching the ground. I was afraid he was going to burn me. I was afraid the horse was going to eat me up."

The flaming horse that came to Robert Segee in his dreams. PHOTO COURTESY OF THE *HARTFORD COURANT*

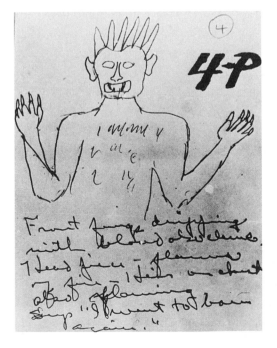

The fiery demon that haunted Robert Segee. "I want to burn again," he said. PHOTO COURTESY OF THE *HARTFORD COURANT*

When he discussed his dreams and his inner life, Segee could supply vivid details, but when investigators questioned him about things that happened, he turned vague.

> *Q.* How about this fire on Market Street?
> *A.* That sounds familiar.
> *Q.* How about the Portland Lumber Company?
> *A.* Yep, it was right down along the pier.
> *Q.* No, it wasn't down along the pier. It was on Hanover Street and started on Friday night or rather early Saturday morning.
> *A.* I remember two or three lumberyards around Portland.

Rather than make Segee provide them with details, his interrogators showed him news clippings of fires, then asked if he recognized them as his work. Beyond this obvious prompting, Segee seemed to acquiesce to any suggestion. He confessed to both the Portland and the Providence circus fires. Of the Portland fire, he said, "It's a sort of a blank in my mind, everything was hazy. I can just remember striking a match." The Providence fire he also set during a blackout. He said the fire was "on the flap of a tent but I don't remember where," echoing newspaper accounts of the time, whereas Hickey's investigation—the notes of which were still sealed—placed the large pinhole on the sidewall. Segee said plainclothes detectives questioned him after both incidents, yet neither fire had prompted any investigation.

His references to Hartford were even less convincing.

> *Q.* The big fire at the circus, how did you set it?
> *A.* I could have set it any number of ways. They had the tents covered with gasoline and oil to keep the rain off. Even the slightest bit of fire would take hold of it very quickly. I don't know why I set it.

His testimony established again and again that Segee did understand what his questioners wanted to hear. He even came to use the psychologist's terms, providing a convenient, knee-jerk trigger for his behavior by saying that he had "unsatisfactory" sexual relations immediately before each fire. In later sessions he referred to this as "the pattern." ". . . that just came about under the same pattern." "I know it followed under the pattern." As the questioning went on, the investigators' coaching grew intrusive. At times Segee didn't give the answers they wanted, so they stopped and continued off the record; when they came back, Segee's answer had changed, now fitting in perfectly.

At the very end, fire marshal Callan asked Segee if he had anything else he wanted to tell them.

"I just have silly dreams," Segee answered.

In Hartford, Commissioner Hickey first heard of Segee's newest confessions from Maine's state fire marshal. Ohio had called them. Callan never got back to Hickey as promised. Three days later, another detective from Maine let Connecticut investigators know the Associated Press had details of the confession, including the circus fire and all four murders.

The news broke nationwide that day, June 30th, backed by releases from Callan's office and the Circleville prosecutor. While Callan's statement laid out the facts, "other sources" filled in Segee's psychological background, paraphrasing the doctor's report. The *Columbus Dispatch* even published one of Segee's drawings—an Indian in full headdress.

Hickey flipped. In his own press release he blasted Callan for purposely freezing the state out of the investigation, failing, in his words, "to render us the ordinary courtesies of interstate cooperation."

Callan responded by finally shipping him the thirty-three page investigation report special delivery. It arrived July 3rd. The 4th, Hickey said, "We have not found anything any different from what we already knew. Until such time as we can further study and investigate the stories Segee has told, there is no corroborative evidence to indicate the truth of his statements."

Hickey's investigation seemed limited to the new information, and functioned solely to confirm or deny the stories, treating Segee as an isolated case. If the commissioner ever tied Segee to red-chested Harry Lakin's suspicious behavior at Municipal Hospital (the Portland man from the light gang crying and telling the Red Cross volunteer that he didn't think it was going to be like this and that he didn't know if he could take it but he wasn't going to squeal) or Blanchfield's men from Portland who quit at noon the day of the fire, he left no record of it. Similarly, he never checked exactly·what job Segee did with the spotlights.

In Columbus, Callan made a show of ripping Circleville officials for leaking information from the report, but clearly not to placate Hickey. "It is up to the communities in other states to obtain details of Segee's confession of crimes other than the Circleville fires. Now everybody's got the information." So far, Callan said, none of the New England states where Segee confessed crimes nor officials in Hartford had contacted Ohio officials—a flat-out lie. "I am perfectly satisfied Segee is responsible for the fires. I wouldn't want to say whether or not we could prove it in court."

But a *Courant* reporter who got through to Segee found a different story. Of his crimes, he said, "A lot of them have been talked into me until I actually believe I done 'em, but now I doubt whether I done half the stuff. Things I was certain of before, I'm not so certain of anymore." He was personable, smiling and shaking reporters' hands. "My life has been full of bad thoughts, bad breaks and bad dreams," he said. "When you got a bunch of brothers who call you dopey all your life, you'd understand a little bit. Actually I never had a happy day in my life." At his hearing he pleaded guilty on two counts of arson; the court committed him to Lima State Hospital for a sixty-day observation.

July 5th, Hickey called and caught Callan, hammering him for the leaks and for not giving Connecticut a crack at speaking with Segee. Callan weakly blamed the Circleville prosecutor.

"You have been offering me those excuses since the thing broke six weeks ago," Hickey said.

"I'm not offering anybody any excuses. I don't have to."

"Well, you are still offering them."

"No, I don't, I don't have to offer any."

"Well, I'm sorry then that you don't have to, because you are still doing it."

"Well, I'm not doing it."

"You're doing it," Hickey said, "and I'm surprised to get such treatment from anybody in the country."

"I don't think you were very courteous when you come out with a press release and then tell me if it wasn't for the press release you wouldn't have gotten a report."

"Well, that's the answer, brother," Hickey said. "I stand on what I say and I'm not afraid of it."

Relations between the two departments never thawed. From here on in, Hickey relied on Maine to provide him with information. No Connecticut authority ever spoke with the prisoner.

In mid-July *Life* magazine printed a story on Segee, complete with his drawings and Spencer Torell's shot of the big top in flames. THE STRANGE CASE OF THE CIRCUS ARSONIST, the headline read, convicting Segee in print just as they had Lemandris Ford. They also published his drawings of three of the killings, leaving out only the now discredited Cape Cottage murder.

Segee stayed at Lima State Hospital into the fall on a sixty-day extension. In late October, inside sources said that doctors would find him legally sane. On Halloween, they did.

The new doctor's diagnosis was perfectly consistent with the original one's Freudian approach. "It is the examiner's opinion that this case represents an acute obsessive compulsive neurosis in which sexual relationships call up the conflicts regarding the Oedipus situation and an acute regression into anal sadistic behavior occurs. The only other possibility is that the sexual act is not in itself completely satisfactory unless fire is also involved in which there is a partial sexualization of fire which brings it closer to a perversion, making it classifiable as an impulse neurosis.

"DIAGNOSIS: Obsessive compulsive neurosis: not psychotic, psychopathic, nor mentally deficient."

The new doctor's findings freed the court to sentence Segee. Asked if he had anything to say before the judge ruled, Segee said, "I have never been in trouble before and ask the court to be lenient." He received two terms of two-to-twenty years in Mansfield Reformatory, to run consecutively—the absolute maximum under Ohio law.

After the hearing, the new doctor told reporters that he believed Segee guilty of some of the crimes, based on answers the suspect gave while under the influence of sodium amytal, a so-called truth serum. In late July, after being injected and asked about the circus fire, Segee "became highly emotional. Then he kept crying, 'I didn't kill anybody, I didn't kill anybody.' He kept going back to talk of the terrible dreams he had. It was always in the course of his dreams that he saw the fiery horse which obsessed him. He would call, 'Fiery horse, don't come after me!' over and over."

When questioned about his early life, Segee had showed fear, crying, "Dad, don't beat me! Don't beat me!"

The doctor described Segee's reactions as those of a confused, bewildered person, the suspect finding it difficult to distinguish dreams from reality—this coming from a man who'd just judged him sane.

Hickey said that Connecticut would take no action against Robert Segee. Neither Maine nor New Hampshire charged him either. Hickey gathered all the information he had on the matter and turned it over to the state's attorney, adding a note that Segee's age made this a case for the juvenile court.

Later that month, two Ohio state troopers questioned Segee about an unsolved murder in Scituate, Massachusetts, thinking this might be the Cape Cottage case. Segee said he'd never spent any time in Massachusetts. Segee then stated "that he at no time set a fire, nor has he ever killed anyone.

"During the conversation Segee stated that all the fires and homicides he is accused of committing came about as a result of his telling about his startling dreams and vivid imagination. All the publicity given Segee's case was based upon his dreams rather than on the actual facts told."

Segee told the troopers that he'd been downtown watching the movie *The Four Feathers* with two companions from the light gang when the circus burned. They returned to the grounds by trolley to find the lot roped off. Whitey Versteeg ordered them to wait until a plainclothes officer questioned them, then after they testified, they were released.

None of this rings true. *The Four Feathers* was released in 1939 and was not playing in Hartford that day (though, a story of a young man wrongfully branded a coward, it's an interesting choice of alibi); there were no trolleys in Hartford in 1944; and among the thousands of pages of testimony, there is no record of Segee's or any of his companions' statements.

The troopers spoke with Segee's parents and aunt again. The family said that for years he'd had dreams bordering on hallucinations. They doubted seriously that he'd set any fires or committed a single violent crime. While the dead girl had lived just a few blocks from them in Portsmouth, the night of her murder the aunt had been baby-sitting the Segee children. Robert was asleep in his bed.

As with everything associated with Robert Segee's confessions, little seemed to fit. It didn't matter. He was in jail, and he would stay in jail. The murders were never proven or disproven, and in the case of the Japanese boy and the Cape Cottage killing, never verified. In 1951, Ohio would deny Segee parole. He ended up serving every day of his four years. In 1954, the psychiatrist at Mansfield Reformatory found Robert Segee to be psychotic, declaring him a paranoid schizophrenic and committing him to the Lima State Hospital for the Criminally Insane.

1950–1990

In November of 1950, Edith Ringling suffered a crippling stroke. In December, John Ringling North signed the last settlement check over to Edward Rogin, making the final price tag for the fire just under $4 million. Despite the bitter infighting between the circus and the receiver, together they had honorably paid off all claims. The claimants, by submitting to arbitration in the first place, had shown themselves not to be greedy. Rogin himself fondly recalled one injured woman who wanted only the price of her ticket.

As the decade began, television swept America, cutting into movie attendance and nearly wiping out live entertainment. Now people stayed home weekday nights. In '51, the show played Plainville again, but attendance was down and there was almost no outcry. The state's defense industries were suffering, and the circus, like the fire, seemed to belong to the past. The big railroad shows were dying, and people knew it.

A sudden nostalgic interest built, shored up by books like Fred Bradna's *The Big Top* and J. Y. Henderson's *Circus Doctor*. In '52, *The Greatest Show on Earth* hit the big screen. It grossed over $20 million—at that time the second biggest box office in history, behind *Gone With the Wind*—and won the Academy Award for Best Picture. The show received over $1 million in royalties—money they desperately needed.

Now that all the claimants had been paid, Edward Rogin applied for his receiver's fee. He asked for $175,000. The circus refused to pay him. Like any good lawyer, he took them to court. Among the facts that came out of the proceedings was Rogin sending Pinkertons after the circus when he suspected the show of underreporting their daily gate receipts (it proved to be true). While Rogin's receivership had been incredibly successful, the court needed better documentation of his work, and in the end awarded him only $60,000. He appealed to the court of errors—and lost.

In another long-standing case, the Coughlans of Bristol won custody of Patty Murphy and her brother. Mr. Coughlan would die just one year later.

The circus grounds changed once again. On Hampton Street, the city broke ground for Stowe Village, a sprawling housing project, part of which encroached on John Sponzo's old property. Within months of its opening, the same ghost stories made the rounds, except now instead of flimsy barracks the spirits of dead children wandered the halls and stairwells of brick lowrises.

In January of 1952, the fund set up to provide flowers for Little Miss 1565's grave ran dry. After a notice in the paper, Thomas Barber received a ten-dollar check from an inmate in the Massachusetts State Penitentiary known as "The Phantom Burglar." Rightfully shamed, the Allied Florists Association of Greater Hartford stepped in and pledged to supply flowers for her in perpetuity.

In November, Democrat James Haley ran for the U.S. Congress and won, representing a newly formed district in Sarasota. His constituents would reelect him to the House eleven consecutive times. In stark contrast to his tenure with the Ringlings, he never lost an election.

Also that year, Barbour Street's John Stewart, who'd discovered in himself an unsuspected courage and urge to help people that day, joined the Hartford Fire Department. One day he would be chief.

Commissioner Edward J. Hickey died in the fall of 1953, with Adolph Pastore and Hugh Alcorn at his bedside. Thousands attended his funeral. The police blocked the streets off. During his career, he'd championed the use of such innovations as radar and helicopters. His obituary didn't mention the circus fire.

As if the two had been mysteriously linked, Edith Ringling died the very next day in Sarasota. Edward Rogin credited her with the success of the receivership, saying she was always on the side of the claimants "when other interests in the circus were opposing us. She was a great woman and a great humanitarian."

Also that fall, Barbara Smith finished her nursing courses at St. Francis, earning her cap. She applied for a job at Municipal Hospital (now called McCook) and got it.

In the summer of '54, just short of the fire's tenth anniversary, the courts awarded Julius Schatz $100,000 for his services as receiver's counsel. Schatz had worked closely with John Ringling North; both exuberant, difficult men, they took an immediate liking to each other. Quiet, steady

Edward Rogin could not help but see the judgment as a slight. Schatz had made himself out as a major player when Rogin had been the one stuck with the daily chores of the receivership. The resulting bitterness between the two men poisoned their lifelong friendship.

Patty Murphy finished her freshman year at Bristol High. An honor student, she belonged to the Junior Red Cross, edited the freshman page of the school paper, and sang in the glee club. She was a typical teenager, her grandmother said. The burns hadn't restricted her at all.

Elliott Smith worked the tobacco fields that summer before heading off to Syracuse in the fall. He planned to major in chemistry. His parents had nurtured his settlement money; he would use it for tuition.

Donald Gale's uncle was a devoted amateur photographer. He roved upstate New York and New England, seeking out picturesque churches. Donald watched him develop his prints, the images magically solidifying at the bottom of the trays. Soon he was doing it, too. He built his own darkroom, and in 1955 landed a job at Newington Children's Hospital in the photography department. He would stay there thirty-three years.

Jerry LeVasseur attended the Gunnery, where all students were required to play sports. He lettered in basketball and captained a football team that lost only one game. In college he would run track; later he raced competitively.

In 1956, Ed Lowe moved with his new family to Westbrook, down by the shore. He'd retired, but in his living room, under the glass top of a tea table, he kept a picture of 1565. Once he had his six-year-old daughter lie down on the couch in the same attitude as the mystery girl—eyes closed, a blanket thrown over her exactly the same way—while he took pictures.

He didn't see much of Thomas Barber anymore. On Decoration Day and the anniversary and Christmas Eve he'd get dressed and drive up to Hartford and meet his old partner at the cemetery, but that was it. He had a new family, a new life.

But the girl didn't let go. She came up in conversation; she was a part of him. A friend from West Hartford who rented a summer cottage near them thought the girl might be Judith Berman. Ed Lowe had known her uncle Bill Berman for years. He used to have the beat in front of their store on Franklin Avenue. The day of the fire Judith's father Hy Berman had been out of town, so Bill Berman and his wife made the identification.

Lowe drove up to West Hartford with the picture and talked with Bill Berman. According to his widow Judith Lowe, Ed Lowe told her that Bill Berman said he thought it was his niece, but asked that Lowe not make it public. The family had been through enough. Lowe promised, telling only his wife. On the back of the photo, he wrote in black magic marker: "JUDY BERMAN? NO QUESTION."

In '56 the circus visited Plainville for the last time. Emmett Kelly was gone, taking his Weary Willie routine to nightclubs and TV. The troupe struggled through the summer until John Ringling North could bear it no more. On July 16th, at Heidelberg Raceway outside of Pittsburgh, North closed down the show, saying the tented circus was "a thing of the past." From now on they would play in stadiums and arenas.

That summer Henry Ringling North received a telegram from a *Courant* reporter (obviously new) wondering if any elephants had been killed in the circus fire. "Some bones have been found near the old circus grounds which scientists are examining," it said. "They believe the bones are either from an elephant or a prehistoric mammal."

In August, State Policewoman Anna DeMatteo made a brief formal inquiry as to the identity of Little Miss 1565. The year before, she'd worked in New Haven with Don Cook, and in the course of their conversations, Don mentioned that he had a little sister who died in the fire and who was never found. Don believed the girl whose grave Barber and Lowe decorated was his sister. At the time, DeMatteo made little of his remarks, but the next spring while attending a lecture on identification at the police academy, she recalled his story. Now an officer, she requested a picture and a sample of hair (snipped, it seems, from the corpse) and quietly took this information to her superiors.

She received a reply within a week. "Your report was reviewed by Chief Michael J. Godfrey, who recalls the persons involved in your report, and he personally talked with Mrs. Cook at the time of the fire.

"The young man Donald, who gave you this information, must be misinformed because Mrs. Cook did lose a child in the Hartford circus fire, but it was a boy instead of a girl. Identification was made.

"This matter can now be considered closed."

All of this, of course, was suspect. Mildred Cook drifted in and out for several weeks after the fire, and according to the records, Godfrey himself never followed any of the missing leads. He was too busy being Mortensen's point man. Also, though Thomas Barber was still working with the city police, and nationally known for his involvement in the 1565 case, it seems that no one brought him in on the investigation.

Barber stayed faithful, visiting Northwood three times a year. Apparently Lowe couldn't make it for the anniversary in 1958, because the AP wire story featured only Barber at the grave with a pot of red carnations. It was Sunday morning; he'd worked graveyard that night and he was tired, but he was there, on one knee, his hat in his hand. "I think I'll go to the grave as long as I live," he said. There was a geranium there too; he wasn't sure who it was from. "I have this funny feeling that people who lost a child in the fire are getting doubtful about Miss 1565. They think that maybe she is their little girl. I've found flowers here before."

AP sent the story out around the country, and a surprising number of papers picked it up. It had been years since people had thought of the fire, and to find this man still honoring that little girl touched them. Barber received a flood of mail, including a few marriage proposals from widows and older women. The majority thanked Barber for restoring their faith in the goodness of man. Many wrote poems or enclosed inspirational literature.

The story also brought out the self-styled detectives and amateur psychics. One who signed herself as Solid Citizen guessed: "My impression is that the girl was named Molly Vincent (or Benson, Bronson, Brinson, Von Zandt or a similar two-syllable name) and that she came from the Upper Linden–Bayonne area of N.J. Magnolia is a clue. Either she lived on Magnolia St., her mother was named Magnolia, or she was born in Mississippi."

Among the stack of letters was one from a Los Angeles columnist. Years before, she'd mentioned the case in her column and a woman had called her, saying she'd lived in Massachusetts at the time of the fire. The woman told her a story about a local girl that now the columnist struggled to recall. "The little girl, about seven, was being raised along with her brothers nine and eleven by an aunt since her widowed mother was employed in Hartford. The day of the fire the mother had taken all three of her children to the circus. During the panic they became separated; she and the older boy were badly burned, the younger boy's body was recovered but the little girl was never found. The aunt viewed Little Miss 1565 but knew she was not her niece.

"Now here comes the weird part. They had a simulated grave next to the little boy's grave and—this young woman told me—on anniversaries would take the children's toys out to the cemetery and even have 'tea parties.'"

The columnist had forgotten all the names, and the young woman had left years back to join her serviceman husband in Japan, but she offered Barber the information, for what it was worth. Whether Barber did anything with the letter or the lead is unknown, but clearly the woman had described, with a few twists and a weird anecdote attached, Eleanor Cook and her family.

The sudden popularity of Barber and 1565 inspired a novel. Connecticut mystery writer Doris Miles Disney's *No Next of Kin* cashed in on the public's interest, solving the case of an unidentified little boy.

A different, far more horrible reminder struck that December. In Chicago, a fire at the Our Lady of the Angels school killed ninety-five people, nearly all children. Three years later, police arrested a teenager in connection with a rash of smaller fires. In the course of his interrogation he confessed to the Our Lady of the Angels fire. Records indicated he attended the school that day. He was introverted, a poor student and—doctors said—derived sexual pleasure from setting fires. His father once punished him by holding his fingers over the flame of a gas stove. The similarities to the Segee case were unmistakable, and as with Segee, authorities could never pin down a conviction. A juvenile, he served time for the other fires.

While the boy's trial was going on, a lit cigarette ignited trash stuck in a chute between the floors of Hartford Hospital's South Building. The chute acted like a flue, filling the upper floors with smoke. People trying to flee couldn't see the exit signs. Among the sixteen patients that died in the fire was Gladys Kokoska, a grandmother who'd recovered from her circus fire burns in the very same building. Her family buried her in Northwood Cemetery.

As the city recovered from the shock, news came from Brazil that a nylon circus tent in Rio de Janeiro had burned, killing more than 320 people, almost twice the Hartford toll. A young former employee whom doctors called mentally retarded admitted setting the blaze for revenge, an older accomplice splashing gas on the fabric. Police played his taped confession for newsmen as a line of more than two thousand relatives formed outside the morgue to identify loved ones.

Officially Thomas Barber stopped his search for 1565's identity the next year, retiring from the force in March. He'd investigated more than two hundred murders, but none stuck with him the way she did. His friends in the department threw a big retirement bash for him at the Statler. His former fellow detective Paul Beckwith—now chief—chaired the committee and gave a brief speech, as did Michael J. Godfrey, now retired. Barber took the podium and said he was leaving the force with mixed feelings. He'd loved the job. He concluded with a few remarks in Italian for his friends who used to live on the Old East Side, recently razed to make way for Constitution Plaza. Everyone lifted a glass.

As Barber retired, Richard Epps—little Richie at the time of the fire—joined the Hartford Fire Department. He didn't think his being at the circus that day had any bearing on his choice of profession. "But, maybe in my subconscious, I don't know." Eventually he would be assistant chief under John Stewart.

In May Barber was back at Northwood. Nothing had changed. In the mail he'd received a packet of seeds from Australia—forget-me-nots a woman wanted him to plant at the grave. The next month *Life* magazine did a spread on him, and the letters piled in again.

Unknown to Barber, the state police were checking into the case of Little Miss 1565—and also 1503. Anna DeMatteo and another trooper had gathered materials on Eleanor Cook and Judy Norris, hoping to identify both. Because the Norrises had all died in the fire, the officers spoke with Barbara and Mary Kay Smith's mother. She could only give them a general description.

They had more luck with Don Cook. At first he'd believed an odd but widespread rumor that a Jewish family from New Jersey had mistakenly claimed her body, having to bury it by sundown that day. He never discussed this with his mother. In the beginning, he felt, she wanted to believe that Eleanor—like Grace Fifield—had amnesia and had gone off with another family; then she favored the idea of the bodies being mixed up.

Don was unsure. He examined the morgue photograph; he'd never seen it before. The teeth looked different, but maybe that was discoloration from the fire. She had the same hair, and the face looked like her, except

Eleanor's cheeks seemed rounder. He was visibly shaken. It could be her, he told Anna DeMatteo. They should have his aunt Marion look at the picture.

Marion Parsons didn't think she needed to look at the picture. If it was just the girl she'd seen at the morgue, she knew for a fact that wasn't Eleanor. That girl had the wrong teeth, the wrong hair, and the wrong clothes. Finally she agreed to look at the picture.

It wasn't the girl she'd seen. She hadn't seen this body, she said, and wanted to know why not. Where was she? This wasn't the same little girl she saw.

She was tearful, but regained her composure. She didn't want to make any hasty judgments, but she thought this was her niece, considering her face had been distorted by the trampling and the heat.

Don's aunt Dorothy also took a look. At first she thought the girl resembled Eleanor, then decided that no, she didn't.

Later, after DeMatteo left, Marion Parsons changed her mind. No, it couldn't be Eleanor. Dorothy already fell into the no camp, so only Don was left saying yes, and he'd been nine at the time and still had qualms about the teeth. Changing their answer now would upset Aunt Emily and Mildred; they weren't strong enough to go through all that again. Right or wrong, Don and Marion and Dorothy would have to protect the family.

With the decision, DeMatteo's second investigation ended—at least on the issue of 1565. The policewoman continued to follow the possibility that Eleanor Cook might be 1503. At eight, her age matched that body, while Judy Norris and 1565 were both six. DeMatteo found out that Talarski's had handled 1503, but came up with no record of clothing or effects. She hoped to secure both a dental and a height and weight chart for Eleanor from the Sheldon Academy. No record exists of her attempt or whether she was successful.

The memory of the fire, like the circus itself, hit the doldrums in the mid-sixties. Local papers noted the twentieth anniversary, but with meager coverage. The show played New Haven every year, an anachronism, just a whisper beneath the constant roar of the mass media. In 1967, Irving Feld purchased the show for $8 million from an ailing, discouraged John Ringling North.

The next year Ed Lowe died of cancer. His widow Judith placed geraniums on 1565's grave. She and Thomas Barber hardly spoke, so he was puzzled when these mysterious flowers showed up. Barber himself was well into his seventies but still made it three times a year. "It's like going to the grave of an adopted daughter."

In 1969, the courts settled the last claim from the fire—the estate of Charles Tomalonis. In '44, Rogin had not been able to locate Tomalonis' next of kin, going so far as to take out ads in Lithuanian papers both in the States and back in his home country. No relative ever claimed him, making him, in a way, a missing person. Probate judge James Kinsella—the same Marine detailed to police the bodies—declared Tomalonis' estate forfeit to Connecticut. His settlement, gaining interest since its award, disappeared into the state coffers.

The twenty-fifth anniversary saw a brief resurgence of interest. WTIC-TV tracked down Robert Onorato's footage of the big top and got permission from his daughter to use it. The documentary "The Day the Clowns Cried" opened and closed with Thomas Barber making his Christmas visit to Northwood. Between these neat bookends, a variety of survivors and officials spoke, including ex-mayor Mortensen, Edward Rogin and Barber himself, shaking his head and saying, "Someone picked up the wrong body." He and Lowe had gone to Middletown in '44 and poked around but came up with nothing, he said, never mentioning Judy Norris by name.

Other than the interviews and Onorato's film, the program was maudlin and awful. The city had built the Fred D. Wish School on the Barbour Street site, fulfilling the plot's original purpose after forty years, and the contrast between today's children running around the playground and what had happened on the spot was too blatant, as was the documentary's ponderous narration—as if the events themselves lacked gravity. There was a nostalgia about the show, and no wonder; the gap between 1944 and 1969 seemed far larger than twenty-five years. The city the fire had shocked—that world—was gone.

So were any objections to the circus returning. In April of 1971, the show's superstar Gunther Gebel-Williams and a baby elephant attended the groundbreaking of the new Civic Center downtown. Four years later, the night of May 6th, the Ringling Bros. and Barnum & Bailey Circus played Hartford for the first time since the fire.

One man and his father had gone back in 1944. In '75, he bought the best seats in the house and treated his father. The show was completely retooled; like John Ringling North in his heyday, Kenneth Feld had tracked down and acquired new and spectacular acts from around the world. The man's father was unimpressed. Leaving, he shrugged. "It's just not the same."

In '76, James Haley retired from politics. He'd won distinction in Congress for his work in veterans and Indian affairs. Mo Udall succeeded him as chairman of both the House Interior and Insular Affairs Committee and the Veterans' Affairs Committee. Haley also fought for water conservation. A friend said, "As a politician he was an environmentalist and anything but a liberal." As a tribute, the VA named their hospital complex in Tampa after him.

In October, the *Times* folded, leaving the Old Gray Lady of State Street a widow.

The next summer, Thomas Barber visited the grave of 1565 for the ninety-ninth and final time. He was eighty-one and needed a cane because of a leg operation. It was a hot, humid day, and his daughter Gloria didn't

Thomas Barber visits the grave of Little Miss 1565, July 6th, 1970.
PHOTO BY DAVID PLOSS FOR THE *HARTFORD TIMES*, COURTESY OF DAVID BOLLIER

want him to go. He was determined; he knew this would be the last time. She drove him, bringing along some damp washcloths and a little brandy, in case. He set a basket of pink carnations by the marker and stood back to say a silent prayer.

"When I'm through," he told a reporter there, "that's it." At home, when another called, he said, "It ends with me."

He died in November. His funeral was on the news. The Bloomfield police had men at every corner, saluting the cortege. Pat Sheehan, the anchor for Channel 3, said, "Well, Lieutenant Barber, now you know who she is."

That Christmas, the Florists Association delivered a holiday wreath to Gloria Vieth's door. She hadn't expected it, but she and Orville and their son got in the car and took it to Northwood, "because I knew he would want me to do it." The weather was bitter and blowing. They had to scrape the snow from her stone.

The circus was supposed to come back to Hartford—the dates were scheduled—but in January the roof of the Civic Center collapsed under tons of ice. Ringling sued the city for $1 million for breach of contract.

In March, Karl Wallenda was walking a wire strung between two resort hotels in San Juan, Puerto Rico, when a gust of wind knocked him off balance. He hung on to the wire for a second, then fell ten stories, still holding his pole, striking a taxicab parked in the hotel driveway and bouncing to the ground, his head and body badly crushed. His last words were: "I'm going to make it." Helen and Herman Wallenda presided over his funeral, with Joe Geiger, Emmett Kelly and Merle Evans honorary pallbearers. Kelly followed him the next year.

A week after the anniversary in 1981, Judith Lowe sent a letter to the *Courant* claiming her husband had found out who 1565 was. "The family asked not to be identified, because of the heartache and agony they had already been through. This is all on record at the Hartford Police Station. My husband gave the information to the then Chief of Police Paul Beckwith."

Though the *Courant* printed it, no reporter ever checked with her until three years later. The reporter was collecting background for his fortieth-anniversary piece when he visited her in Westbrook. Judy Lowe told him the Judith Berman story. He went straight to the Berman family, who denied it angrily, confirming that Judith had been identified by dental records. Later, the reporter repeated the story to Mildred Cook in Southampton. He felt that Eleanor was 1565. Mildred said if he wrote that it would kill her sister Emily. His published story ultimately contained none of it.

WPOP's fortieth anniversary radio documentary "Someone Yelled Fire!" aired at 2:35 that afternoon, to duplicate the timetable of the day. It was during interviews for the piece that Mayor Mortensen's dissatisfaction with Chief Hallissey came to light, as well as the *Times* reporter's mistake concerning the three dead performers.

That year, Hartford finally allowed a tent show to play within the city limits—the Big Apple Circus, in Bushnell Park, right around the corner from fire headquarters on Pearl Street. Chief John Stewart himself signed the authorization papers.

For several years, things were quiet. The circus played the Civic Center every spring, and people hardly noticed. The survivors of the fire had grown older, and the city had other problems. Articles on the fire were rare.

In late July of 1987, a neighbor couple taking their evening walk through Northwood Cemetery discovered near the Allied Florists' latest offering to Little Miss 1565 six mysterious notes. The stem of an artificial flower anchored each piece of paper to the ground; on the one by 1565's grave, a woman had scrawled in fine red pen: "Sarah Graham is her name!"

The notes described a single, large party—one of the more common hypotheses.

1503 was "Michael Graham, twin, 6 yrs, 7/6/38."
1510: "Michael, Sarah's mother."
2200: "Michael + Sarah's stepsister or friend, somehow related, 4512's daughter."
4512: "Michael + Sarah's stepfather."
2109: "Michael + Sarah's step-grandmother Ann Fox-Smith."

The case went to Hartford police lieutenant James Looby—an excellent choice. The department's self-appointed historian, for years he'd fielded calls from all over the world about the circus fire. He immediately dug into the official records at the Connecticut State Library. They'd just been made public, attorney Henry Cohn the first civilian to leaf through them, researching a book on Edward Rogin's receivership.

From the beginning, Looby doubted the notes' credibility, but just a glance at the record of the unidentified dead proved them a hoax. Michael and Sarah's stepfather, 4512, was a woman; their stepsister or friend, 2200, an old man; their mother, 1510, a boy. Looby went back to the office, convinced.

But the fact that the notes were wrong didn't answer the question: Who were these people? Looby read deeper into the state library archives, poring over old reports, trying to fit things together. He began making calls. He talked with Judy Lowe and heard the Judith Berman story.

In the middle of this, Mildred Cook called him. She'd seen the story in the paper and figured he'd get around to her. No, her daughter wasn't Little Miss 1565. She repeated the Judith Berman story and suggested he speak with the reporter from the *Courant.* If there were any further developments, she'd appreciate it if he contacted her.

But there were no further developments. He didn't have the luxury of time, and the trail was cold. Other cases waited. The notes were a hoax, yes, but from the existing files and his legwork, all he could reasonably say was that there were several misidentifications made at the State Armory, a conclusion Dr. Weissenborn had come to the Monday the six had been interred.

The next investigator after Looby would say something different, shocking Hartford, in the process reviving the fire and becoming—decades after the fact—one of its heroes.

1990–1991

Like Looby, Hartford arson investigator Rick Davey answered a lot of phone calls on the circus fire. Every time the anniversary rolled around, the switchboard lit up. "How did it start?" people wanted to know. "What about the guy from Ohio who confessed to it? Did those two cops ever find out who that little girl was?" Lieutenant Davey studied fires both as a professional and for a hobby, and he was tired of not being able to answer their questions.

Because Hickey's state police had assumed jurisdiction over the fire, the city fire department only had scattered records on it. When Davey began his research, the state police explained that they had no files either, which was true; they were at the state library, and not yet available. Davey went to the public library and looked through books on disasters. At most, they had a chapter on the fire. Again and again, the picture of Little Miss 1565 turned up. The girl's story intrigued him. He remembered seeing the picture when he was a child of seven or eight; she was the first dead person he'd ever seen.

Davey began keeping his own files, photocopying anything he could find on the fire in his spare time, collating and highlighting it, taking notes. He tracked 1565 to the morgue at Hartford Hospital; he was leafing through their reports when the archivist there suggested he should look at the material at the state library, recently declassified.

They had boxes of it—folders and lists and reports, and pictures of everything. They had Robert Segee's confession and his drawings of the Red Man. They had Anna DeMatteo's notebook with her visit to Marion Parsons, and the family photos of Eleanor Cook she'd requested, all of it in one place. Davey copied hundreds of pages, putting together his own private library on the fire, indexed in numbered looseleaf notebooks.

The reports and photos convinced Davey that Hickey had gotten the origin of the fire wrong. The grass by the jack where the commissioner claimed the fire started hadn't been touched, and neither had the jack right beside it. None of the reports had the fire at the base of the sidewall; all the witnesses said it started higher up. Articles published the next day offered the possibility that it had begun in the men's room. And a cigarette? Davey knew a cigarette had to smolder a long time to catch anything on fire.

The cause was unclear, but he'd investigated more than two thousand arson cases, and Segee's confession rang true to him. The difficulty—as with any set fire—was proving it. The only physical evidence left was pictures, and even these might not help because so many people had combed over the scene.

The picture of pretty Eleanor Cook, smiling, hair in ribbons, haunted him. In '44, the nurse's aide and the social worker at Municipal and the two troopers at the armory and Weissenborn had all thought she was 1565. The only thing that stopped the medical examiner from making an ID right there was Emily Gill's assertion that her teeth were wrong. In '56, the state police had blown off DeMatteo, and in '63 both Don Cook and Marion Parsons seemed to think the girl was Eleanor. Davey believed she was, but again, he needed to prove it.

The girl in the morgue photo was far from a perfect match for Eleanor Cook, but Davey knew firsthand what fire could do to the body. Heat shrinks cartilage in the tips of the ears, pugs the nose upward, pulls the lips back from the teeth. And she'd suffered some kind of blunt head injury; her forehead bulged. Davey doubted she'd died of her burns; it seemed more likely she'd been trampled, her skull fractured. Weissenborn had just given burns as the cause because he was in a rush that Monday.

The Cook children, (from left) Edward, Eleanor and Donald. This shot of Eleanor would be cropped and used in the 1963 and 1991 reinvestigations. PHOTO COURTESY OF THE COOK FAMILY AND THE *HARTFORD COURANT*

The time on her death certificate was wrong as well; 1565 died in Municipal Hospital at 6:04 P.M., but here the doctor had her at the circus grounds at 2:45. How many of the other records were suspect?

Davey turned up a report matching Eleanor Cook's hair to that of 1565. While not conclusive, it stated that both specimens may have come from the same scalp. Just the fact that the state police had done the test five days after the mass burial at Northwood meant that they most likely considered her to be the girl.

It still proved nothing. The science of the time couldn't match physical markers the way they could today, and now any forensic evidence was long gone. All Davey had were the physical description, the dental chart, and the photos.

The photograph of Eleanor he kept in his desk, looking at it at least once a day, sometimes more. "Over a period of time I just kind of fell in love with a little girl, the photograph of a little girl, someone I never knew." He couldn't get the picture out of his mind. For Davey, the identification became an obsession. He had kids of his own but was divorced. Like Thomas Barber and Ed Lowe, he could devote time to the project, and he did.

He concentrated on the evidence he did have. The original nonidentification made sense. Marion Parsons had told DeMatteo that she'd never seen 1565, and Don Cook described Emily Gill as the family member least capable to identify Eleanor. Physically, both aunts seemed to think the girl was similar to their niece except for the teeth. There was a chance both had been in either shock or denial, using the teeth as an excuse not to confront Eleanor's death. Davey needed more physically. From the two pictures, he measured the distance between the top of her upper lip to the base of her nose—they matched. Next he compared the earlobes, both strangely shaped, and found they matched as well. Perhaps they could identify her by the Bertillon method, a process invented last century by a Frenchman who held that people's ears were as unique as their fingerprints. It was a start.

Now, if others might have doubts, Davey was convinced. A professional, he wanted others to test his theory before going public. Little Miss 1565 was a big deal, and he expected a lot of heat. He brought in two foils to bounce his ideas off—his arson squad partner, Hartford police detective Tom Goodrow, and *Courant* reporter Lynne Tuohy. He asked them to look over his voluminous files and then try to punch holes in his case.

Tom Goodrow shared with Davey a connection to the circus fire. His wife Joan's uncle had been William Curlee.

Goodrow took a box of his partner's files home and went through it. The evidence seemed to be all there, already in file. Why hadn't this kid been identified? He told Davey they should shore up the case before they went public with it. Together they made duplicates of all the photographs the state library had in its archives. Goodrow knew that Jimmy Looby had done some work on the case back in the eighties, so he got ahold of his notes as well.

Goodrow was methodical, a plodder, a meat-and-potatoes guy, just the facts, ma'am. Davey was strong on details too, but in this instance he was close emotionally, and Goodrow helped to ground him. The detective came up with a simple list of goals they needed to pursue: 1. ID the girl. 2. Reassess the fire. 3. ID the suspect.

Meanwhile Davey had met with Lynne Tuohy, who covered criminal justice for the *Courant*. Tuohy found Davey credible, not a wing nut. He'd been quiet with his project, he wasn't talked out on it. He patiently laid out his theories, showing her paper evidence. At first he wouldn't let her take any of it, but once he saw she was genuinely interested, he dumped a dozen file boxes on her. Tuohy had just delivered twins. After getting her other kids to bed, she sat in her living room, delving through the thousands of pages.

To support Davey's contention that the blaze could not have started from a cigarette, Goodrow turned up a report on grass fires done in the seventies by another fire investigator. In high humidity, cigarettes would not start grass fires. The normal range in which they would was 17 to 23 percent. At 2:00 in the afternoon the day of the fire, the humidity was 41 percent.

Tuohy discovered that Robert Segee was still alive and living in Columbus. She pulled his address and phone number from directory assistance and gave it to Davey, letting him have first crack. Later she called Segee herself.

"I can't talk to anyone about that," Segee said. "It's happened too long ago. I don't want to. I've been tested enough, and they ruined my life. I didn't set the fire. I was had."

Davey and Goodrow reviewed the testimony of witnesses and concluded that the fire first appeared inside the tent approximately two-thirds of the way up the sidewall. The NFPA had put the origin of the fire between the back wall of the men's room and the sidewall, but Davey and Goodrow ruled that out because there wasn't enough fuel there. The fire had to have started in the men's room, radiated heat from the blaze on its rear wall catching the big top's sidewall. Once the flames reached the treated roof, it was all over.

Goodrow saw 1565 as a missing persons case that involved a fire. In his mind, it was open and shut. "The information that we needed, that I needed to do an assessment and to come to a reasonable conclusion . . . there was no investigation—it was easy, it was all on file. Nothing to it. I wish all the investigations were this easy."

To officially make the identification, they needed the help of Eleanor Cook's family. When Davey tried to contact Mildred Cook, she didn't want to talk. They had to find Don Cook, now in Iowa, and have him speak with his mother. He convinced her to confront the issue. Marion and Ted Parsons and Emily Gill were all gone now. It was time.

Don Cook provided Davey and Goodrow with family photos of himself and Edward and Eleanor. He answered pages and pages of questions about the timing of the original identification—when exactly Emily Gill and Marion and Ted Parsons and James Yee had been to the armory. It was Davey's contention that as Eleanor's body moved from Municipal Hospital to the armory to the morgue at Hartford Hospital and then to Taylor & Modeen that it had somehow eluded her family. Also, as Dr. Weissenborn found, that Emily Gill had been incompetent to ID the body.

They nailed down the loose ends. They double-checked that there was no body under Eleanor's stone in Center Cemetery. They interviewed the Berman family, who told them a dentist, not her uncle, had identified Judith.

Even then, Mildred Cook was still not convinced until Rick Davey laid it all out for her. Once she agreed, Don Cook made an identification from the pictures. Goodrow brought in State Medical Examiner Dr. H. Wayne Carver and his assistant Dr. Ed McDonough to examine the new evidence, and, if convinced, to formally issue a revised death certificate. The doctors thought they might involve the famed forensic expert Clyde Snow.

As the 1565 case was winding down, Davey and Goodrow packed their evidence on Segee and the new point of origin and flew to the FBI Academy in Quantico to deliver an all-day presentation in front of a panel of federal arson investigators. Segee fit the profile of a serial firesetter/serial killer, and there was talk of their VICAP unit tracking and interviewing him in the future. Davey and Goodrow returned to Hartford, ready to take their case to the state.

All this time, Lynne Tuohy had been sitting on the story. She told them she had to break it soon; she was afraid someone would scoop her, and she'd put in too many hours for that to happen. Davey was fine with going public, but Goodrow wanted to hold back. In early March of '91, Tuohy said she was going to run with it that weekend. The story was large, and all hers. The main bar—the arson—hadn't been written, but the side-bars were done, edited and nearly ready. On the basis of supplemental circumstantial evidence and Don Cook's signature on the back of the morgue picture, Dr. Carver issued a new death certificate. Little Miss 1565 was Eleanor Cook.

The next day Goodrow called a practice press conference at police headquarters downtown, with the medical examiner, Fire Chief John Stewart and others. Tuohy's ex-husband, Channel 3 reporter Brian Garnett, noticed all their cars and figured something big was up.

He got part of the story out of an assistant police chief standing in the hallway. That night, Garnett and Channel 3 scooped Tuohy. His details were skewed, but the gist of the story was on target. 1565 had been identified.

Tuohy worked all night to get her story finished. It hit the stands the next morning, the front page, with promo cards for the honor boxes. The reaction astonished her—not just the number of calls and letters, but how many of them were critical of Mildred Cook. How could a mother not come forward and claim her child? they asked. What kind of a person was she?

Mildred Cook's loss had moved Tuohy. A mother herself, she appreciated how Mrs. Cook had found the strength to continue after losing both Edward and Eleanor. She was a religious woman, and a hard worker, and the criticism she now faced made Tuohy angry. She wrote a scathing defense of Mildred Cook, making plain the reasons she'd never claimed her daughter.

Mildred Cook leafs through her scrapbook of Eleanor's letters and spelling tests. PHOTO BY JOHN LONG, COURTESY OF THE *HARTFORD COURANT*

Mildred Cook herself said she'd believed Emily and Marion when they told her Eleanor wasn't at the armory or the morgue. She'd never seen the picture of 1565—a claim her critics disputed, saying it was on the front page of the paper every year. But it wasn't; it had never been on the front page. It had run right after the fire, in the *Times*, when Mildred Cook was unconscious in the hospital, and it had run in 1946, but by then she'd moved back to Southampton, beyond the circulation range of the Hartford papers. After that, Barber and Lowe and then just Barber were featured on the anniversary. Plus, her relatives actively insulated Mildred from news of the fire. Every July 6th, they distracted her with trips and outings. As Mildred said, "We didn't talk about it. We just kept on living the best we could."

Another part of the response that surprised Tuohy was the survivors. Dozens wrote to say they wanted her to write something on the fire besides Little Miss 1565. Elliott Smith was disappointed that she'd become the whole story when there were heroes like the man who lifted him out of the pile, and the doctors and nurses. Raymond Erickson's sister Joann Bowman wrote, wondering why Eleanor Cook had gotten so much attention and Raymond so little. Tuohy decided there was a big story here. She would see if she could interest her editor in a feature. The anniversary was coming up.

Davey and Goodrow became celebrities for a time—or Davey did. It

Hartford Fire Lieutenant Rick Davey (left) and Hartford Police detective Tom Goodrow, receiving a commendation from the city for their work on the 1565 case. Seated at left is Fire Chief John Stewart.
PHOTO COURTESY OF TOM GOODROW

was his fifteen minutes, and he grabbed it, going on the local news, doing talk shows and documentaries for A&E and the History Channel. The two took a slideshow around for a while to volunteer fire departments and the University of Hartford, but the bloom soon faded.

The cause of the fire the state's attorney's office would only change from "Accidental" to "Undetermined," not "Suspicious" or "Incendiary," as Davey and Goodrow had hoped. They could prove it wasn't a cigarette dropped in the grass, as Hickey had guessed, but beyond that, who knew? A match was possible, or a cigarette catching paper. The state didn't go for Segee's confession. They did say the case was open, though, and that they would look into it.

In June, Talarski's disinterred the body of 1565 at Northwood Cemetery. The coffin had fallen apart, and the frontal lobe of her skull was a hole—confirmation that she'd been trampled. Davey and Goodrow were both there, helping the sexton and the funeral director fit the bones into a new white coffin.

The next day her family buried her beside Edward Cook in Center Cemetery. It was humid, and the small crowd of family and friends huddled under a blue canopy. With Mildred and Don Cook and Davey and Goodrow looking on, one of Eleanor's childhood friends sang "Jesus Loves Me, This I Know," accompanying herself on the autoharp. Reverend James

(Above) Center Cemetery, Southampton, Massachusetts. 1565 awaits reburial as Eleanor Cook. PHOTO BY TOM GOODROW, COURTESY OF MR. GOODROW HIMSELF
(Right) Mildred Cook with her daughter's headstone. PHOTO BY JOHN LONG, COURTESY OF THE *HARTFORD COURANT*

Yee spoke briefly before the mourners retired to Southampton Congregational Church for punch and cookies. It was a homecoming for many of them, with lots of good talk.

Back at the cemetery, Talarski's funeral director spooned dirt from a jar into the grave. Yesterday he'd filled it at Northwood, so Eleanor would always have a part of Hartford with her.

· · ·

The identification of Little Miss 1565 was a great story with a perfect ending, but that doesn't make it true. Lost in all the supplemental circumstantial evidence is the fact that the dental charts don't match.

1565 had only two permanent teeth, the lower middle incisors, typical of a six-year-old. Eleanor Cook, at eight years four months, would normally have had at least her six-year molars. Marion Parsons, her guardian, said that Eleanor had eight permanent teeth.

Rick Davey never mentioned the problem of the charts to Lynne

Tuohy (or DeMatteo's 1963 investigation, it seems, though that one file contained basically everything he needed). Drs. Carver and McDonough never verified that Eleanor's teeth matched 1565's; Carver said only that X-ray equipment of the time might have failed to pick up adult teeth below the gumline—a valid point but off topic. Pediatric dentist Jack Kenney and noted forensic dentist Lowell Levine, who worked the Ted Bundy and Woodchipper murder cases, both say 1565's teeth are those of a significantly younger child.

More convincing is the fact that at 3'10", forty pounds, 1565 falls well off the low end of growth and development scales for an eight-year-old. Her height fits a girl six years six months; her weight a girl five years three months. And Eleanor Cook, as the *Times'* description of the missing girl said, was tall for her age.

Furthermore, the clothes on 1565 were the same ones Marion Parsons identified on the girl she saw at the armory—a white dress with flowers and brown shoes. Eleanor had been wearing the red playsuit and white shoes.

Davey's identification also assumes that only Emily Gill looked at 1565 at the armory, when in fact Emily Gill, Marion and Ted Parsons and James Yee all saw her and said she wasn't Eleanor.

It's possible the clothes were mishandled, but the dental X-ray and the height and weight were taken in the quiet of the Hartford Hospital morgue, with an eye toward a permanent record. The charts and figures are consistent, and there is no way anyone would confuse the relatively untouched 1565 with the only other girl there, the charred 1503.

Of the two unidentified girls, 1503 is more likely to be Eleanor Cook. Like Eleanor, she's listed as having eight permanent teeth. At 3'11", she'd also be too short for Eleanor, but her feet were burned off, making her true height the right size for a tall eight-year-old. Her weight, fifty-five pounds, is also consistent with the age.

Eleanor Cook may be neither. Both Thomas Barber and Anna DeMatteo put together identical lists of girls killed in the fire between the ages of four and nine. There were twenty-one of them. One mistake at the armory would throw the whole chain into chaos.

The evidence the current identification is based on is slight at best. At a glance the pictures don't quite jibe; they do only after a great deal of explaining, taking things into consideration. Don Cook naturally wanted to find his sister. The Bertillon method is not conclusive, and is rarely—if ever—used anymore. Drs. Carver and McDonough never called in Clyde Snow. When 1565's body was disinterred, no one collected any forensic evidence.

Asked whether he himself instantly saw a resemblance between the photos of the live Eleanor Cook and 1565, Dr. McDonough said, "I think that the history was much stronger. Again, there was really little doubt that it was this little girl, and then we looked at the photographs in order to just confirm that. It would be the same as if you're in your house and a fire breaks out and it has to be you type thing. You're missing, it's your house, and there's a body in there that is the same size and shape and gender and anthropologically the same, then it's you. By history alone."

But, as William Menser and Dr. Weissenborn and Thomas Barber and Ed Lowe all found out, that was not the case in the circus fire. You couldn't match the six missing with the six dead. Here, it seems, people tried to, disregarding hard evidence to the contrary.

The misidentification may have been the well-intended product of compulsion. For Davey, it may have been unthinkable to admit 1565 wasn't Eleanor Cook. As he said, "I didn't work that long for that. She had to have a name."

Currently the State Police Forensic Science Lab is reviewing the case, looking once again at the collected evidence. They seem open to a reinvestigation, but only Don Cook himself can set one in motion.

Lynne Tuohy and Don Cook seemed surprised by the noncompliant dental charts and height and weight, as if hearing about them for the first time. Don said he'd be glad to give blood for a mitochondrial DNA test. Rick Davey will not discuss the case.

These revelations put Mildred Cook's behavior in an entirely new light. The reason she never came forward to claim Little Miss 1565 was simple. She was not her daughter.

1991–1999

That July, Lynne Tuohy's "Eternal Flame" piece for the Sunday *Courant's* *Northeast* magazine collected the memories of circus fire survivors for the first time. With the interest stirred up by the 1565 case, she had her pick of stories. Emmett Kelly lugging the bucket made the cover. Inside, Spencer Torell's shot of the tent burning earned a two-page spread. And after forty-seven years, the paper finally ran the cub photographer's shot of the dead piled by the grandstand rail. The interviews were compelling, and the manner in which Tuohy intercut them satisfying.

New York publishers approached her, asking if she'd thought of writing a book, but by then, emotionally, she'd gotten too close and given too much. She'd just finished another intense piece for the anniversary, a feature on Raymond Erickson; his sister Joann still had his shoes and socks. At that point, Lynne Tuohy needed a break. And anyway, Rick Davey was putting together a book, and she considered it his story.

Later in the year, Yale University Press released the first important book on the disaster, Henry Cohn and David Bollier's *The Great Hartford Circus Fire*. An examination of the arbitration agreement, it followed Rogin, Schatz and Weinstein through the convoluted process of setting up and then executing the receivership. Cohn and Bollier had done their homework, and the results were fascinating legal scholarship.

Playwright Anne Pié explored a more personal side of the fire in her drama *Front Street*, a nostalgic look at an Italian family from the neighborhood where Thomas Barber first walked a beat. In the play, the youngest son goes to the matinee and the family doesn't know what's happened to him. Pié was eleven at the time of the fire and lived next to Northwood Cemetery. That afternoon she and her friends heard sirens and saw the sky over Keney Park fill with black smoke; Monday they attended the mass burial. When a producer in L.A. did a staged reading of *Front Street*, a woman he didn't know got up and walked out of the theater. When he saw her at another reading, he asked why she'd left toward the end of the second act. She told him she'd been in the bleachers the day of the fire and the play evoked such an emotional response that she started to cry.

By now the FBI had given up their plan of interrogating Segee. The state police reopened the case, but Davey and Goodrow, both with the city, were officially not involved. For political reasons, the state called it a reexamination rather than a reinvestigation. The case had low priority. Davey had planned on going to Ohio and speaking with Segee—it was going to be a chapter in his book—but since the state didn't consider this a criminal investigation, they told him no.

While Davey was sure Segee was guilty, and Goodrow strongly suspected it, in lieu of new evidence all they had was mere suspicion, not probable cause. The only thing new they'd turned up since the original investigation in 1944 was the fact that a cigarette wouldn't have caught the grass on fire that day. They'd moved the point of origin, but that was it.

The media hassled Segee, knocking on his door, shining their lights in his eyes. He'd gone gray, and his place was decorated in an American Indian motif. "I'm telling you the truth, I did not set that fire," he said. "I'm not guilty of the charges, but nobody ever believed me."

Then why did he confess?

"If you was hassled as much as I was, you'd tell them anything to get them off your back."

In March 1993, the state police sent two men out to Columbus to talk to Segee—the first time Connecticut had access to him. He'd moved since the news broke. They found him living with his daughter in a poor part of town. His hair was long and he wore a headband. They interviewed him at his kitchen table with his daughter present.

Segee said his name was Chief Black Raven and that he was a shaman. He talked and talked. They asked him point blank if he'd set the fire. He denied it. He'd gone to see *The Four Feathers* and when he came back on the bus the tent was down. His foreman with the light crew didn't like him and he became a suspect.

He explained the Circleville convictions as politically motivated; the sheriff was trying to get reelected and was related to the judge. They'd interrogated him nonstop for twenty-four hours. He agreed to what they said because he wanted to rest. They didn't want the truth because he was an Indian, and different. Segee said he was between two cultures and that when the Ohio police interviewed him they brainwashed him and muddled up his mind. He was of two realities now, one being the white man and one the Indian. When he made his statements back in 1950, he was either brainwashed or insane.

When the detectives asked him how someone might have set the tent on fire, Segee said someone could have used a mirror or a magnifying glass to set the grass on fire. He had visions of the fire, but he had so many vision quests that he had a hard time separating reality and fantasy. He was telling the truth, he said. He had to make peace with his spirit Wonka Tonka. Now he'd told the truth and made peace. Last night he had a vision quest of his own death, and it was a good quest, and he did not start the Hartford circus fire.

The men returned to Hartford with nothing concrete on Segee. With no further evidence, there was no arson. The cause remained "undetermined."

· · ·

In January 1994, echoing a scene from *The Greatest Show on Earth,* a Ringling Bros. train derailed near Lakeland, Florida. A witness observed the train go by and saw two pieces of a wheel fly off a passenger car and land in the nearby woods. The train continued nearly three miles, across five grade crossings, before it slipped off the rails. Two circus workers died. In Hartford, people remarked that it was a strange way to start the fire's fiftieth anniversary year.

Popular author Mary-Ann Tirone Smith timed it right, releasing her novel *Masters of Illusion* in June. Subtitled *A Novel of the Connecticut Circus Fire,* it followed the family life and loves of a woman who'd survived the fire as a child, the fingerprints of her rescuer seared into her back. The heroine marries a firefighter who, like Rick Davey, becomes obsessed with the mysteries of the fire. The author said she based her main character on a friend of a cousin—Barbara Smith. At one local reading, Rick Davey—supposedly still working on his own book—sat in the front row with a lawyer by his side.

The fire department marked the fiftieth anniversary with a ceremony at the Wish School. It was Captain Charles Teale's idea. Since he was a child, he'd listened to his grandmother's stories of the fire. He couldn't imagine the anniversary passing without some commemoration, so he asked the chief if he could organize an official gathering of survivors—in his spare time, of course. Teale wanted something small and intimate, but the media discovered his plan, and the weekend before the 6th, the *Courant* did a big spread on it.

Teale sent out invitations to special guests. Two couldn't make it: Lynne Tuohy, up in New Hampshire on an assignment, and Mildred Cook, who thanked him in a letter. "Transportation might be a problem," she wrote, "but I would not care to attend anyway—there are too many painful memories connected with July 6th."

More than two hundred others showed up. It was a hot, humid day, and survivors made nervous jokes about how the air felt the same. Few had been back to Barbour Street. Over the years the neighborhood, like Hartford, had changed. Stowe Village was drug-infested, a place where car-jackings and drive-by shootings happened; that day police swept the projects, arresting fourteen members of the 20 Love gang. Teale thought some people stayed away not because of bad memories but the place's new reputation.

Outside, camera crews caught the early birds. Some stood in the grass out back, pointing to where the big top had been, and where they'd made their escape. People brought their crumbling newspapers and programs and ticket stubs. They hadn't forgotten; they'd been saving them all along.

The ceremonies were supposed to start at 2:00, with a moment of silence scheduled for the exact time of the fire, but emcee Charles Teale couldn't get the survivors to stop talking among themselves, and soon he didn't want to. People were amazed there were so many left. No one wore name tags, making everyone a surprise. Barbara and Mary Kay Smith came, and Jerry LeVasseur, and Donald Anderson. Jennie Heiser was there, and Bill Cieri, Judy Lowe subbing for her late husband. Retired chief John Stewart felt doubly obligated to come. People thanked Captain Teale with tears in their eyes.

The air-conditioning broke down, and the auditorium was stuffy. Katherine Martin remarked that the weather was tough on her; her scarred skin didn't exchange heat well. Ladder Company 3 solved the problem, setting up smoke ejectors and blowing air through the open doors.

A TV crew finishing an interview up front delayed the program, but finally Teale got things under way. A piper played, former fireman and mayor Mike Peters spoke, as well as survivor and Lieutenant Governor Eunice Groark. The fire department presented a plaque to the Wish

School's principal. It read: "In loving memory of those who perished on this location 50 years ago, July 6, 1944, and with heartfelt condolences to their survivors." Charles Teale had chosen those words; years later he could repeat them by heart.

"Those people," he said, "they made me want to cry, each and every one of them. I wasn't really up to the task emotionally of putting this thing together, but I'm glad I did."

After the program, Rick Davey gave his slide show and answered questions. He didn't come right out and say Segee did it, but survivors could tell he was carefully dancing around it.

When the ceremony finally broke up, Charles Teale drove Jennie Heiser back to her retirement village at Avery Heights. He would continue to visit her for years. He would also pay his respects to the dead at the grounds and at Northwood every anniversary, putting on his dress uniform and bringing flowers from his garden.

That afternoon, while the survivors reminisced, the Clyde Beatty–Cole Bros. show paused during their matinee in Old Saybrook at 2:44 and observed a moment of silence. At the end of the tribute, the announcer gravely listed new fire safety laws and emergency medical procedures that had improved conditions since 1944.

In Las Vegas, the Greatest Show on Earth had the day off.

• • •

In August of 1997, as if connected, both Robert Segee and Mildred Cook died, their brief notoriety and fame largely forgotten. Lynne Tuohy, though, remembered Mildred Cook, and wrote a moving tribute to her. In Columbus, where Robert Segee had lived for more than forty years, he didn't even rate an obituary in the paper. In Hartford, the *Courant* missed his death completely.

• • •

At this writing, Ringling is poised to open their first American show under a top in more than forty years—the one-ring Barnum's Kaleidoscope. While Ringling's Gold Unit briefly toured Japan with a tent in the late eighties, other troupes have played here under vinyl for decades without mishap, the two largest being Carson & Barnes and old favorite Clyde Beatty–Cole Bros. Whether Connecticut will allow the new and nostalgic Kaleidoscape near Hartford isn't certain. In 1996 the state fire marshal closed down the Royal Hanneford Circus in Newington minutes before showtime because their tent failed a laboratory burn test. The Shriners, who'd hired the circus, lost thousands of dollars.

Hartford has changed drastically since 1944. G. Fox sits empty, as do hundreds of buildings throughout the inner city. On Washington Street, blocks from Bull Hickey's old headquarters, signs on telephone poles warn drivers that cars stopped to solicit prostitution will be seized. The signs are wrong, neighbors say; the prostitutes have moved and the crack dealers rule the corners.

Since the fiftieth anniversary, the press hasn't bothered with the fire, some Julys letting the anniversary slide by without comment. But people like Charles Teale still bring flowers to the graves; survivors still finger their curled newspapers.

The Connecticut State Library sees a few researchers every year, leafing through Hickey's and Healy's brittle reports. The boxes are filled with lists and horrible photos, paper clips bleeding rust. In a tiny manila envelope stapled to Trooper Francis Whelan's notes, the nickel Felix Adler gave him as a souvenir waits, an extra treat.

The Circus World Museum in the Ringlings' adopted hometown of Baraboo, Wisconsin, has more: three chairs from the fire donated by a good friend of Merle Evans. Their paint is blackened and cracked like desert mud, the undercolors of earlier seasons peeking through the tomato soup red: a milky orange, a dull sea green. The library there also has three pages of sheet music from "The Changing of the Guard," the theme for the closing spec that season, its edges burned black, singed thin. Their collection of rolling stock boasts a number of cage wagons that survived both Cleveland and Hartford, and the flatcars they came in on. The crown jewels though, are Mack water truck 132/133, which fought the fire, and the red and yellow ticket wagons that sat in the front yard. In summer the museum hauls in a solid crowd; tourists fill the parking lots and flock to two shows daily, beaming under the big top, reveling in the circus as it was meant to be.

The Wish School—like the transplanted barracks and Stowe Village—is supposed to be haunted. Water faucets turn on and off by themselves, followed by the diminishing patter of feet. In summer, laughter echoes through the empty halls, and the bright piping of a calliope.

Municipal Hospital, renamed McCook, closed decades ago. Now its buildings are home to the Burgdorf Health Center.

The armory houses the city's minor-league basketball team, the Connecticut Pride. The lobby where parents gave their children's names has a ticket window, and upstairs, purple bleachers line the court on the drill floor. High in the girders, leaking Mylar balloons nudge the ceiling. When I visited, a power forward was out on the court, alone with a coach, working on his moves. "No," the coach said, "see, that's just what you're doing."

While the rest of the world forgets, the circus fire remains the property of the survivors. To this day, Timothy Burns of South Windsor carries a small pocket knife. At his father's wake, he slipped his dad's knife into his jacket pocket, as if he might use it in another life. Frances Cook has the little beaded purse she carried that day; Harry Lichtenbaum of Wethersfield keeps a bag of peanuts.

Eunice Groark speaks for many when she says, "I guess the one indelible imprint I have is that fire is something one should respect. Make sure wherever it is that you go that there are ways of getting out." Survivors staying in hotels take rooms on the lower floors and count the doors to the fire exits; in nightclubs they search for red exit signs. Some are still queasy in crowds, like Charles Nelson Reilly: "To this day, I am never comfortable being a member of the audience." Others are claustrophobic, and can't ride elevators or stand CAT scans.

Their aversion to flames makes them brick up fireplaces and distrust candles. Harriet Globman says it drives her crazy to see people toss away a burning cigarette; she'll go out of her way to stomp it out. If another woman hears fire trucks converging, she'll drive the opposite direction, no matter where she's headed.

Lorna Hastings still goes around the house checking for fire whenever she thinks she smells something burning. For years she wouldn't turn the heater on in her car and dreaded the arrival of winter. Her children tired of her endless fire drills.

Most won't stand under a tent, even at a wedding; they'll wait outside. Others won't watch a circus on TV, or shiver when they hear circus music. Forget "The Stars and Stripes Forever."

Just writing about the fire makes you look at your loved ones differently, memorizing not their features but their teeth. Lynne Tuohy says she knows every inch of her kids' bodies.

The most common sentiment about the fire I heard from survivors was that it was something they'd never forget as long as they lived. Some still wake up screaming, fifty-five years later. Nightmares were said to have plagued Mayor Mortensen until his death in 1990. Nurse's aide Eileen Fitzgerald Hennessy's memories have the same intensity: "What I tell you is fact, like it was yesterday. You think it goes away. It does not go away."

In 1969, Emmett Kelly said, "I think of it, it's like a movie running in my mind. I try to forget it. I don't like to talk too much about it."

Dorothy Bocek Strzemieczny, who lost her sister Stella Marcovicz and nephew Francis, describes the effect Mildred Cook knew well and Don Cook knows today: "Through the years you kind of forget about it. You do but you don't really. We try not to think too much about it."

Life and time don't stop. People carry on somehow, learn to endure. As Elliott Smith says with pride, "I'm not a victim, I'm a survivor." That in itself is inspiring, a lesson to take away.

As for the mysteries of the circus fire—the missing and unidentified, the possibility of arson—they will probably always be mysteries, unsolved and unredeemed. Likewise, the desire to make sense of what happened, to find some justice and peace of mind by ordering and documenting the events, will always tempt us. But the fire is not that kind of story. Look close and it breaks up, it falls apart. As Joann Bowman wrote to me of her brother Raymond Erickson, "Sometimes you just don't know."

That is not to say there is nothing we can do for the dead or their families. All stories teach us something, and promise us something, whether they're true or invented, legend or fact. The reason 1565 and Thomas Barber stood in for the whole story of the circus fire for so many years is no mistake, and no slight to those who survived, though it must have seemed that way sometimes. To be lost and forgotten—to be abandoned—is a shared and terrible fear, just as our fondest hope, as we grow older, is that we might leave some part of us behind in the hearts of those we love and in that way live on. Perhaps, in the end, we will not be lost. In that respect, she has received the only gift we can give her, a gift we wish desperately for our loved ones, a gift we all want, finally: to be remembered.

Acknowledgments

First and foremost, I would like to thank Lynne Tuohy of the *Hartford Courant,* whose feature work on Little Miss 1565 and whose 1991 cover story "Eternal Flame" in *Northeast* magazine remain the best accounts of the fire. Without her legwork and her fine eye and ear, this book would be that much poorer.

The brunt of the paper research was done with the assistance of Mark Jones and the staff of the History and Genealogy Unit of the Connecticut State Library in Hartford. Alice Pentz and the Avon Public Library kept me supplied with books on Hartford, circuses, and all aspects of fire. Other folks who provided invaluable assistance were Fred Dahlinger, Erin Foley and Bernice Zimmer at the Circus World Museum in Baraboo, Wisconsin, Joan Barborak at the Hertzberg Circus Museum in San Antonio, Janice Mathews at the Hartford Collection of the Hartford Public Library, Marsha Lotstein at the Jewish Historical Society in West Hartford, Rhonda Green at the Cleveland Research Center of the Cleveland Public Library and Deborah Pfeiffenberger at the New Britain Youth Museum.

Art Kiely procured and printed many of the photographs in the book, as did John Long at the *Courant.* Paul R. Shafer shared his photos and his memories, and so did Judith Lowe and Gloria Vieth. Nancy Finlay at the Connecticut Historical Society arranged a special printing of never-before-seen shots. Maurice and Thelma Allaire contributed their negatives of the Portland stand, and Robert F. Sabia sent along his videos of William Day's films of the New Haven and Providence dates, among others, and also checked the manuscript for factual errors. Likewise, Leda and Gordon Partridge gave me total access to Christina K. Brand's spectacular pictures of the circus setting up the lot on July 5, 1944. Spencer Torell, who took many of the most famous shots of the fire, helped identify which pictures belonged to which photographer and donated a full set of his own prints.

Donald G. Horowitz came up with rare views of the Cleveland menagerie fire and also parsed the manuscript. The Prints and Photographs Department of the Library of Congress provided hard-to-find photos, and Larry Hughes at the National Archive and the staff of Grinberg Worldwide Images unearthed rare newsreel footage. Donald Bowden at Associated Press did his usual fine job, coming up with prints that never made the papers. Ralph Emerson Jr. gave me permission to reprint his father's great shot of Emmett Kelly.

Shanee Stepakoff shared her research and taught me far more about the North End of Hartford at that time than I ever could have found out on my own. Allegra Hogan shared the special collections table and her own fascinating project.

Both Henry S. Cohn and David Bollier, whose *The Great Hartford Circus Fire* (Yale University Press, 1991) plumbs the intricacies of the arbitration agreement between the circus and the survivors, generously contributed their expertise. Mary-Ann Tirone Smith, author of the popular novel about the fire, *Masters of Illusion* (Warner Books, 1994), pointed me to several informative sources. Semina De Laurentis of Seven Angels Theatre brought Anne Pié's *Front Street* to my attention, and the playwright herself trusted me not only with her drama but her memories. Rich Hanley of Connecticut Public Television kept me abreast of his progress on his documentary of the fire and shared his ideas. Craig Constantine at Towers Productions recalled putting together his features on the fire for A&E and the History Channel, as did Ken Rowe—also Art Donahue at WCVB.

Fred D. Pfening Jr. of the Circus Historical Society supplied me with Ringling Bros. and Barnum & Bailey route books from the era, and Dave Price and *Bandwagon*, the society's monthly journal, helped me get a better feel for circus tradition. Jim Foster at *The White Tops* came up with solid leads, and Maxine House got the word out to subscribers; Terry and Dick Abbot kept me current with back issues. Treasurer Gordon Taylor and many members of the Circus Fans Association of America lent a hand as well. Don Marcks at *The Circus Report* and Cherie Valentine at *Back Yard* helped beat the bushes. Gordon Carver with the Circus Model Builders lent needed expertise. Bob Peckham of Windjammers Unlimited and Richard Whitmarsh, leader of the South Shore Circus Band, helped with questions on Merle Evans, as did Richard Snyder and his encyclopedic knowledge of and devotion to circus music. Mike Martin supplied me with many fine videos of the show from that era.

Tom Goodrow, formerly of the Hartford Police Department, Detective Bill Lewis with the Connecticut State Police, Mike Simmons at the Ohio State Fire Marshal's office and Jim Looby, former HPD and now with the state's attorney's office, acquainted me with the official side of the mysteries surrounding the fire. Florence B. Sinow, communications officer with the Connecticut State Police, broke loose crucial investigative documents, and Susan Savage at the State Corrections Department tracked down some very dusty files. Charles Teale of the Hartford Fire Department, who conceived of and organized the fiftieth anniversary commemoration, graciously shared his recollections of that day. Kenneth Crooms, unofficial historian of the Wish School, thrilled me with his stories. Cynthia Coulter-Reichler of the State Commission on Fire Prevention and Control filled the gaps.

Special thanks also go to Dr. Robert Sheridan of the Shriners Burn Hospital and Mass General for his patience and generosity, archivist Steve Lytle for his assistance at Hartford Hospital, Pete Mobilia at St. Francis Hospital (and for his fine 1984 WPOP radio documentary, "Someone Yelled Fire"), Drs. H. Wayne Carver and Ed McDonough at the Connecticut State Medical Examiner's Office, Dr. Lowell Levine of the New York State Police, Dr. Jack Kenncy in Chicago, Dr. Gus Karazulas with the Connecticut State Police Forensic Science Laboratory, forensic pathologist Dr. Doug Ubelaker of the Smithsonian Institute, Dr. Peter Knowles at the Avon Dental Group, Eugene Kowalczyk at Talarski Maple Hill Chapel and Alex Marcellino in Vital Records at Hartford City Hall.

Thanks also to Jocelyn McClurg at the *Hartford Courant*, Bill Ryan of the *Courant*, Jim Fowler of the *Sarasota Herald Tribune*, John Crockett of the *Hartford Times*, Dave Stevenson at the *Columbus Dispatch*, Harry Atkins at *Emergency Medicine* and Erin Newman at *Emergency Medical Services*, and to the research bureaus of the *Sarasota Herald Tribune*, *Cleveland Plain Dealer* and *Yankee Magazine* (and Jody Saville and managing editor Tim Clark there).

Likewise, Peggy of Firefighters Bookstore and Bill McBride of The Jumping Frog deserve credit, as do Susan Audette of Mansfield Middle School, Amy and Bill Gerrish, Johanna and John Murphy, Giovanni

Iuliani, Gordon Clark Ramsey of the University of Hartford, Dennis Barrow at the Aetna Archives and the staff of the National Baseball Hall of Fame Research Library. Thanks too to Art Selleck and Larry Ford of the Manchester Fire Museum, and Jack Kuras and Suzanne Macy.

Thanks also to Elizabeth McCracken for her wise counsel—good advice at just the right time—and to Cindy and Luis Urrea for their keen readings and big hearts. Brian Hall generously trained his fine eye on the manuscript, as did longtime readers Paul Cody and Amy Williams, and of course Trudy, who not only read it but who had to listen to circus fire trivia the entire time I was working on the project.

And an especially big thank you to David and Mabel Carter and Barbara Thompson at Mailboxes, Etc. for keeping #1944 open.

. . .

The number of people who shared their memories of the fire and the days surrounding it was astonishing. I would especially like to thank Donald Anderson, Don Cook, William Epps, Donald Gale, the late Jennie Heiser, Jerry LeVasseur, Judith Lowe, Barbara Smith Mangan, William Menser, James J. Rice, Elliott Smith and Joan (Smith) Lindell, John B. Stewart Jr. and Gloria and Orville Vieth for their endless patience and openness.

In a way, this book is a memory book. The following are all those who made it possible; without them, this history would not exist: Gary Agasi, Vivian Alfano, Richard Anderson, Virginia Anderson, Sue Andrews, Betty Arthur, Dr. Richard Bagnall, Ken Ballette, Rivy Beizer, Corinne and Kathy Bellingham, Phyllis Benoit, Evelyn Bernstein, Sandra Blazensky, Edith Lefkin Bloch, Frances Blumenthal, John Bock, Richard Boulanger, Joann Bowman, Walter M. Brown, Iva Burnham, Timothy M. Burns, Sally Butler, Irene (Bessette) Calkins, Nancy Cannon, Dolores Cardillo, Don Carmody, J. Bruce Carrier, Tony Casiano, Moe Cattanio, Dr. L. Adam Chotkowski, Nancy Chunan, William Cieri, John and Madge Cofiell, Stanley Cohen, Doug Cole, Ned Coll, James P. Connolly, Frances Cook, Pat (Maguire) Cook, Anna Cote, James Counihan, Chris (Ellis) Courtney, Mary Culligan, Lewis Davidson, Robert Day, George De Franzo, Leonard De Maio, Jerry DeMeusy, Bradford Dennler, Amelia and Art Desrosiers, Teresa DiCorleto, Joe Donato, Katherine Donohue, Doris Dooley, Robert

Drayton, Dr. Frank Dully, Jr., Juanita Dutton, Marion (Lefkin) Eisenberg, Whitney Ellis, Rachel Elman, Clifford Emery, Peggy Fabian, Bill Faude, Arthur L. Fern, Eleanor Flynn, Fernand Forgeur, Loretta Francis, William E. Francis, Louise Garewski, Molly Garofolo, Edward J. Garrison, Jerry Gilbert, Nan Glass, Harriet Globman, Joan Goodrow, Bill Goralski, Violet Goshdigian, Marion Gossling, Mary Gribauskas, Eunice Groark, Meredith Guiness, Sloan Harger, Lorna Hastings, Fred Heatley, Lloyd Heavenor, John Hlavati, Zosh Hoffenberg, Joan Conlin Homa, Alice Horst, Joe Horvath, Miriam Howland, Bennett Hyne, Bud Jacobs, Whitey Jenkins, Bruce E. Johnson, Edna Johnson, Susan Smith Johnson, Diane Jonardi, Jerry Kaplan, Ann Kearns, Tim Kelliher, Joan Kelly, Wally Kelly, Patrice Killian-Brauer, Albert Kimball, Bernice Kleinman, Leo Kleinman, Jo Korten, Alvin Kotler, Kathleen Krein, Laura Kubick, Karl Kuzis, Arthur Lassow, Roseanne Lawrence, Asahel Lee, Len (at the MacGray Company), Harry Lichtenbaum, Barbara Lukens, Ed Lukstas, Albert W. Lynch, John Madden, John Mahoney, Richard Mahoney, Kathleen Martindale, Joseph Martinelli, Thomas Maskery, Rick McDonald, Bea McHugh, Bob and Elise McKay, Mike Meehan, Linda Meyers, Donna Michelini, Lewis J. Miller, Mary Jane Miller, Gail and Sandy Mirabile, Beatrice Mitlak, B. Albert Montella, Carolyn Moon, Susan Snelgrove Moore, Algert Mordas, Susan Morelli, Jean Myers, Angela (Yacavone) Newell, Dana Newell, Nancy Norton, Margaret Porter O'Brien, Robert H. O'Brien, Harvey Ofshay, Naomi Factor Papa, William Papetti, Irene Z. Pardo, Patricia Parente, Carol Parrish, Maureen Walsh Payton, Joe Pazzanno, George Pearse, John Pearse, Katheryn Pearse, Jane Peck, John Pedro, Marita Plikunas, Donna Ploss, Barbara M. Porter, Jack Powers, Patricia (Colman) Pratt, Alice Pringle, Elizabeth Reed, Eileen Regan, William Reid, Richard Renert, Lorain Reyor, Robert Ribera, Barbara Bacon Richard, Joan M. Rivers, Russ Roden, Eleanor Rodrigue, Eugene Roy, Joseph Ruggiero, Mildred Safin, Cathy Salvatore, Michael Salvatore, Dick Sanford, Janet Moore Sapolis, Micki Savin, Gerry Scheide, Iris Schlank, Ellen Schuman, Cele Seeley, Sandra Sharr, Lois Sheehan, Herbert Shook, Michael J. Silvester, Milli Silvestri, Robert A. Smith, Helen Kennedy Sonneman, Bob Steele, Rabbi Israel Stein and Roz (Berkowitz) Stein, Lee Steinberg, Dorothy Bocek Strzcmieczny, Velma B. Sullivan, Marilyn Young Tarasuk, Armen Tavy, Dorothy (Boardman) Teffs, Roosevelt Terry, Marna (Young)

Acknowledgments

Thoma, Joan Thompson, Don Tinty, Ronnie Tolson, Lois Wasserman, Dorothy Waterbury, Margery Weed, Patricia Weiman, George Weimann, Jack Weinberg, Helen and Jack Welch, Connie Westfort, Douglas Whinnem, Betty Wickham, Dr. Chet Wiese, Bob Wilson, Carrie Wilson, Barbara (Tallman) White, Ruth Neistat Whitman, Rev. James Yee and Joseph Zukowski. Thank you all.

RINGLING BROS

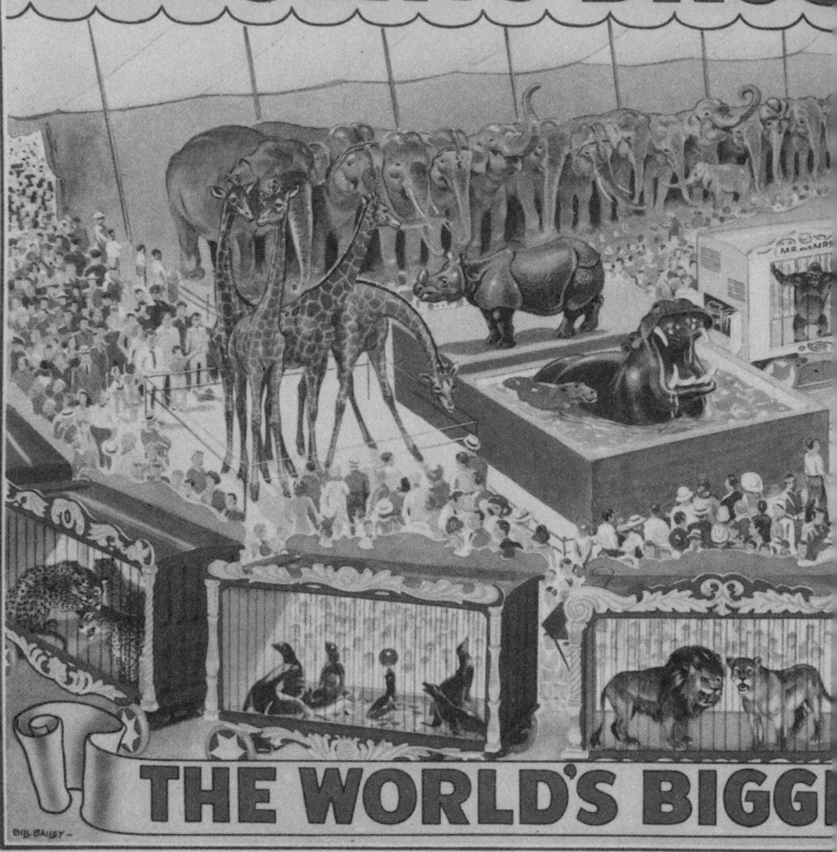

AFTERNOON
& NIGHT

HARTF

WED. JULY 5